COURTLY INDIAN WOMEN IN LATE IMPERIAL INDIA

THE BODY, GENDER AND CULTURE

Series Editors: *Lynn Botelho*
Amy Froide
Elizabeth Hurren

FORTHCOMING TITLE

Paracelsus's Theory of Embodiment:
Conception and Gestation in Early Modern Europe
Amy Eisen Cislo

www.pickeringchatto.com/body

COURTLY INDIAN WOMEN IN LATE IMPERIAL INDIA

BY

Angma Dey Jhala

MUNDUS
INTELLECTUALIS

LONDON
PICKERING & CHATTO
2008

Published by Pickering & Chatto (Publishers) Limited
21 Bloomsbury Way, London WC1A 2TH

2252 Ridge Road, Brookfield, Vermont 05036-9704, USA

www.pickeringchatto.com

BRITISH LIBRARY CATALOGUING IN PUBLICATION DATA

Jhala, Angma Dey, 1978–
Courtly Indian women in late imperial India. – (The body, gender and culture,
1450–1900)
1. Women in politics – India – History 2. India – Court and courtiers – History
– 20th century 3. India – Politics and government – 20th century
I. Title
305.4'89621'0954'0904

ISBN-13: 9781851969418

Typeset by Pickering & Chatto (Publishers) Limited
Printed in the United Kingdom by MPG Books Ltd, Bodmin, Cornwall

CONTENTS

ACKNOWLEDGEMENTS

This book could not have been conceived, written nor completed without the encouragement, support and patient indulgence of so many. This is as much a testament to their belief in me as it is my own work, and I owe them much in the writing of this history.

This topic first emerged out of my senior honours thesis at Harvard University and I am indebted to the guidance of my undergraduate mentors in the Sanskrit and Indian Studies and History departments, who first saw the potential in this work, most importantly Stephanie Jamison and Donald Fleming. They have remained unflagging supporters throughout this process. My thesis readers Caroline Elkins and Diana Eck helped my research evolve from a nascent undergraduate thesis to a doctoral prospectus, and Pratap Bhanu Mehta served as an inspiration to continue my work on history and South Asia in general.

The project evolved into a D.Phil. dissertation at Oxford University, where I was most fortunate to have the steadfast mentorship of my supervisor, David Washbrook, who both wisely advised me when I was swerving off course and reassured me at those rare moments I happened upon an (unexpected) intellectual find. His keen humour and kind support helped me to remain focused and undaunted despite the inevitable adversities of graduate research and writing. Maria Misra, Nandini Gooptu and John Darwin gave insightful and probing suggestions at both earlier and later critical moments of composition, and the generous comments of David Cannadine were particularly appreciated during the last phase of writing and revision. Norbert Peabody read early drafts of chapters and was very supportive throughout my graduate studies. At Harvard Divinity School, Leila Ahmed was an incomparable advisor, reading early drafts of papers, which became chapters of this book, encouraging me in the writing of this book as well as others and guiding me on the academic path. I thank her and Afsaneh Najmabadi for introducing me to the wider study of gender in a comparative context. Nur Yalman and Amartya Sen kindly read earlier versions of essays or chapters, which evolved into the final manuscript. I would also like to thank Sugata Bose, Sunil Khilnani, John McLeod, Barbara Ramusack and Robert Travers for their general interest in my research.

I wrote and revised this book in various locations. At Oxford, I was lucky to compose much of this work in the convivial and beautiful environs of Christ Church. Most of the revisions were completed while I was teaching in the History Department at Tufts University, where I received a kind welcome from Ayesha Jalal.

Writing a book requires the help of many people, not least funding agencies and libraries. At Harvard College, travelling grants from Radcliffe College, the Asia Center and the Dean's office enabled me to spend a summer recording several oral histories, which went into this book. At Oxford, the Clarendon Fund, American Friends of Christ Church fellowship and several grants from the Beit Fund enabled me to commence my studies and pursue many fieldwork trips to India. In addition, I would like to thank the numerous librarians who assisted me on this long journey into the archives, most notably the staff members of the Oriental and India Office Library, London, the Indian Institute Library, Oxford, the South Asian Studies Centre Library, Cambridge, Widener Library, Harvard, and the Dhrangadhra Raj private archives. Their unstinting patience in aiding in all bibliographic matters, forgiving late library fines and finding obscure manuscripts greatly aided in this project and revealed to me the deep satisfaction to be found in the process of archival research.

Several people were gracious in sharing with me their time and memories, and humouring my many questions and lines of inquiry, most unstintingly, in particular HH Maharaja Meghrajji of Dhrangadhra and HH Maharani Brijraj Kumari of Dhrangadhra. HH Rajmata Gayatri Devi of Jaipur, HH Rajmata Krishna Kumari of Jodhpur, the late Ranisaheb Sita Devi of Kapurthala, Rajkumar Martand Singh of Kapurthala and Rajkumari Moitri Roy Hume of the Chakma Raj also gave greatly of themselves. I thank them for providing me with a lens into a world few historians have charted, that of a lived experience which has largely been absent from the written archive. Their stories have deeply enriched and enlivened this work.

The hospitality and love of Aunty Buri and Ina, Joannie and the Penniman family, Nicholas Scott and Barbara Isaac provided me with homes away from home and made my stay in England that much sweeter and more memorable. I shall not soon forget their kindness in taking me in at all times and hours, and for supporting my studies in the most tangible way; it reflects the wonderful legacy of friendship between families which crosses the expanse of generations. The love of Richard Cash and Maria Hibbs Brosio has been with me ever since the cradle, and I am most blessed in their unswerving care, not least attendance at numerous university commencement services and experimental dinner feasts. Mapu Chacha's boundless love and energy in all matters, from mailing books at the last minute to listening to endless concerns of the heart, will always be deeply cherished beyond words.

My grandparents were a constant fount of support and noble emulation. From my grandfather Dadabava, I discovered the delicious delights of scholarship, and his stories of a youth spent in Oxford inspired my own journey to the city of dreaming spires. Badamama's unconditional love and deep sense of faith always made me grateful for life and reassured me that home was never far away, and ever waiting.

My sister Liluye gave me many moments of laughter and optimism. I shall always remember our summers filming in Oxford and Gujarat, London and Rajasthan, and the snake that breathes life eternally. Despite boisterous arguments and much melodrama, she has remained my most loyal advocate and discerning critic. Such are the gifts of sisterhood.

My parents encouraged me to pursue a life of the mind and reap the fruits of quiet scholarship. Their selfless devotion and dedication to parenting have made me who I am. My virtues are a blessing from them; my vices are singularly my own. My father's good humour and forceful yet gentle probing got me through some of the most difficult parts of the writing process. To my mother, especially, I have an enormous debt and words are ill served to express how seminal she was in this work. She is to me the most special companion, intellectual colleague and *mater* I could have asked for. In ways, both metaphorical and literal, she has been with me on every step of this journey and language is but a crude way to celebrate her part in this endeavour.

Lastly, this book could not have commenced nor concluded without the smiling favour of my kuldevi Shaktima, without whose divine grace, I would not be nearly so fortunate.

INTRODUCTION

One day long ago a young Maharani sat at a latticed window in a palace of white marble and looked out over the silver lake and beyond to the low hills whose slopes the ray of the late afternoon sun had transmuted into purple and gold. But the eyes of the Maharani were not drinking in the glories of the sunset: they were fixed on a crowd on the opposite shores of the water where the lake narrowed to a valley in the hills. She knew what the scene meant, although she could not clearly distinguish the people. For had not her lord and master made a wager with his favourite dancing-girl that she would not walk the width of the lake on a tight-rope, a wager made in a drunken delirium and the reward to be half his kingdom? How she hated the girl and yet shuddered at this cruel test![1]

This 1934 image of the secluded Indian royal woman locked within the stultifying confines of her palace zenana is a recurrent vision of late colonial princely India. The writer paints this Maharani with all the trappings of eastern lore and western voyeuristic fantasy. She is hidden behind the 'latticed' window from the masculine gaze of the imperial observer, and languishes within the hot bed of intrigue, vying with a nautch girl for the favour of her husband. The Maharani is both disturbed by the image of her husband's mistress, yet empathetic to the 'cruelty' of the wager she is playing. In such portraits, courtly Eastern women appear to be the passive, sexual objects of lascivious Eastern autocrats or the pawns of the liberating, enlightened British occupier. Mythologized by colonial literature as lascivious and sensual and reconstructed by the nationalist discourse as silent and secluded, courtly Indian women have invariably been depicted as the object of male desire and conquest, with little or no agency. The English novelist E. M. Forster described the beautiful Hindu Maharani of Dewas Senior as languid and mute, while giving audience to her European guests in only a negligee.[2] Indian nationalists such as Mahatma Gandhi and Jawaharlal Nehru purported that veiling or *pardah* was a 'barbarous custom' doing incalculable harm on the state of India's women.[3] Often portrayed as a dependent and victimized creature, bejewelled and dressed gorgeously only for the eyes of her king and male kinsmen, she is the screen upon which both colonial and nationalist imaginary longings play themselves out in forming conceptions of the Indic 'traditional' or indigenous. Indian women who practised the customs of the zenana and the veil were believed to be 'confined to a life of languid idleness in closed rooms, hidden from view ... suffused with an unhealthy sexuality and a disabling passivity'.[4]

Courtly Indian Women in Late Imperial India poses a challenge to such conventional narratives by arguing that female members of princely households were in fact significant players in colonial governance and postcolonial politics. By probing into the blurry line between the private and the public, the familial and the political, this book attempts to complicate the study of gender, race, royalty and politics in late colonial and twentieth-century South Asia.

Before India's Independence from Great Britain in 1947, two fifths of the subcontinent and one third of the population lived within some six hundred semi-autonomous kingdoms of varying geographical, religious, ethnic and linguistic diversity. Dubbed by the Raj as the 'native states' of princely India, they spanned the foothills of the Himalayas to the southernmost tip of the Indian peninsula.[5] Although the rulers of the princely states controlled significant wealth and power, they have remained largely neglected in mainstream scholarly histories. Perceived as Oriental despots or puppets of the colonial regime, they fall outside the dominant territorial spheres of historical inquiry in British India, where both imperial officials and South Asian nationalists were geographically located.[6]

While the princes have gained recognition with a small cadre of scholars, who have worked assiduously in bringing their histories and contribution to Indian politics out of the archives since the 1960s, these scholars will readily admit that there has been little emphasis placed on courtly women as actors and symbols in the relationship between native states and British paramountcy and, later, independent, republican India. Such an observation has spurred this investigation into the private domestic world of the Indian court, what is termed the 'zenana', and the role of women in it.

The zenana, which translates from the Persian as the 'women's courts' or 'quarters of the palace', was the strictly female sanctum within the larger arena of the Indic kingdom and was an institution adopted by Muslim, Hindu, Sikh and Buddhist ruling dynasties. In such a structure, women lived behind *pardah* (literally translated as the 'veil' or 'curtain') in seclusion. This book focuses predominantly, but not exclusively, on Hindu Zenanas and the ways in which courtly women displayed and negotiated power during the late nineteenth and twentieth centuries. During the colonial period, Zenana women were significant agents in matters of state succession, dynastic alliance and the question of colonial law versus indigenous practice. They served as subtle resistors against British imperialism as well as local, patriarchal hierarchies. In post-independent India, a number of former Zenana women have entered electoral politics and occupy local and national seats of influence, playing a significant role in matters of royal, dynastic marriage and in popular culture, where the mystique and lore of the Zenana lifestyle features in current novels, films and music.

This book argues that the zenana is a crucial arena to critique the intersection between gender, colonialism and modernity through three seminal relationships of power in late imperial and twentieth-century India. First, it serves as a prism to analyse and elaborate upon the dramatic encounter between the indigene and the foreign imperialist. The meeting between the female 'native leader' and the British was one of dialogue and mutual exchange, far from an essentializing tale of unilateral domination. Second, the politics of the zenana provides a revealing exposition into the shifting strategies courtly Indian women used in resisting local patriarchies, which yields a far more complicated portrait of female political strategy from behind *pardah*. Third, as the later part of the book will explicate, Zenana women play a role in independent India as members of the republican government. While the princely states officially lapsed with Independence, their political ideologies remain alive in those erstwhile members, male and female, who are active in the public life of the nation in the fields of government, tourism, diplomacy, education, law and historic and cultural patronage, among others. In contrast to the image of the passive, subordinate female, this book aims to re-establish the courtly Indian woman as a principal actor and potent symbol in Indian society and history during a crucial century of transformation, from 1890 to 2000.

A Footnote in History: The Indian Princely States

Until 1947, India was divided into two distinct regions: the territories of British India and approximately six hundred semi-autonomous kingdoms. These 'native' or 'princely' states, as they were termed, formed a diverse and powerful polity. Some states were as large as European countries and as wealthy, such as Kashmir and Hyderabad.[7] Indian kingship itself was not static or homogenous, and each princely state often had its own history, culture, religion, language and kinship groupings, which differentiated it from other 'little kingdoms' as did the zenanas within them. Some upheld primogeniture; others were matrilineal in succession, such as the South Indian kingdoms of Travancore and Cochin.[8] Certain states had centralized governments (for example Travancore and Mysore), thereby incorporating smaller kingdoms in their way. Others only became clearly established through the influence of the East India Company (such as Jammu and Kashmir).[9] Their rulers relied on military troops and the support of jagirdars, who received hereditary revenue in return for providing soldiers. For these rajas, alliances with the British were one way to lessen their dependence on the jagirdars.[10]

With the treaties of 1818 and the defeat of the Marathas and the Pindaris during the decline of the Mughal Empire, the East India Company emerged as the single paramount power in the subcontinent. The aim of British paramountcy, however, was not to directly rule the whole of India, but rather only those areas which were financially profitable and politically expedient, such as Bengal and the presidencies of Bombay and Madras. For the remaining 'terra incognita', the British implemented a policy of 'indirect rule', which provided 'a cheap means of pacifying and subordinating regions not under their own direct control' by forming subsidiary alliances and treaties with the native rulers.[11]

When asked by the princes for a definition of the vague meaning of paramountcy, the 1928 Butler Commission merely stated, 'Paramountcy must remain paramount'.[12] The idea of paramountcy itself was constantly in flux, and acquired different meanings in varying contexts. As Sir William Lee-Warner, an authority on paramountcy at the end of the nineteenth century, suggested: 'Even if the whole body of Indian treaties, engagements and sanads with all the Native states were carefully compiled, with a view to extracting from them a complete catalogue of the obligations or duties that might be held to be common to all, the list would be imperfect'.[13]

Under the umbrella of the Pax Britannica, the princes held full authority in internal matters of state governance such as taxation, state revenue collection, criminal and judicial law and the development of educational and cultural institutions.[14] However, they could not conduct foreign policy and were obliged to maintain a body of Company troops, which would be stationed in their kingdoms under the control of a British political officer.[15]

By the mid-nineteenth century, the crisis of the 1857 Mutiny highlighted the vital role of the Indian princes in Britain's policy of 'indirect rule'.[16] While it can be argued that Dalhousie's earlier strategy of annexing Indian princely states was one of the many grievances leading to the mutiny, some princes also served as important allies for the British at this time of crisis. During the revolt, certain 'patches' of the native states, such as Gwalior, Hyderabad, Patiala, Rampur and Rewa, proved to be 'breakwaters in the storm' which would have otherwise 'swept away' the British, in the words of the first Viceroy Lord Canning.[17]

Henceforth, the princes were 'accorded a permanent position as part of the British Empire'.[18] The Queen's 1858 Proclamation which was announced shortly after the events of the Mutiny, sought to "respect the rights, dignity and honour of native princes as our own', because they were the quintessential 'natural leaders' of South Asian society'.[19] In shifting from Company to Crown rule, the statement aimed to establish a new social order with the British monarchy as the focus of sovereignty, capable of structuring into a single hierarchy all its subjects, Indian and British.[20] It encouraged and embellished a 'language of feudal loyalty' among the Indian princes.[21]

After the Proclamation, the head of the British Government in India acquired the dual title of Governor-General and Viceroy. As Viceroy, he was the Crown's representative in its dealings with the princes of India and their subjects. As Governor-General, he took over control of foreign affairs, defence, communications and coinage for British India, while the princely states were left 'internally autonomous' and guaranteed protection from enemies 'foreign and domestic'. The political agent or resident served as such a representative of the British Raj within the territorial boundaries of the princely states.[22] There were less than twenty residences and agencies scattered across India, generally located in the capitals of the larger states.[23] The agencies maintained large staffs, employing both British and Indian workers.

For this reason, the native Indian rulers saw themselves as being in treaty with the Crown not the administration of British India. As the present Maharaja of Dhrangadhra explains:

> The two were distinct, categorical entities. There was no overlap. British India (shown as red on the map) was governed by the Governor-General and it was under the *sovereignty* of the British Crown/Monarch. Indian India (yellow on the map) was overseen ('overawed', if you prefer) by the Crown Representative (a later designation), and it was under the *suzerainty* of the British Crown/Representative. Ruling Princes were sovereign in and over their States.[24] [Italics in original].

In 1876, Prime Minister Benjamin Disraeli proclaimed Queen Victoria Empress of India during an opening of Parliament. In his speech, Disraeli emphasized the heterogeneity of the princes in regards to race, religion and legal tradition, and eulogized their rare histories as 'highly gifted and civilized'. He claimed that the lustre of these royal lineages rivalled the antiquity of the English monarchy itself. The princes, he intoned, 'occupy Thrones which were filled by their ancestors when England was a Roman Province'.[25] Disraeli suggested that these kingdoms represented India's extraordinary cosmopolitanism, which could have no 'coherent community' unless it was incorporated into the 'integrating systems' of the Empire.[26]

The Delhi Imperial Assemblage held one year later in 1877 to officially crown Victoria 'Empress of India' served even further to associate the Empress's authority and that of the British with India's 'traditional' rulers.[27] Lord Lytton, the newly appointed Viceroy and Governor-General, orchestrated the highly ornate ceremony. His hope was that the public pageantry would establish the Queen's authority by placing her rightfully 'upon the ancient throne of the Moguls'.[28] Lytton believed that the strong support of the Indian princely order was crucial to the interests of the Crown. The 'native aristocracy of the country', he wrote to Queen Victoria, 'whose sympathy and cordial allegiance is no inconsiderable guarantee for the stability ... of the Indian Empire'.[29] Those who attended, some three hundred princes, were seen as the 'flower of the Indian nobility', thanked for their participation in the suppression of the Mutiny and awarded new honours for meritorious service in a similar tradition of 'nazar' or fealty as that which was performed earlier at Mughal durbars.[30] The ceremony combined both Anglo-Norman and Mughal conceptions of royalty and visual display.[31] In Lytton's opinion, the princes were not so much 'representatives of their subjects' but collaborators celebrating their 'sentiments of attachment to the Crown'.[32]

In the subsequent period, a system of 'personal' relationships between the Indian rulers and their British sovereigns, as romantically portrayed in the literature of the late nineteenth and early twentieth century began to emerge. The adoption and gifting of imperial 'honours', such as medals, gun salutes, seating placement at durbars, orders and knighthoods further tied the Indian princes to their colonial masters. Royal Indian women, such as wives and other female relatives of Indian rulers, were included in this process of 'ornamentation' and were awarded The Order of the Crown of India for meritorious acts of service.[33] At the apex, Queen Victoria had a gun salute of 101, followed by the Viceroy, as representative of the monarch, at thirty-one guns, commensurate with some members of the British royal family. The Indian princes were awarded gun salutes, numbering from twenty-one to nine. The highest-ranking Indian princes at twenty-one guns were Hyderabad, with the greatest population; Kashmir, the largest in territory; Mysore, third in size and population; and Baroda and Gwalior, as remnants of the Maratha legacy.[34]

As David Cannadine argues, the British Empire was therefore not motivated so much by racist definitions of the Orientalist Other but by class distinctions, hence the Raj felt a natural affinity towards the hierarchically ordered Hindu caste system. The incorporation of the princes into the imperial government was one means towards recreating and perpetuating the ranked stratification of the metropole in its colony.[35] At the same time, many of the princes were disinterested and even hostile to this imperial honours system. In 1869, Maharaja Ranmallsinhji II of Dhrangadhra was the first prince in Saurashtra to be awarded a knighthood, which he was reluctant to accept and 'only acquiesced after much urging by his courtiers who pointed out that refusal would grossly insult the Paramount Power and Queen Victoria'.[36] Maharaja Sayajirao of Baroda famously turned his back on the English monarchs, King George and Queen Mary, during the 1911 Delhi durbar as a sign of resistance in addition to refusing to wear his Order of the Star of India, the greatest award given to an Indian prince by the British government.[37]

In 1921, the princes founded their own body, The Chamber of Princes, which provided a forum of dialogue and cultivated 'an environment in which good government became more fashionable'.[38] As 'modern' statesmen, they attempted to combine indigenous forms of *rajadharma* (kingly duty) with British models of good governance. Some exercised vital powers in local, regional and all-Indian imperial politics during this period.[39]

However, the differences between the princes, which Disraeli had eulogized earlier, proved to be too great. Rajput Kshatriya kings in Jaipur and Jodhpur looked down upon the Sudra-descended Maratha kings of Gwalior and Indore, as well as the Jat-Sikh kings of Punjab (such as Patiala, Nabha and Kapurthala). In equal measure, the Maratha kings, such as Gwalior, retained aged resentment against the Rajputs for siding with the East India Company, which lead to their own demise. Even closely related dynasties 'were not immune from vendettas'.[40] Morvi and Cutch in Kathiawar were locked in a dispute over a piece of the Rann; Patiala with his Sikh kinsman Nabha over the rulership of the *Khalsa*.[41] The ruler of Indore, Tukoji Rao, noted that 'on account of the differences in the education, training, methods of thought, status and position of the Indian Princes, it would be impossible to secure ... unanimity ... on any subject placed before the council'.[42]

This inability to maintain cohesiveness arguably led to the wane of the princely order and its weakened place in Indian politics by the mid-twentieth century. The period of rapid metamorphosis, which brought modernization, independence and democracy to the new nation, can be interpreted as the twilight years for princely India. The princes were generally characterized as the losers in the battle for power between the British Empire and the Indian nationalists with the resolution of Partition in 1947.[43] In the thirty-year period from 1919 to 1947, the lives of the Indian princes were forever altered. At the end of World War I, the princely states were still relatively secure. Indian rulers were admired by their subjects and even by nationalists. In the 1920s, Mahatma Gandhi, whose father and grandfather had served as chief ministers under Indian princes, was himself 'positive' towards the states, which were close to his ideals of Ram Rajya, the 'acme of swaraj'.[44] Yet, a few years later they were virtually extinct and nonexistent players in the construction of the Indian republic.[45]

While the nation won Independence from foreign rule, the princely states lost their autonomous identities. Rulers were stripped of their executive rights and their territories merged with the new democratic republic. In 1971, under Prime Minister Indira Gandhi, the erstwhile princes lost their last major entitlement, their constitutionally granted incomes, the 'Privy Purse', which was based on an annual percentage of the revenue from their former kingdoms. With the absorption of the princely states, their systems of administration and land tenure were gradually abolished. Nonetheless, many of these erstwhile sovereigns remained active in the public life of the nation, and several women associated with the zenana emerged from *pardah* and entered the body politic.

The Weltanschauung of the Zenana

Since medieval times, the homes of most Indian rulers, both Hindu and Muslim, had two distinct living spaces: the zenana and the mardana. Men resided in the Mardana and women in the zenana. The zenana was the sequestered female quarters of the palace. Originally a Persian institution, which entered India with

Muslim invasions, it altered local customs as Hindu dynasties emulated the mannerisms of the Muslim court. Although the concept of gender segregated living spaces was ancient to India, finding reference in the Sanskrit epics and the *Kama Sutra* as well as Hindu architecture, such as the Rajput fort of Chittor in Rajasthan, it was not rigidly enforced until the arrival of Islam.[46]

During Emperor Akbar's reign there was a marked move towards the confinement of women and the creation of a harem structure.[47] As he and a number of his descendents married Hindu Rajput princesses, Mughal courtly life and architecture was in turn imitated.[48] Norman Ziegler notes that the Mughal ruler had great influence over Hindu princes for he 'held a position of high rank and esteem, and the traditions often equate him with Ram, the pre-eminent Kshatriya cultural hero of the Hindu Rajput'.[49] The traditions of seclusion also influenced Buddhist and Sikh royal dynasties, which came into contact with Mughal imperial forces, such as the Chakma Raj in the Chittagong Hill Tracts and the Punjab kingdoms.

Just as the princely states were diverse as a group, the zenana itself housed women from several kingdoms, regions and religions, serving as what can be described as a microcosmic 'united nations' within the sphere of the court. This is in marked contrast to the twentieth-century image of the princely states as diffuse and polarized. As the exclusively female quarters in the ruler's palace, each zenana had its own unique history and socio-political identity. It brought together women with different religious, caste, regional, linguistic and clan affiliations, creating a heterogeneous, cosmopolitan world within the already cosmopolitan universe of princely India. Hierarchical and polygamous institutions, Hindu Rajput Zenanas for example, were presided over by predominantly Kshatriya women who were supported by females from Brahmin, Sudra and Vaisya castes as well as Muslims and Jains. During the twentieth century, Christian women also entered the zenana as wives and mistresses of Indian rulers and the courtly aristocracy, and as governesses, nurses and teachers for the children of the household. The zenana was a fluid world of shifting alliances, and, within the span of one reign, unique coalitions of power could emerge. Until the middle of the twentieth century, many royal Indian women still continued to live within the bounds of the palace zenana.[50]

This multi-layered, stratified world inherently blurred the boundaries of the private, sequestered arena of the royal family and the public, political realm of the court within the kingdom. Royal families, by the nature of their histories, lead highly politicized roles. Hence, the 'domestic' or familial sphere, symbolized by the private lives of Zenana women and their children, indirectly or directly influenced the public engagements of the ruler, the affairs of his ministers and the mechanisms of state governance. The 'politics of reproduction',[51] as Leslie Peirce notes in her work on the Ottoman harem, was integral to the underlying dynamics of a royal household, which practised polygamy where there were several sexual partners for the king, including wives, courtesans and women in service capacities. The private rites of women, such as menarche, marriage, courtship, sex and love, pregnancy, mothering and widowhood affected the broader state apparatus of government. When an unmarried princess began to menstruate, it was not purely a private event. It signified the importance of wedding the king's daughter to a ruler of equal or higher rank and the accompanying concerns over spousal selection and the necessary financial expenditure for the ceremony with the requisite pomp and circumstance, which would be deducted from the kingdom's coffers. Certain kingdoms could become bankrupt, if they suffered the marriages of several young royals followed in quick succession.

In addition, a ruler's sexual or personal preference for a particular wife or mistress rearranged the hierarchy of the court around the favoured woman and, in a similar manner, power circulated around the mothers of the future heir and the current Maharaja. The dynamics within the bedroom, the family and the household directly influenced the wider politics of the court. As Ruby Lal notes in her work on the domestic world of the early Mughals, these two spheres invariably overlap: 'everyday activities intersected with historic 'events' in ways which make it difficult to separate the 'private' and the 'public', the 'personal' and the 'political'.[52] Although traditionally perceived as passive and impotent, Zenana women affected the public transfer of power in both the colonial princely state and the modern republic.

The Political Agent in the Palace: The Colonial Zenana

During the colonial period, the British official gradually came into contact with the workings of the zenana, sometimes acting as a third party observer or participant in succession disputes and marriage alliances. Nineteenth- and twentieth-century political officers, such as George Le-Grand Jacob and Kenneth Fitze, whose work will be cited in later chapters, provide eye-witness accounts of such 'intrigues' and 'rivalries' between feuding factions within the polygamous zenana and the wide network of informants women behind *pardah* had to maintain and augment political authority. These succession rivalries became particularly contentious when the young ruler was a minor.

Furthermore, the practice of *pardah* did not prevent Zenana women from engaging in politics. The Begums of Bhopal, in particular, are examples of powerful female rulers, who governed from behind *pardah* during the nineteenth and early twentieth centuries. Over a one hundred year period, four successive women ruled Bhopal state despite numerous threats. They 'were able to distinguish themselves as warriors, scholars, builders, and social reformers' and ensured 'the independence and prestige of their state under British paramountcy'.[53] While it should be noted that the Begums were Muslim heads of state and thus not inherently related to the theme of Hindu Zenanas, their political achievements are expressive of the power of which women were capable of behind seclusion. They also reinterpreted Islamic Koranic law to question the legal precedent for primogeniture.

In addition to appearing unskilled in the tactics of statesmanship, women behind *pardah* were perceived as uneducated and illiterate. On the contrary, a number of Zenana women were important contributors to the arts and letters. Sunity Devi, Maharani of Cooch Behar in the late nineteenth century, was the first Indian woman to write her autobiography in English.[54] In 1911, her contemporary, the Maharani of Baroda, wrote an important treatise on the role of women, focusing on issues of labour, work, politics and family.[55] The late Rajmata of Gwalior's mother was the first Nepalese woman to matriculate to university.[56] They were also influential in educating their children.[57]

The colonial legacy of rule through diplomacy rather than warfare also altered the motivations for marital alliances among the princely families. There are several instances of British government officials who arranged weddings in view of 'westernizing' Indian rulers during the late nineteenth century. In particular, there is the example of the Maharaja of Cooch Behar who married the daughter of the Bengali reformer, Keshub Chandra Sen, a leading member of the Brahmo Samaj, in 1878. The Maharaja's British advisors, Mr Dalton and Mr Kneller, had arranged the meeting between the two families and prospective partners, and it was their approval which sanctioned the union. The marriage is also a striking case of a king who relinquished traditional codes of polygamy in favour of monogamy.

Nripendra Narayan Bhup Bahadur, Maharaja of Cooch Behar, had been a ward of the British Government since his infancy and was carefully being 'educated' as a model ruler.[58] His English tutors wanted the young ruler to attend public school in England, but his mothers and other female relations would not agree to his voyage across 'the black waters' unless he was first married in India.

In search of an 'enlightened', educated Hindu bride who was no longer in *pardah*, the Cooch Behar contingent pursued leading Calcutta figure, Keshub Chandra Sen. Keshub Chandra Sen's reformed view of Hinduism, with its emphasis on a theistic philosophy and the abolition of caste, appealed to an Occidental, Christian sensibility. He was also a staunch advocate of the virtue of monogamy, and would not accede to give his daughter without a written promise from the groom to ascribe to this main tenet of his philosophy and convert to Theism. The adolescent Maharaja of Cooch Behar wrote in 1878 this reply to his future father-in-law:

> My Dear Sir,
>   I have been asked to let you know what my honest opinion is on the subject of polygamy.

In reply, I beg to inform you that it has always been my opinion that no man should take more than one wife, and I can assure you that I hold that opinion still.

I give below a statement of my religious views and opinions. I believe in one God and am in heart a Theist.[59]

The influence of British views on morality and conjugal life is evident in this marriage of state. By marrying this eastern Kshatriya ruler to the Sen daughter, the British Indian government believed it was one step closer to modern progressivism and western enlightenment. Indeed, even members of the British aristocracy and royal family became involved in the politics of 'arranged marriage' for Indian princes, and their ideas of companionate marriage changed the motivations for personal unions. These alliances are expressive of the linking of two parts of India, the autonomous tracks of the princely states with the suzerainty of the British paramount powers. They are also indicative of how disparate and distinct communities and regions of the sub-continent could be joined under the unifying banner of the imperial Raj.

Zenana women also manipulated colonial intervention and resisted regional patriarchies in making and breaking marriage alliances for their children. At the turn of the twentieth century, the widowed Hindu Rajput Ranis of Rajkot and Palitana in peninsular Gujarat successfully leveraged the influence of the paramount power in their favour to fend off the male relations of spurned bridegrooms. They worked with various levels of the Raj bureaucracy, at times culling the support of higher ranked members of the colonial government if their own local British administrators were not supportive of their views, even petitioning the Viceroy. They simultaneously co-opted the language of western conjugality and romance to justify the suitability or inappropriateness of certain marital matches. In such discussions, the British official was often caught in a dilemma whether to support 'modernist' ideals of the European, companionate marriage or uphold customary (often patriarchal) tradition.

In addition to new ideas relating to the appropriate brides for Indian princes, the role of the colonial subject in arranging unions and Zenana women's own manipulation of the language of anglicized love and courtship, Indian royals began marrying European men and women. As early as 1800, a Muslim aristocrat had married an Englishman,[60] and the late nineteenth and early twentieth century saw more than twenty Indian rulers, Hindu, Muslim and Sikh, marrying Caucasian women.[61] The role of race became contentious in the nuptials of Indian princes to women who did not belong to their same religious, class or caste background. White women were particularly problematic as they often defied all four categories, which affected dynastic succession. The British colonial administration did not favour miscegenation at any time, and tried to prevent such weddings with harsh warnings. The Maharajas of Indore, Pudukkottai and Kapurthala, among others, chose love over political prudence. In certain cases, they abdicated their sovereign powers, entered morganatic marriages, altered the line of succession and lived abroad in order to marry such 'impermissible' brides. As Rosalind O'Hanlon notes, sexuality was not merely a private or individual sensibility: 'Sex and gender, public and private, masculine and feminine were linked in the processes through which colonial states could transform sexual identities and the moral realms in which they lived'.[62]

With Independence, marriage alliance-making went through further transformations, with the socialist agenda of the Nehruvian state and later the growing emphasis on business enterprise and commercialism fostering novel translations of the desirable conjugal partner in royal circles. At the same time, Zenana women entered electoral politics and more visibly influenced the new political theatre.

Emerging out of *Pardah*: Zenana Women in Postcolonial Politics

Although the princely states are described as having faded away from the political scene, many erstwhile rulers remain active in modern South Asian politics. The zenana itself evolved with the emerging change in the status of the Indic kingdom. Women who once lived behind *pardah* gradually came into public life and a number embarked upon political careers as elected members of government, such as Vijaya Raje Scindia, Rajmata of Gwalior, and Gayatri Devi, Rajmata of Jaipur. Both born in 1919, they lived in hierarchical, polygamous zenanas behind *pardah*. In the wane of empire, they performed the duties of Maharanis while their husbands were still rulers in the 1940s, and experienced the transfer of power, when the princes were stripped of privileges and rights. In their later years, they became politicians in democratic India, campaigning for election, scoring records in the polls with the number of the votes they garnered, and effecting party policy. Both women experienced the horrors of the 1975 Emergency and were incarcerated in the infamous Tihar jail as members of Indira Gandhi's Congress Opposition. The zenana worldview has been described as often outmoded and anachronistic in the post-Independence period, no longer applicable to contemporary India. The life histories of these women, as only two of many examples, question this view. Representing the Bharatiya Janata Party, the Jan Sangh, Congress, Swatantra and other independent political parties, former Zenana women appear to represent a wide spectrum of political thought and its attendant constituencies.[63]

In pre-Independence India, women of the zenana mainly acquired power through covert and subversive means. Behind *pardah*, there existed a sophisticated system of political intelligence and intrigue, as noted earlier. In contrast, since Independence, the political arena has dramatically altered. Former Zenana women no longer maintain implicit, *pardah* rule, but instead operate through the public display of campaigns, elections and politicized dialogue through the vehicles of film, the media, autobiographies and fiction.

Even after the demise of the princely state, these women and their families continue to hold the symbolic and sometimes the real power of an erstwhile ruler, affecting policy and change in contemporary India. These observations have led to the following questions: what was the worldview of the zenana? How did women during the colonial period augment and finesse power both within traditional patriarchal circles and against a foreign, colonial force? How did female rulers as regents or ruling sovereigns manifest authority? How did private rites such as marriage and childbearing affect matters of 'state' importance such as succession and political alliance? What was the education of Zenana women as natural 'leaders'? In the postcolonial period, how have Zenana women who have entered a political sphere shaped contemporary Indian politics and gender identity? Did the traditions of hierarchy and power dominance played out behind the zenana walls help or hamper these women to be affective politicians and leaders in a democratic system? These are among some of the many questions this book shall pose, which have not been addressed in the existing literature.

Framing the Debate: Critiquing Orientalism and the Hollow Crown Paradigm

A crucial element of this study is the way in which indigenous courtly women were objectified by colonial legal and social systems even while being made into subjects by them. It inherently critiques the project of orientalism and the 'Hollow Crown' paradigm, in examining the relationship between native rulers and the paramount power, which was more nuanced than a simple story of dominance and mimicry, pageantry and parody or silence and objectification. The meeting between the British and the peoples of the empire was that of an encounter, however skewed.[64]

Recent contributions in the fields of literature, psychoanalysis, anthropology, gender and culture, which have been categorized as 'postcolonial' or 'postmodern', have delved more into the experience of colonized people, and have deconstructed the relationship between the Occident and the Orient within a paradigm of hegemonic domination.[65] With the publication of Edward Said's influential *Orientalism*, the western academy has focused predominantly on Europe's rewriting of the East. As Said wrote: 'It is Europe that articulates the Orient; this articulation is the prerogative, not of a puppet master, but of a genuine creator, whose life-giving power represents, animates, constitutes the otherwise silent and dangerous space beyond familiar boundaries'.[66] While this work does not wish to undermine the atrocities and abuses associated with empire, it hopes to suggest that the relationship between imperial nations and those they encountered was more heteroglossic, hybrid, ambiguous and paradoxical.

Certainly, the 'impenetrable' courtyards of the sequestered zenana appeared to be a 'dangerous space' (as was much of princely India) for western observers and colonial officials, in part because they were inaccessible. Popular colonial writings deftly 'orientalized' the Hindu Maharani or the Muslim princess as much as they did their male royal compatriots. This Orientalist interpretation of an indigene robbed of his 'voice' by the colonial 'author' fuels the perception that the Indian prince was emasculated during the colonial encounter. Nicholas Dirks' earlier groundbreaking work on the 'little kingdom' of Pudukkottai in South India, while bringing the Hindu kingdom into central focus within the fields of history and anthropology, has been a leading proponent of the hollow crown theory. He has argued that the colonial Indian kingdom was a 'hollow crown' upon an empty political stage.[67]

Such analyses, while significant in highlighting the neuroses of empire, eclipses the possibility that the colonizer and colonized were engaged in a much more spirited dialogue of mutual exchange and dialogue.[68] Several scholars have questioned this 'hollow crown' model.[69] John McLeod in his work on paramountcy in the princely states of western India observed that the princes were neither puppets nor collaborators with the British. With rulers collecting revenue at pre-colonial rates and no longer needing to upkeep military expenditures, they became 'real kings', far from the Dirksian hypothesis. As he suggests: 'even those who saw the princes as in some way illegitimate holders of power had to recognize that they did indeed possess real power, although its nature was changed from pre-colonial days'.[70] Manu Bhagavan's work on education, modernity and the princely states suggests 'that denizens of princely states had the ability to map nationalist imaginaries within and onto their state and state-supported institutions, to initiate internal improvement and change to envision their own modern realities, and to thereby contest colonialism in ways that were distinct to the particular local context'.[71] More general works such as Ian Copland's *The Princes of India in the Endgame of Empire* and Barbara Ramusack's ambitious volume, *Indian Princes and Their States* brings the subject into mainstream South Asian historiography.[72] These works highlight the relevance of the Indian kingdoms as real, political forces in colonial and postcolonial India.

Thus, the story of the colonial encounter was not one-sided but in certain instances resulted in a dialogue of reciprocal rapport. Similarities of class tied Europeans with non-Europeans rather than differences of race. A prince was seen as a prince, whether he was a Hindu Maharaja or a Hawaiian chief, and was therefore perceived to be a social equal to a European monarch. In this respect, the British royal family, from Victoria to Elizabeth II, mixed comfortably with Indian princes both in Britain and the native states (at least in the setting of the dinner party if not that of the bedroom). In July 1999, when Prince Charles eulogized the recently deceased King Hussein of Jordan, he described his friend as a 'social equal whose high rank dissolved racial differences: "a wonderful combination of the virtues of the Bedouin Arab and, if I may say so, the English Gentleman"'.[73] In certain instances, class thus served as a greater indicator of power than race.[74] According to David Cannadine: 'We should never forget that the British Empire was first and foremost a class act, where individual social order took precedence over collective racial othering'.[75] Indeed, the relationship between Zenana women and British officials reflects this more fluid exchange of cultural attitudes, religious practices and legal provisions during the high noon of empire.

Placing the Zenana in the Context of the Debate on Tradition versus Modernity

Alongside this discourse on the 'hollowing' of royal power, South Asian historiography has focused on the invention of tradition and the challenge of modernity in late colonial India. For British administrators, Orientalist scholars and South Asian nationalists, the debate on tradition 'marked the study of Indian Society and culture'.[76] Indeed, both the Indian prince and the eastern woman were contested sites in this debate, and the Zenana female was therefore doubly the object of colonial and nationalist constructions on what fundamentally represented the 'Indic' spirit.

Several scholars have argued that Indian social tradition was largely a nineteenth-century British colonial invention.[77] Ronald Inden, following in the wake of Said's *Orientalism*, has argued that there were certain 'essentials', which constituted Indian 'tradition'. Divinely construed kingship was one such essence.[78]

Early British officials ranked and graded Indian social hierarchies in an effort to understand them.[79] The work of colonial historians and political administrators such as James Mill or Edmund Burke attempted to get at the heart of what defined Indian tradition. James Tod's *Annals and Antiquities of Rajasth'an* came to be read as one such foundational history for Hindu kingship and Rajput 'feudalism'. James Tod (1782–1835) was the first political agent for the western Rajput states in 1818, having earlier served as the British Resident at the court of Daulat Rao Sindhia of Gwalior from 1805.[80] During his time in Rajasthan, he was deeply moved by the mythic history and fiery courage of the Rajput aristocracy and royalty. A keen ethnographer, he wrote a compendious multivolume work on the histories of the Rajput dynasties based on his travels, which provided detailed clan histories and lineage charts, arguing that the Rajputs were descended from Sanskritic heroes and Hindu gods. For him, the Rajputs reflected the 'essence' of the Hindu political state.[81] He believed them superior to the European feudal families in their expression of chivalric virtue and as emblematic of a dying heraldic age. He wrote in the *Annals*:

> If we compare the antiquity and illustrious descent of the dynasties, which have ruled, and some, which continue to rule, the small sovereignties of Rajast'han with many of celebrity in Europe, superiority will often attach to the Rajpoot. From the most remote period we can trace nothing ignoble nor any vestige of vassal origin. Reduced in power, circumscribed in territory, compelled to yield much of their splendour and many of the dignities of birth, they have not abandoned an iota of the pride and high bearing arising from a knowledge of their illustrious and regal descent.[82]

As Varsha Joshi suggests, Tod's main objective was 'to introduce Rajputs to western readers and to portray them in a romantic, adventurous and at the same time often cruel light ... [which] reflected nineteenth-century notions of medieval feudalism and chivalry'.[83] Inden corroborates this view: 'Tod depicted the Rajput 'system' as an early, pristine form of governance, the essence of which was princely feuding, thick-skinned and hot-headed'.[84]

These critiques of Tod perpetuate the very relationship between the colonizers and colonized which orientalism exposed and attempted to deconstruct, by keeping India 'eternally ancient and passive'.[85] If the colonial subject was responsible for the construction of the Indic Other, in such methods as the 'historicizing' and ranking of indigenous rulers in Tod, the arrangement of vice-regal durbars or the gifting of orders of merit, then ultimately the colonized, even those of an elite group such as the Indian rulers, were silenced actors in a colonial political drama.[86]

Such an interpretation of Tod, as reflecting the essence of Hindu kingship and rendering it vulnerable to the colonial Self, is incomplete. It remains 'blind' to how the colonized borrowed categories from the Indological discourse for their own purposes. Tod highlights a multiplicity of distinctions between varying local indigenous groups not any one 'essence' of traditional kingship.[87] As David Washbrook expands, the colonial translation of such 'traditional' components did not 'simply invent them: if they were products of the 'imagination', it was of an imagination shared between colonizers and certain groups, at least, among the colonized'.[88] Not only was the relationship between the paramount power and the indigenous prince far more complicated than a simple oppositional paradigm, but so were the relationships between varying colonial subjects themselves.

By virtue of being female, Zenana women were doubly the objects of this investigation into tradition, both as women and as princely members representing the 'essence' of indigenous leadership. In an environment where tradition and modernity are both carriers of patriarchy and thus artificial constructs of colonialism,[89] women became 'emblematic of tradition'.[90] In her insightful critique of colonial and indigenous patriarchal readings of *sati*, or widow immolation, in nineteenth-century Bengal, Lata Mani articulates that the identity of the Indian woman is lost in a larger debate on tradition, where tradition becomes equated with scripture.[91] Both colonial administrators and indigenous male elites advocated the prohibition of *sati* by privileging scriptural evidence over customary practice.[92] Either as victims or pathetic heroines, Mani suggests, Indian women become emblematic of tradition for both the colonialists and the emergent nationalists. But women themselves were lost in the debate; they had no voice in a discourse, which was about them but did not include them.[93]

The subaltern critique on gender studies has furthered this distinction between discussions about women and their own ability to participate in such debates. Gayatri Spivak in 'Can the Subaltern Speak?' proposes that the woman literally 'disappears' and is written out of the text or the lived historical experience. She challenges that 'between patriarchy and imperialism, subject-constitution and object-formation, the figure of the woman disappears, not into a pristine nothingness, but into a violent shuttling which is the displaced figuration of the 'third-world woman' caught between tradition and modernity'.[94] Partha Chatterjee extends Lata Mani's conclusions in his discussion on women in the Indian nationalist movement. He argues that Indian nationalists in an attempt to reject westernized values created separate spheres, which preserved an Indic nature as distinct from the European self. He conceptualizes this paradigm in the symbolism of inner/outer, *ghar* and *bahir,* or the world and home. The outer arena is material, rationalist and ultimately masculine; in contrast, the inner world of the home embodies the feminine spiritual integrity of the nation.[95] Nationalists, such as Mahatma Gandhi, saw Indian women's qualities of self-sacrifice thus as expressive of the nation's spirit itself, which was neither 'weak' nor 'effeminate'.[96] As the mother of Indian men who will people the nation and as the living manifestation of religious observation, the woman is a foundational figure in the nationalist cause. Thus the preservation of the 'traditional' woman corresponds to the protection of Indian values from the impurities of the West, and reflects indigenous men's moral superiority over European imperialists.[97] While Chatterjee's arguments are important, they are problematic as they define the political and private in a model of masculine and feminine spheres, which do not overlap. In his critique, the woman still lives within the feminized realm of the family, which is divorced from the outer space of state governance, *realpolitik* strategy, and engagement with the colonial power or resistance to local patriarchies. Spivak's reading is highly sophisticated in placing the woman squarely at the heart of the tradition versus modernity debate, but it fails to acknowledge that women did speak as active agents. As Durba Ghosh notes in her work on native women in colonial India, Spivak suggests that the absence of female subaltern subjectivity in the colonial records poses 'insurmountable obstacles' to writing subaltern histories, but provides no insights into how these kinds of archival shortcomings can be overcome or how the exclusion of women's names could be 'historically informative about native women's encounters with various parts of the colonial enterprise'.[98] In many ways, these theories keep the woman in 'shadows' even by noting that she is in the shadows. Rather, the literature on the zenana reveals that women did speak and are still speaking.[99]

Indeed, the private sphere of the family was very much part of the outer political realm of the Indian kingdom, sometimes obliquely, other times explicitly. Tanika Sarkar in her work on Hindu women and nationalism suggests that nineteenth-century Bengali household management mirrored external politics; just as a king ruled a dominion, so did a woman her household.

> Management of household relations becomes a political and administrative capability, providing training in governance that one no longer attains in the political sphere. The intention is to establish a claim to a share of power in the world, a political role that the Hindu is entitled to, through successful governance in the household. A possibly unintended consequence, however, is that, in the process it also renders household relations into political ones.[100]

Royal women in particular lead innately politicized lives and actions within the 'household' are not merely ones of an internal, 'spiritual integrity' but affect an external system of governance.

In part the problems associated with this historiography on the colonial invention of Indic tradition rests on the kind of sources available to South Asian historians or the ways in which scholars use these sources.[101] Much of this history is situated in British India, particularly Bengal, and does not reference the princely states, several of which until Independence maintained internally autonomous governing structures and resisted colonial paramountcy both by upholding their treaties of non-intervention with the British and by subverting them. In addition, there are problems with the mode of literary analysis being used. As Peabody and Mani argue, the misreading of so-called fundamental or 'essential' texts leads to incomplete conclusions. Following along the lines of Durba Ghosh's innovative and important work on sexuality, domesticity and race in early colonial India, this book reinstates the voices of indigenous women 'to inhabit their own histories' and thus 'break down and resist, rather than reinstate, some of the gender, class, race hierarchies that constituted the structures of colonial societies'.[102]

At the same time, the colonial project of essentializing Indian tradition went hand in hand with a modernizing agenda. The two concepts were not mutually exclusive.[103] Several scholars have argued that the 'modern' was expressed in relationship with 'tradition' not as its fundamental opposite but as a constitutive element of being modern. Saurabh Dube critiques the essentializing aspects of these constructed oppositions between East and West, Modernity and Tradition. As he suggests:

The implications of these binaries and the seductions of this blueprint have constituted the undersaid and the under-thought of academic disciplines, a part of reigning
metageographies. They inculcate dispositions toward mapping modern peoples and
places in history and charting traditional communities and customs out of time. They
cultivate inclinations toward plotting native peoples in their passage to progress, the
grand transition from enchantment to disenchantment, from tradition to modernity.
They generate sensibilities toward rendering 'authentic' communities as changeless
and entranced, already before history and always beyond the modern.[104]

As Dipesh Chakrabarty has argued the past is an integral element in understanding South Asian modernity.[105] He notes in *Provincializing Europe* that Bengali
nationalist thought on colonial domesticity and women's education combined
elements of the public and the private, domestic and national, modern and
traditional. The *grihalakshmi*, the ideal prototype for the nineteenth-century
Bengali woman, was meant to adopt European virtues of household cleanliness,
health and hygiene, post-industrialist conceptions of time and Victorian ideals for women's education while at the same time maintaining the family unit
and traditions of the *kula* or clan. Advocacy of western education for Bengali
women was premised on this idea of balance. These women would have enough
European-stylized learning so as to be 'pleasant' and diminutive in speech with
their in-laws but not so much that they might defy the traditional (patriarchal)
authority of the *kul* through outspokenness, selfishness or laziness. Thus western
education reconstructed the Bengali woman as cultivated and pleasant, unlike
her uncouth, uneducated compatriots, but at the same time situated her within
the boundaries of traditional feminine modesty and domestic roles, unlike her
feminist western counterparts.[106]

In his examination of the middle class in colonial Lucknow, Sanjay Joshi
extends this argument, revealing 'multiple, often contradictory, pressures' in
which 'traditional' ideas played a role in the construction of 'modern' ideas about
religion, community, gender relations, and the nation'.[107] For instance, Joshi
notes that middle class men's ambitions to 'improve' women through 'modern'
ideas about female education and emancipation emerged alongside initiatives
to reiterate older patriarchal norms, notably the idea of the woman as *patrivrata*
who lives to serve her husband.[108] Such narratives on colonial constructions of
womanhood drew upon both the vocabulary of western liberalism and indigenous patriarchal traditions.[109] While bringing together the traditional and the
modern, and the Indian and the European, colonial middle class interventions
'created a modernity where both Manu as well as Mill and Macaulay could be
points of reference'.[110]

Thus British paramountcy not only incorporated aspects of tradition, such as
the Indian feudal system lauded by Tod into its policy of 'indirect rule', but also
advocated British forms of progress and modernity to transform native socie-

ties, just as traditional societies incorporated western practices while preserving other constitutive elements of the 'traditional'. The British sought to 'maintain India as a feudal order' while simultaneously 'looking towards changes which would inevitably lead to the destruction of this feudal order'.[111] They needed Indian aristocracies to legitimate crown rule in India. At the same time, they endorsed modernizing tendencies, which would provide a new kind of 'civic or public order'.[112] Towards this aim, British administrators encouraged princes to adopt progressive measures in the administration of their states. These projects for 'good government' included the building of public health facilities based on western medicine, instituting legal reform for women, particularly in regards to *sati*, widow remarriage and the marital age of consent, constructing railways, telegraphs and ports, opening European styled schools and universities, and laying the foundation for representative assemblies.[113]

However, the British were not always pleased by the outcomes of such hybrid modernizing trends. In certain cases, princes who were educated in English styled public schools sympathized more with western mores than their own. They subverted the hierarchy of difference between East and West, Other and Subject, by marrying white women or adopting more anglicized attitudes to dress, behaviour, language or alcohol consumption than the British themselves.[114] The Indian prince, who neglected ruling his own kingdom to sunbathe on the beaches of the French Riviera or socialize with Hollywood glitterati, became the bane of existence for many a British political officer and native state minister, let alone the women of the courtly household. Such native princes crossed the racial and ethnic divide of superiority/inferiority, believing themselves Englishmen in mind and thus equal to the colonial ruler himself politically and socially. Simultaneously, he was, by virtue of rank, a monarch outside the bureaucratic policies or legal systems of British India and thus above and beyond it.[115]

The paramount power was similarly contradictory in its position towards 'modernizing' Zenana ladies. The British endorsed 'traditional' practices in regards to marriage alliance and succession law, but introduced western ideals of conjugality and education. In the same instance that they tried to prevent European women from marrying Indian princes, they encouraged indigenous rulers to marry anglicized high caste and class Indian women. Like the Mughals, British administrators upheld 'traditional' primogeniture in relation to religion, yet the Anglo-Indian legal system, which gave equal rights to women in the courts, created the basis by which Zenana women questioned legal precedence. They critiqued *pardah* as a custom, which rendered Zenana females docile and subjugated in their eyes, yet they simultaneously were scandalized by those palace ladies who broke with the veil. They encouraged widowed Ranis to serve as regents during the minority administrations of their sons, and yet distrusted the influences of the zenana on the upbringing of young princes.

Thus, as both prince and woman, the courtly Indian female was seen as an outmoded and anachronistic member of an 'antique', political structure at odds with the modernizing tendencies of colonialists and nationalists. Nonetheless she retained political importance for both groups: as repositories of 'tradition' for the British, and as the inner space of the 'indigenous' for the nationalists. These descriptive evaluations, however, still based the discussion of the zenana upon masculine discourses, whether colonial or Indian. The voices of Zenana women themselves are full of even greater paradoxes, which do not fit into neat classifications.

The Use of Sources

As the fields of women's history, gender studies and feminist historiography are growing so are the sources available to historians. Non-literary materials which were earlier deemed questionable for scholarly investigation, such as oral histories, interviews and song lyrics, are becoming more accessible, particularly to academics and lay historians studying groups, like women, who were previously marginalized from broader debates. Disciplines including social anthropology, literary criticism, psychoanalysis and history have challenged the emphasis once placed on 'high culture', print forms, articulated by dominant, empowered elites.[116] In addition, literary sources which have ordinarily remained exclusively within the domestic sphere, such as women's memoirs, diaries, letters, poetry and fiction, are being incorporated into socio-political histories. As Antoinette Burton points out in *Dwelling in the Archive*:

> What counts as an archive? Can private memories of home serve as evidence of political history? What do we make of the histories that domestic interiors, once concrete and now perhaps crumbling or even disappeared, have the capacity to yield? And, given women's vexed relationship to the kinds of history that archives typically house, what does it mean to say that home can and should be seen not simply as a dwelling-place for women's memory but as one of the foundations of history -history conceived of, that is, as a narrative, a practice, and a site of desire?[117]

In trying to bring the lives of Zenana women into a discourse on history, this project mines the archive as much as it can by utilizing a wide variety of sources. For colonial material, it references inventories and histories of British India and the princely states. In particular, it draws on the work of eighteenth-, nineteenth- and twentieth-century writers, who served in some capacity within the princely states as British officials. In addition, the Political Department Records of the Residents' Reports from the Princely States have revealed an ocean of material including oral evidence from law trials in the Bombay courts, letters between Hindu Ranis and British officials regarding the making and breaking of marriage alliances in western Indian kingdoms, and expenditure lists for various public duties, including the annual allowances for royal women, the costs for betrothals, marriages and coronations and the state funds required for the education of minor princes. These records are particularly useful for accessing private events, customs and ceremonies during the colonial period, which often go unrecorded. It must be kept in mind, however, that the political residents' reports were official correspondence and are thereby invariably coloured by the political motivations, cultural prejudices and social objectives of the imperial protocol established at Delhi or Calcutta. As much as is possible, this book cites the original letters, speeches or depositions of courtly women and Indian princes found within the residents' reports to allow their voices to be heard directly.

For twentieth-century materials, the study incorporates anthropological accounts, biographies, autobiographies, oral histories, journalistic interviews, letters, diaries, exercise notebooks and educational records. Oral histories, in particular, dramatically bring to life the hierarchy, customs and day-to-day life-style of women in zenana structures. It seeks to address questions about royal women's lives, which have been missing from an academic discourse, especially their private marital and sexual experiences. While such histories are limiting in their time frame and highly subjective, they are nonetheless helpful for chart-ing the changes that evolved in the twentieth-century zenana. As Bernard Cohn notes in *An Anthropologist among the Historians and Other Essays,* 'history can become more historical in becoming more anthropological', particularly in regards to modern South Asian studies.[118]

Biographies and autobiographies are equally important. This study princi-pally incorporates the memoirs and biographies of Zenana women from the late nineteenth and twentieth centuries, such as the Maharanis of Jaipur, Gwalior, Cooch Behar and Baroda. These are illuminating works, providing rare descrip-tions of experiences, familial, political and private, of women who have lived in *pardah* through their own eyes. Interestingly, a number of these women who wrote autobiographies were also interrelated through marriage or birth, and thus shed light on a whole generation of women across India.

It is worth mentioning, too, both the advantages and limitations of personal historical narratives as source material. Mary Chamberlain and Paul Thompson provide an useful analysis of oral history and memoir in their introduction to *Narrative and Genre.* With the advent of a move from deconstruction to post-modernism, advocated by a small but influential group of radicals in the 1980s, the autobiography became interpreted as a purely literary and subjective genre, 'in which there was no longer a biographical self capable of reflection, or a biographical reality upon which to reflect. Hence reflection itself was merely ideology; and autobiography totally fictional'.[119]

This observation highlights the autobiography's nebulous place between fact and fiction. As Chamberlain and Thompson question, 'How far should it be read as a narrative of real experience, and how far as a form of fiction?[120] This is one of the principal problems an historian faces when dealing with the memoir as a source. As any source, the memoir is neither infallible nor objective, and a scholar must be aware of the subjectivity of these personal histories. On the other hand, nearly every life is heightened by colourful anecdotes. Who can legitimately be the writer of a categorical truth? If the memoirist cannot tell her tale without some embellishment, no one can. We must merely keep this in mind as historians. The autobiographies cited in this work focus on the personal relationship between the female author and her audience. They simultaneously strive to tell stories, which are private, of families, romances, marriages and mothering, and highly public, the roles of queens in courtly affairs, the agendas of elected politicians and the doctrines of political parties.

This rich array of diverse sources in dialogue with each other begins the process of unearthing the lives of courtly women at the height of empire. There are many stories, which, due to the limitations of this book, cannot be fully told here. It is the hope that this work will be the catalyst for yet more histories of this understudied area.

Filling a Scholarly Lacuna

While an interest in princely India has been growing, there are few histories of the zenana. Pamela Price's research exposes the role of royal Hindu women in litigation trials over succession and property disputes, but does not establish its larger implications for the nature of female royal charisma in colonial South India.[121] Varsha Joshi's *Polygamy and Pardah* provides rich material on Hindu Rajput women, but is focused predominantly on medieval and early colonial Rajasthan.[122] Lindsay Harlan's ethnography on *Religion and Rajput Women* provides a window into the role of Hindu ritual and devotional practice for contemporary Rajput women, but she does not place her work within specific historical paradigms, state formations or political processes.[123] There have been revealing histories of Muslim royal dynasties, such as the work of Ruby Lal and Siobhan Lambert-Hurley, which focus on the Mughal harem and the Begums of Bhopal respectively, but they do not address more broadly the role of courtly Indian women in the period under investigation.[124] In addition, this work builds upon the recent contributions of historians in complicating the narrative on interracial relationships between indigenous men and women and Britons in early colonial India, such as Durba Ghosh. But unlike Ghosh's work, this book focuses predominantly on late colonial indigenous women who did not enter colonial households as companions to Englishmen.[125] As Barbara Ramusack admits: 'the agency of elite and non-elite women in princely states during the colonial era begs for further analysis.'[126]

Courtly Indian women are more likely to be found in the pages of popular histories than their academic cousins. A slew of recent historical biographies, which read with the ease of investigative journalism, have focused on the romantic lives of princely women, Hindu and Muslim, Indian and European.[127] In addition, a number of Zenana women have written memoirs, educational tracts and fictional works.[128] However, neither these biographies nor autobiographies have critically examined the political worldview of women in the zenana, as mentioned earlier.

Royal Indian women have also found themselves in the plotlines of historical fiction and the films they have engendered. While several of these novelistic renditions have been based upon oral histories of living descendents of the zenana, they do not analyse the time in which these women lived nor the concerns they faced.[129] Others have been adapted into films to critical and popular acclaim, by portraying the lives of English women and men who married Indian royals, but they have often played into the orientalist misconstruction.[130] Films such as Ivory/ Merchant's *Hullabaloo in Pictures* and Shyam Benegal's musical *Zubeida*, both about the current Jodhpur royal family, have perpetuated the image of the zenana in the popular imagination. In many ways, the 'imagined communities' of princely women have survived more in the realm of fiction than history. Indeed, history has shut out the courtly Indian woman even as she appeared to be shut in by seclusion. This work aims to begin the project of addressing this lacuna. It argues that charting the transition of the zenana during the late nineteenth and twentieth centuries serves as a vibrant kaleidoscope into observing systems of regional power, as *pardah* women subverted not only male hierarchies within their kingdoms but also resisted the panopticon-like surveillance of the external, European occupier, and later played a part in postcolonial politics in South Asia.

Schemata

This book is arranged into six chapters. Chapter 1 explores the complexities of zenana politics in the late colonial state, *c.* 1890–1947, by focusing on issues of male succession, women serving as regents, rivalry within a polygamous institution, and the colonial encounter with the sequestered female ruler. Questioning orientalist and patriarchal readings of the zenana, it argues that royal Indian women resisted both colonial and indigenous male hierarchies, by leveraging political, social and sometimes military power as well as legal intelligence in their favour. It elaborates upon the history of the princely states, the internal hierarchy of the zenana and colonial and indigenous accounts of the interactions between Zenana women and British officials.

Chapter 2 focuses on the role of women in disputed dynastic successions, by examining closely Kenneth Fitze's *A Review of Modern Practice in Regard to Successions in Indian States* from 1947. It investigates examples from Hindu Rajput, Buddhist, Muslim and Sikh kingdoms, as well as eastern Kshatriya and Maratha states. These histories reveal how women, either as arbiters of disputes or as mothers of future heirs, controlled and affected dynastic successions within Indian princely states. They often manipulated the intervention of British administrators and Anglo-Indian law to push for succession outcomes that favoured them, while simultaneously displacing indigenous male members of the courtly family.

Chapter 3 addresses the politics of marriage alliance for Zenana women in the late colonial state and during the twentieth century. Under the umbrella of the Pax Britannica, the motivations for royal alliances changed, and unions between ruling dynasties, which ordinarily did not intermarry, became more prevalent. Love marriages such as that of Indira Devi of Baroda began to appear; British colonial administrators and members of the English royal family including Queen Victoria became involved in affiancing Indian rulers, serving as intermediaries; and western women arrived in India as royal brides. In addition, this chapter discusses the ramifications of the revolutionizing 1956 Hindu Marriage Act, which prohibited polygamy, and engendered more 'deviant', less traditional, 'love' matches and its implications for dynastic marriage in nationalist, postcolonial India.

Chapter 4 turns to the disputed marriages of the Hindu Rajput princesses of Rajkot and Palitana in peninsular Gujarat, *c.* 1901 and 1908, respectively. It analyses the ways in which Ranis co-opted the language of western romance and companionate marriage and used Anglo-Indian law to break off unwanted marriage alliances for their daughters. In the process, they contested both British intervention into Zenana courtly affairs and curtailed the influence of local male scions. It is a vital lens into how Zenana women worked across different levels of the colonial bureaucracy, often pitting local officials against their superiors in Delhi or London.

Chapter 5 develops further issues of sovereignty, law and sexual politics through an examination of two rulers from the central Indian kingdom of Indore. Spanning the reigns of Tukoji Rao Holkar and his son Yeshwant Rao Holkar, from the 1920s to the 1940s, it examines how the personal choice of women, as mistresses and royal brides, affected the political status of Indian princes, in one instance leading to the ruler's abdication and in another compelling the Maharaja to rewrite succession law by instituting a female heir. It will argue that the 'wrong woman', as defined by traditional circles or the British, affected a ruler's ability to remain sovereign.

The sixth and concluding chapter investigates broadly the politics of Zenana women in postcolonial India. In particular, it analyses the lives of two former Maharanis who have subsequently become elected democratic politicians, Vijaya Raje Scindia and Gayatri Devi. This chapter addresses issues of the political family, female agency through widowhood and the development of the Rajvanshi, or princely politician, in post-Independence India. In certain cases, Zenana women had greater authority as members of elected government than previously, particularly when their elected constituencies were larger than the territory of their erstwhile states.

The Epilogue links the 'Zenana mentality' to contemporary twenty-first-century South Asian politics and highlights its currency and relevance to this day. In addition, it discusses the appropriateness of the construction of a 'colonial confusion' in critiquing how British officials perceived the roles and identities of courtly Indian men and women at the high noon of the Raj.

1 PALACE POLITICS: ZENANA LIFE IN THE LATE COLONIAL PRINCELY STATE, *c.* 1890–1947

> It is not unusual to consider Eastern women as a down-trodden, poor-spirited race, and yet cases are numerous in which they have been the actual rulers, whilst fathers, husbands, and sons were of small account.[1]

So Major General Sir George Le Grand Jacob, an aide to the Resident in Kathiawar during the 1830s, vividly described *pardah* queens in a memoir of his years spent in western India. In this account, Zenana women appear far from the docile, orientalized figures they have been portrayed in the European and Indian travelogues and novels of the period. This chapter elaborates upon the fraught relationships between British political officers, like Le Grand Jacob, and royal and aristocratic Indian women in colonial princely states, from 1890 to 1947.

As way of introduction, it first investigates the political climate of late nineteenth- and early twentieth-century India, and then delineates the role of the British Raj and its representatives in the affairs of the princely states, particularly the nature of 'indirect rule' through the Residency system. In addition, it examines the internal hierarchy of the female court and the negotiations between British political officers and the *pardah* women they came in contact with. It then critiques how princely women controlled and acquired power as influential regents and players in succession disputes.

Examining the colonial encounter with the sequestered female ruler sheds greater light upon the contentious relationship between European imperialism and indigenous royal leadership. The meeting between the Indian sovereign and British political officer was one of constant dialogue and tension. Indian princes and courtly women resisted, coerced, avoided, fought and even co-opted British officials into their own courtly agendas, and, in certain cases, manipulated different levels of the imperial bureaucracy. Relying upon the archival writings of Political Agents in the princely states, the work of British historians and indigenous histories, these records reveal the significant and real authority of Zenana women in late imperial politics.

As referenced in the introductory chapter, the zenana has often been portrayed as a world governed by impassioned rivalries, dangerous, wild exercises in power and romanticized love unions focused on sating the needs of the eastern male despot. The writings of European travellers in India have produced an exoticized portrait of the women's courtly world. Ann Morrow paints the Zenana as a sexual haven, where women lived in harmonious solidarity and enjoyed the simple pleasures of sisterhood within a polygamous institution:

> The zenana was like a convent dedicated to sex. There was a relationship between the wives, like sisters. The modern equivalent is the Mormon religion. There was a childlike gaiety, the laughter of women together. In the exaggerated sexuality of a purdah culture, it was also a shared cocoon against the outside world and emotional vulnerability.[2]

Ania Loomba elaborates upon this metaphor of the princess in Orientalist studies. She suggests that the sequestered Maharani as 'the veiled Asian woman' becomes 'a recurrent colonial fantasy, as does the recurrent figure of the Eastern Queen, whose wealth testifies to the riches of 'the Orient' and whose gender renders those riches vulnerable to the European self'.[3] Rana Kabbani recounts the thirsty curiosity of Europeans who peered over the palace walls to watch the sheltered, private world of the seraglio and the sexual practices of the Turkish sultan with his queens.[4] These travelogues by western voyeurs confirmed the fact that 'Easterners were fanatical, violent and lusty souls'.[5] Such essentialist depictions of the Eastern royal woman kept her in shadows as the mere screen of the occidental imagination; the tableau upon which desires and dreams were presented and played out.

In such depictions, courtly Eastern women are seen as 'obstinate old dowagers or intriguing regents who have somehow to be got rid of for their feminine incompetence or sexual misdemeanours'.[6] As Reina Lewis writes of the colonial Ottoman harem, western observers described it as a polygamous space dominated by tyranny, excess and perversion. Tyranny was defined by the unequal relationships between the eastern 'despot' and women, eunuchs and women, mistresses and slaves. Excess expressed itself in the large numbers of women within the harem, the luxury of the interior space and the sexual passions of the eastern ruler; and perversion manifested itself through the 'barbarity' of polygamy and the 'sapphism' of women locked up without access to the pleasures of 'real' men.[7] In the Indian context, a similar gloss was placed upon women of the zenana.[8] In contrast to this image, several women rulers not only manipulated political alliances within the male court of the indigenous ruler, but also artfully counteracted the authority of the British Crown representatives for their own ends, which at times garnered grudging and, in rare cases, the enthusiastic admiration of British political officers.

Described as cunning and crafty by some colonial observers, the adroit tactics of courtly Indian women can be categorized as politically astute, skilled in *realpolitik* strategy and far more worldly wise than the nature and the architecture of the zenana might presuppose. As historian Joan Scott has noted, history has often excluded women from political discourse: 'why (and since when) have women been invisible as historical subjects, when we know they have participated in the small and great events of human history?'[9] This chapter argues that zenana women, both from behind *pardah* and by challenging it, were able to augment power within the inner sanctum of the female court, the larger male arena of the kingdom and further out into the wider boundaries of the princely state and beyond.

Royal and aristocratic Indian women were successful in creating political networks with key partners, such as financiers, military entrepreneurs, and centres of religious power and patronage. In the pre-colonial period, Maratha women had served as diplomatic emissaries for their husbands, travelling to receive titles from Mughal Emperors or arranging conciliations between rival, warring Maratha kingdoms. Some, such as Tarabai Bhosle, Ahilyabai Holkar and Tulsibai Holkar, were well known for long periods of stable rule as regents and widows.[10] Others took to the battlefield, whether to fight neighbouring kingdoms, Mughals or the British. The Maratha Rani of Jhansi confronted the British during the Mutiny, and was seen as performing the duty of her dead husband by taking on the role of a man.[11]

Courtly women, as mothers, wives and powerbrokers, were effective wielders of influence through access to the minor princes by securing official appointments, ousting rivals and bequeathing expensive gifts or bribes.[12] As Rosalind O'Hanlon notes, 'Whatever formal seclusion there was in the *zenana*, then, it did not cut women like these off from politics, but rather the opposite. The half-humourous references of nineteenth century observers … to 'domination behind the curtain' may actually have reflected what was once a serious historical reality'.[13] This book goes a step further to argue that the political manoeuvring behind *pardah* was not merely a late pre-colonial phenomenon, but continued under the Pax Britannica. In some cases, courtly Indian women had more access to regnant powers with the advent of British imperial rule than in the past.

Regency and succession were the primary political processes that courtly women were involved in. Scions of the princely family were in a continual dance of competition and rivalry. Being a polygamous institution, the zenana was governed by personality politics with ranked women promoting the interests of their own sons and courtly factions over those of other females and members of the royal family.

> They sought to achieve dominance in succession disputes, to establish a superior posi-
> tion vis-à-vis their kinspeople, and to gain needed support in military confrontations
> with other regional states. Succession disputes occurred before, during and after the
> entrance of the British into India. Multiple wives and concubines and the lack of
> any firm commitment to primogeniture among both Hindu and Muslim rulers could
> precipitate a contest among sons, each allied with mothers, male relatives, and ambi-
> tious job-seekers. Despite or perhaps because of assorted sexual relationships, some
> rulers and dynasties repeatedly lacked direct male heirs. In those cases the struggle
> would be among illiterate or adopted heirs and cadet branches of the ruling family.[14]

Polygamy engendered a tiered hierarchy within the zenana. Mothers of the ruler, his co-wives, the entourage they brought with them from their natal homes, the hosts of concubines and the many *davris*, women in service capacities, all con-tributed to this complexity. While royal women left their father's homes, they ferociously protected and advocated the traditions of their own families, clans or *kuls* in the married homes. In certain cases, they laboured more for its prestige than their husband's family and clan.[15]

While primogeniture was the convention in many dynastic homes, it was not always stringently enforced as the ruler sometimes appointed a younger son or daughter as successor and at other times the nobility interfered to appoint their own candidate as heir. Ranis occasioned the most common type of interven-tion against primogeniture when advancing the claims of their sons, particularly younger ones. Each queen's self interest lay in her child becoming king. As mother of the heir, the *Rajmata* would be at the apex of the zenana social order.[16]

In part due to the nature of these 'assorted sexual relationships', some dynas-ties did not have direct male heirs repeatedly which led to difficulties deciding the successor.[17] In the pre-colonial period, the Mughal emperor often adjudi-cated such disputes.[18] During the colonial period, intervention in succession politics was one of the main reasons for British indirect rule in the 'native states' of India. From the beginning, the paramount power vacillated over the meaning of its relationship with the Indian kingdoms and, in particular, the women of the royal courts.

Courtly, secluded women were skilled in fighting succession claims and ruling in the place of male members of the dynastic family. They were also persuasive, forceful and intractable in resisting the British Raj, at times using military might and knowledge of Anglo-Indian law to promote their own interests. Women who served as regent mothers in princely states during the late colonial period had a particularly complex relationship with the British Indian government. Even though they were perceived as sexually voracious and politically inept, they often frustrated and eluded the censure of colonial administrators.

Observing the zenana not only serves as an important exercise into the illu-mination of female sovereignty in South Asia, but also as a particularly nuanced locus for the colonial encounter. As Norbert Peabody has argued,

> native agenda and actions (which hitherto have been ignored as inconsequential to colonial history) thereby find greater importance, and 'the colonial' becomes somewhat less European and more fully the product of an encounter (however asym-metrical) between European and non-European societies.[19]

Ann McClintock in her work on race, gender and colonialism makes similar assertions. She suggests that imperialism is shaped both by the colonizer as well as the colonized, the 'metropolitan policy' and the 'conflicts within colonial administrations'.[20]

Manu Bhagavan in his recent work on education and the Indian princes sug-gests that the princely states, by the nature of their geography, local histories and politics, remained both within the public and private spheres, straddling the arenas of 'native' India and the Eurocentric modernity of British India. He articulates that this indigenous spirit ultimately served as a conduit for intermix-ing both western and Indic models into a particularly fascinating amalgamation. He writes:

> The princely states, by definition, were simultaneously both public and private realms, the latter vis-à-vis the states' 'native' space within India. The reified private sphere of such states generated a 'pure national' space untouched by colonialism that allowed for the articulation of the public, state and civil society as *native*, the possession and conversion of a variety of 'Western' ideas into 'Indian' ones.[21]

Women within *pardah* crossed an additional boundary between the public and private landscapes. Not only were zenana females by virtue of being princes, step-ping in and out of the private enclave of the native states and British India, but as women they were also entering and exiting the private sphere of home. The physical space of the zenana and the iconic depiction of the Indian female as connected with family and home have often relegated courtly Indian women to an exclusively domestic role as mothers or sexual deviants, as lovers or wives, in relationship to male rulers. This study argues that the involvement of Zenana women in matters of private 'events', such as marriages, pregnancies and love trysts, is vitally connected to issues relevant within the public sphere of state governance, in particular the legalities and regulations of succession practice.

Palace politics in the zenana during the late nineteenth and twentieth cen-turies reveals a multifaceted dynamic between the paramount power and its non-European subjects. The line of control was not unilateral and unidirec-tional, from the foreign imperialist to the secluded female queen, but also from the interior of the zenana walls out to the Residency and beyond.

Princely India and the Paramount Power

The interaction between princely India and the British paramount power has been described as a policy of 'indirect rule'. Indirect rule was an administrative solution for Europeans as it reduced the civil and military expenditures and manpower required to govern large tracts of the subcontinent, which were more easily controlled by incorporating the services of indigenous rulers. In certain locations, local rulers even paid the salaries and expenses of the Europeans involved in indirect rule.[22]

The number of Britons in India was always rather small. For India as a whole, including both British India and the princely states, there was only one British official in the Indian Civil Service for every one quarter million Indians.[23] As an entity, the Indian Civil Service was a cadre of one thousand officers at a time when there were three hundred million Indians.[24] As British taxpayers refused to fund either the military or civilian branches of the Raj, there was not enough financial capital to import large numbers of British personnel to India. This was one of the primary reasons that India never became a colony of white settlement and why indirect rule appeared an efficient policy. By 1921, the total European population in India was just under 157,000, of which 45,000 were women. By 1929, the number of British in the Indian Civil Service, the top level of civil government, was only 894.[25]

Indirect rule was possible in part due to the indigenous systems of governance provided by the princes. Indian rulers had long established traditions of kingship and law which predated the arrival of the European imperial powers, but the signing of treaties during the early nineteenth century with the British would redefine their territorial boundaries, interaction with neighbouring kingdoms, and, in some cases, the administration of their states and their relations with their own ministers and clansmen. The treaties extracted tribute in the form of revenue, soldiers to constitute imperial forces and goods that were useful for the East India Company to benefit their directors in London.[26]

Edward J. Thompson argues that the Indian 'prince' as characterized by the British therefore only emerged in 1806, with the signing of the first treaties, and received his full position in the Indian polity by 1819.[27] The treaties allowed shades of autonomy to the indigenous rulers for the internal governance of their states, and often varied from kingdom to kingdom.[28] Before the Mutiny, members of the Company bureaucracy took differing attitudes to the role of intervention within princely states. The Court of Directors in London, 'desiring cheap administration, enjoined its servants 'not to interfere in the internal affairs of other states'. However, British officers on the ground in India 'often thought otherwise'.[29] During the 1830s and 1840s, there was a constant tension between 'intervention and laissez-faire' which continued until well after the 1850s. While attempting to play an inconspicuous role, the British administration felt it had the 'right and responsibility to mediate to ensure good government'.[30] In certain cases, it intervened to control princely successions, minority administrations and regencies as part of this policy. However, with the events of 1857, the relationship between the British in India and the princes acquired a new form with the transition from Company to Crown rule.

During the tumultuous events of the Mutiny, the native states proved to be invaluable allies to the British. The rulers of Nepal, the Sikh kingdoms of the Punjab and certain Rajput and Maratha principalities provided essential assistance.[31] After the 'suddenness' of the widespread rebellion, the Company's men, led by Governor-General Canning, reassessed the significance of the princes for Britain's future role in the subcontinent. They had learned a major lesson: that while Dalhousie's earlier practice of annexation had turned some 'peaceable' rulers into foes, the princes as a body were faithful allies and had proved to be vital breakwaters in the storm of mutinous activity. Thereafter the policy of annexation, which was, in any case often far too expensive, was replaced by one of indirect rule through a system of mutual alliance.[32]

With the Government of India Act in 1858, Crown rule was officially established. The East India Company and its Board of Directors in London were disbanded and a system of counterbalances was simultaneously inaugurated. In India, the Viceroy or Governor-General governed the Council, but could be overruled by the Secretary of State in Whitehall, who in turn could be trumped by the Council of India, which met at the India Office, on issues relating to finance and legislation; all of which was ultimately answerable to the Prime Minister and his Cabinet.[33] Thereafter, all tributes, revenues and covenants between the Company and the princely states were handed over to the Crown who in turn provided internal safety and security to the states.[34]

The British realized that they had to woo their princely allies if they wished to protect and strengthen this symbiotic relationship. In return for services rendered during the Mutiny and with the hope for continued future partnership, the Crown devised a system of gifting honours to Indian dignitaries, such as gun salutes, knighthoods and titles, in a similar manner to that with which it favoured its own aristocracy and gentry in England. Such badges of merit emphasized the construction of a 'feudal hierarchy'. Those loyal during the Mutiny in 1857 and in its wake for instance were rewarded The Order of the Star of India, which aesthetically represented the marriage of the Crown with its Indian jewel. While an image of the Queen lay in its centrepiece, the necklace interspersed Tudor roses with the Indian symbol of lotuses.[35]

The ceremonial of the durbar, where members of the British administration officially met native princes, was perhaps the most telling public display of the Raj's incorporation of the symbols of indigenous leadership. Such grand occasions reflected the theatricality of imperial power and the relationship between the Crown and its subsidiary allies, which was in emulation and imitation of the pageantry of both Mughal and European royalty. In such settings, appropriate etiquette and deportment were essential elements of political dialogue and exchange. Seating placements, ceremonial dress, and stylized modes of speech between Indian royals and British proconsuls were all of great importance.[36] The 1877 Delhi Durbar, where Viceroy Lytton officially declared Queen Victoria Kaiser-I-Hind or Empress of India was expressive of this trend of visual ornamentation, replete with both Anglo-Saxon and Indic symbols of kingship.[37]

The Viceroy, as a Crown representative, transplanted the majesty of the Queen or King-Emperor to India and effectively symbolized the British monarch's suzerainty over India's own leaders. Curzon, who served as Viceroy from 1899 to 1905, took Lytton's concept of pageantry to a more ornate level. He was a man who epitomized his historical age; he thrived on spectacle and was captivated by the aristocracies of the East.[38] While on tour in Asia, he wrote detailed descriptions of royal palaces and royal etiquette. In his opinion, India's grandeur lay in its princes and titled wealth, which made England, in comparison, appear 'dingy and unimaginative'.[39] Curzon particularly appreciated the pomp and show of the Raj, which he believed would preserve India's princes from the diluting influences of the west.

In 1903, he personally organized and orchestrated the imperial durbar at Delhi to announce the coronation of Edward VII. He wrote to a friend that it would be the 'biggest show that India will ever have had'.[40] He believed it would bring together people from all over the subcontinent and radiate the glory of the Empire through the unity of India. The symbolism of kingship was forefront in his pageantry and he wanted the princes to be 'prominent actors in the ceremony' not 'mere spectators at it'.[41] He invited twice as many princes as had arrived for Lytton's 1877 assemblage, and his festivities lasted two weeks, with around 150,000 people gathered.[42] The Duchess of Marlborough who was present described the occasion as something out of the *Tales of the Arabian Nights*.[43] As David Cannadine suggests, these were markers of a clear link between the traditions of monarchy and the power of Empire: 'the relationships between the aristocracies of the metropolis, and the aristocracies of the periphery ... [are] integral to our understanding of any patrician order and any imperial system'.[44] In such a manner, the Raj manufactured a hierarchy along British lines and transported it to India, while simultaneously incorporating local elements. Princes mingled easily with members of the Raj bureaucracy, as social equals through the honours system, which tied them with the British.[45] As Viceroys represented the awe of majesty and had the dual role of sovereignty over India's indigenous kings and administrative governor-general of British India, they were generally selected from members of the British aristocracy in large part because it was commonly known that an Indian ruler would only show fealty to another man of his own or similar social status. Thus, between 1856 and 1947, twenty Viceroys to India were members of the British peerage.[46]

Acquiring the support of India's traditional leadership helped to legitimate Britain's paramountcy in South Asia. As Michael Fisher observes, 'by ensuring the loyalty of India's 'princes' and the continuity of its traditional institutions – primarily through the careful guidance of the Resident – the British Empire was intended to be eternal'.[47] In her famous proclamation, Queen Victoria emphasized her hopes for indirect rule by underlining the Crown's tolerance towards the religious traditions and customs of the princes.

> We hereby announce to the native Princes of India that all treaties and engagements made with them by or under the authority of the Honourable East India Company are by us accepted, and will be scrupulously maintained, and we look for the like observance on their part. We desire no extension of our present territorial possessions ... We shall respect the rights, dignity and honour of native Princes as our own; and we desire that they, as well as our own subjects, should enjoy that prosperity and that social advancement which can only be secured by internal peace and good government.[48]

Queen Victoria herself was fond of her Indian subjects. Indeed, it has been argued that she was more 'passionate' about India than any earlier British monarch and that she openly reproved those who disparaged Indians on the basis of race for she, herself, was indifferent to issues relating to colour. She once compelled Lord Salisbury to apologize for describing Indians as 'black men'.[49]

In particular, the Queen was enamoured by the princes, whom she regularly invited to Windsor and Sandringham, and she incorporated them into her larger kinship networks, in several cases acting as godmother to the children of rulers and their wives.[50] David Gilmour suggests that some princes were so 'petted by the Court and London society that they were often reluctant to return to India and govern their states'.[51]

The princes were accepted as integral elements in the project of paramountcy for several reasons. Indigenous leadership was an inexpensive method for the British to patrol and administrate large areas of land, which were often inaccessible: an essential element of indirect rule. The princes were also important contributors to the British imperial military by financing campaigns and providing recruits, not only for battles on Indian soil but also overseas. They symbolized the grandeur of the empire and the eloquence of ancient monarchies, when played out in the setting of 'public consumption' such as durbars, viceregal visits and tours by the English royal family when visiting the crown colony. Lastly, the princes provided support at the all-India level and in British wars abroad.[52]

Such active collaboration fostered what Ian Copland has described as the 'romance of the princely courts' during the late nineteenth and early twentieth centuries.[53] To European observers, their martial prowess, at 'once fierce and outlandish', added to their glamour as rulers.[54] The customs of the native courts appeared to the 'untutored gaze of English romantics, immensely old', leading Disraeli to admiringly reflect that their dynastic lineages were far older than that of the English monarchy itself.[55] The lifestyle of pageantry appealed to certain European travellers as well. During Lord Irwin's 1929 viceregal visit to Kolhapur, a *Times* correspondent described the Zenana ladies as adorned in gorgeous saris, peering through 'nebulous curtains' and the courtiers as dressed in 'vivid sashes and pagris and jewelled swords'.[56]

Throughout, however, the definition of paramountcy was largely ambiguous. William Lee-Warner described the relationship between the Crown and the princes as 'undefined'.[57] The princely states themselves came under the jurisdiction of the Political Department of the Foreign Office. The Foreign Office along with the Political Department in Bombay had wide reaching responsibilities from 'Aden to Bushire, up to Kashgar and down to Sikkim'.[58] Within the hierarchy of the Political Department, the Residents of Hyderabad and Mysore were at the apex. One step below were the Residents and the Political Agents of Bombay, Central India, Rajputana and the frontiers. After the Residency of Baroda was removed, the Agent to the Governor in Kathiawar was the most significant position within the Bombay Political Department.[59]

Outside the perimeters of their kingdoms, native princes could not hold diplomatic ties with other states or countries.[60] While they could maintain standing armies, they could not exceed a predetermined number nor employ Europeans, Americans or members of other Asiatic countries in their ranks.[61] They were also barred access to foreign capitalists. When the Nizam of Hyderabad sought aid from European merchants for the construction of his railways, his British advisors categorically rejected the plan.[62] Rulers themselves could not leave their kingdoms without first informing their Residents and Political Officers of their travel itineraries.[63] Paramountcy effectively stripped the princes of external influence outside their kingdoms, and they were dependent upon the Crown in matters relating to foreign policy and defence of their states.

At the same time, many of the princely states were internally autonomous, and the presence of the paramount power was rarely felt within their borders. As Lee-Warner noted: 'In a Native State, large or small, the Queen's writ does not run; that is the main point: it is foreign territory in the midst of the Queen's dominions'.[64] The nineteenth-century treaties allowed the princes to maintain a fair degree of autonomy within their principalities and by the early twentieth century, they pushed for greater visibility in all-India affairs. In 1909, Viceroy Lord Minto limited British intervention in curbing the sovereignty of the princes. He encouraged his officials to accept the legal systems and traditions of native states and to limit any interference.[65] By 1916, Viceroy Lord Chelmsford acceded to demands by the princes to host conferences in Delhi. Two years later the Montagu-Chelmsford Report of 1918 served as the basis for the 1919 Government of India Act, which gave 'formal recognition to many of the rulers' claims to autonomy'.[66] As Vijaya Raje Scindia, Rajmata of Gwalior suggested, it was in this period that in many ways 'the princes had become real kings'.[67]

Due to their support of the First World War, the princes argued in favour of greater recognition for their services in the form of land grants as in 1858. They hoped to reinstitute their lost rights, protect themselves against further infringement and be consulted more regularly regarding the affairs of empire.[68] In 1919, London established the Chamber of Princes to assist the Viceroy on matters relating to the Indian states.[69] By 1921, the Chamber of Princes was officially formed. However the Indian States Committee, appointed by Viceroy Lord Irwin in 1928, 'refused to define paramountcy'.[70] Chaired by Harcourt Butler, the committee merely advocated minimal interference within the princely states.[71]

The vague language of paramountcy disillusioned a number of the rulers, who became thoroughly 'disenchanted with British constitutional processes'.[72] Before 1929, many of the princes had happily contributed to the projects of empire, such as the three imperial durbars and the war relief during WWI. After the Butler Committee's report, several refused to participate in the political process, which historians have suggested led to their eclipse by 1947.

Between 1928 and the mid-1930s, the British government, native princes and Indian nationalists argued for an independent, integrated India.[73] In 1928 Motilal Nehru, President of the Congress, advocated for the creation of a commonwealth of India with dominion status and a similar system of paramountcy with ties towards the princes as was established under the Raj. Although later the Congress, under the leadership of Jawaharlal Nehru and then his daughter Indira Gandhi, would become an opponent of the princes, at that time it aimed to protect their semi-independent status. Between 1930 and 1932, London invited the princes to participate in three Round Table Conferences, which were assembled to consider an All-India federation along the lines of Canada or Australia.[74] Due to a lack of unanimity among the princes, which shall be discussed further in a later chapter, they were unable to maintain a unified front, divided by divergent loyalties on the lines of religion, language, ethnicity and culture.[75] Often 'personal rivalries' negatively affected hopes for political cooperation.[76] The 1935 Government of India Act gave the princes the right to nominate members for a third of the lower house of the Indian legislature. The authority offered was in direct proportion to the territory they held and each ruler could determine whether to accede his state to federal India or not.

From 1909 up to 1930, the paramount power had actively cultivated the support of Indian rulers, at times by giving greater autonomy to the princes in the administration of their internal affairs.[77] They were particularly keen to please those who played dominant roles within the Chamber of Princes. The round table talks of 1930–2 and the Government of India Act in 1935 effectively changed Britain's relationship with India.[78] Thereafter, the British government needed to cultivate goodwill with several members of the Chamber of Princes, not only those few who were active leaders.[79] Concessions were made not only to the most powerful princes but also to varying levels of the princely hierarchy as bargaining tools to encourage them to join the future federation. Originally, the leading princes in the Chamber championed the idea of federation and the British government worked hard to secure the willing agreement of all parties in a constitution.[80] But there was no consensus within the Rajwada ranks.[81] Nor did the princes' 'obstructionism' during the writing of the bill in 1932–5 win them support in Britain, especially after they rejected the terms of federation. In 1939, Viceroy Lord Linlithgow gave up trying to lure the princes with the onset of WWII. In addition, the growing antipathy within the Indian National Congress to princely governments may have made the rulers more willing to continue to accept paramountcy as it stood and hence the British felt less of a need to actively cultivate their support.[82]

From 1939 onwards, it became evident that India's Independence was imminent and a Congress ruled Government would ensue. For the period between 1939 and 1947, the paramount power tried to control the situation and 'discharge whatever of Britain's self-defined obligations in India were salvageable'.[83] It attempted to protect its promise of sovereignty to the princes, laid down in their earlier treaties. However the last few years witnessed an 'abrupt reversal of British policy' towards the native states. The British became far more interventionist; reverting to practices not seen since 1909. Viceroy Lord Linlithgow encouraged his officials to interfere in the affairs of the princes and to resist accepting their demands.[84] As John McLeod suggests, during the last few years of British paramountcy, the princes' sovereignty was limited in a manner it had not been for the past three decades.[85] Inevitably, by the time of the signing of the Indian Independence Act, they would be almost absent in the making of the new republic and nation.

For the purposes of a discussion on the politics within the zenana, it is most relevant to observe how paramountcy operated at the local level within princely states. Until Independence, the Political Department interacted most directly with princely India and Zenana women.[86] The Indian Political Service recruited heavily from both the Indian Civil Service and the Army.[87] The Civil Service was seen as the 'steel frame' of Imperial rule and its officers controlled districts often the size of English counties.[88] The Viceroy, assisted by the Political Secretary, led the Political Department.[89] By the early to mid-twentieth century, the Political Department was a sophisticated diplomatic corps. After the statute of 1935, the Viceroy's role changed to Crown Representative while the Political Secretary became the Political Advisor. Residents, supported by Political Agents, were answerable to them.[90]

Political officials were scattered over India in less than twenty Residencies or Agencies, usually located at the capital of the important states. Single, large states such as Hyderabad, Kashmir, Gwalior or Mysore had a Resident of their own. Other territories were composed of several smaller states, such as Rajputana and Kathiawar in mid-western India, which had one Resident who was assisted by one to three Political Agents.[91] As Sher Ali Pataudi, descendent of an erstwhile Muslim princely state, observed:

> In a single-state agency (such as Baroda or Mysore) the Political Agent might attend the palace up to twice daily for talks with durbari officials and, occasionally, with the Chief himself. In a multi-state agency (such as Eastern Rajputana, Budelkhand or Rewa Kantha) his personal visits were likely to be less frequent: weekly, monthly, or perhaps even yearly in the case of really tiny out-of-the-way principalities. At other times contact was maintained through correspondence, and in the twentieth century increasingly by telephone. One of the Political Agent's more time-consuming occupations was dictating and answering letters and telegrams. If political work was sometimes boring it was in the office chores that made it so.[92]

Generally, the agency itself maintained a large staff, employing half a dozen European and Indian assistants and an even larger office staff. Besides for the European members under their employ, it was particularly important for the British that they cultivate the support of their Indian subordinates. Key men in the native establishment were the *daftardar* or *seristador*, the Registrar, who 'doubled as the Political Agent's confidential advisor and foreman over the other Indian staff'.[93]

The Role of the Resident

The Political Office and those who made up its corps of Political Agents and Residents were not always held in the greatest esteem. As early as 1875, the Prince of Wales, when touring India, was alarmed by the rudeness of the Bombay Government's political officers. He addressed Viceroy Lord Lytton with concern: 'I am at present far from satisfied (with the performance of the Foreign Department)'.[94] Similarly, Sir Tej Bahadur Sapru, a distinguished Liberal leader and an eminent jurist, queried: 'Why do you send to India Viceroys who are third-rate and Governors who look like engine drivers?'[95] A number of Britain's leading statesmen rejected invitations to serve as Viceroys, including Winston Churchill, Anthony Eden and R.A. Butler.[96]

The Indian Political Department emphasized physical might over intellectual prowess. 'An athletic frame, even if encased in a dim mind, was an undoubted asset'.[97] Furthermore, the privileging of bodily strength over mental

aptitude resulted in greater recruits from the armed forces than civilians. As Sher
Ali Pataudi notes, 'Given the government's prejudice against using civilians in
political posts and their preference for athletic attainments over learning skills,
it is no surprise that the Indian Political Service became a by word for intellectual mediocrity'.[98] According to Clive Dewey, they hid their intellectual selves
behind a more physically active persona. ICS officers, who joined the ranks of
the Politicals, had to 'pretend' to be men of action to 'escape the stigma attached
to cleverness by the late-Victorian middle class'.[99] In such an environment, character counted for far more than brains.[100]

Any military officer, who had passed his promotion exam, was unmarried
and under 26 years old, could apply for a permanent posting in the Political
Service, and any Civil Servant, who had passed his exam, was unmarried and had
less than five years service could similarly apply. A complex formula was devised
whereby 6.3 officials were accepted per annum at a ratio of 70 per cent military
and 30 per cent civilian.[101]

The men of the Political Department were predominately middle-class,
educated at English public schools, had Oxbridge degrees or were trained at
Sandhurst.[102] They were expected to master a number of subjects, including English, Greek, Latin, French, German, Italian, mathematics, science and others.[103]

Whether recruits went to crammers to pass the board exams or universities,
often the vital years of their education were spent in the public school. It was there
that character, rather the cultivation of the mind, was foremost in the training of
young men for the purposes of being sent out to lead the Empire. At Haileybury,
students were encouraged to become cricketers or the leaders of fagging parties
rather than gain a Double First at Oxford.[104] As David Gilmour suggests,

> the fagging system taught them how to command and how to obey; the cricket and
> football pitches taught them about discipline and team spirit; the classroom, with its
> concentration on history and the classics, gave them an idea of imperial responsibil-
> ity; and the ambience of the place provided a muscular ethos of courage, endurance,
> loyalty and self-control.[105]

The leading schools to prepare young men were Cheltenham College, Marlborough, Rugby and the new Haileybury (which reopened after 1862). Eton,
Harrow and Winchester effectively drew fewer recruits; in certain circles, especially among middle ranking Civils, an Etonian background could be a decided
disadvantage. In other circles, particularly the highest level, it could be a singular
advantage.[106]

Those hoping to become Politicals from the ICS often went to the front or
a native state for a training of about six months; others from the army spent a
period of eighteen months studying revenue and judicial structures. At the conclusion of this period, they were examined on Indian history, law and penal codes,

the treaties with the princes and vernacular languages. 'Bookish knowledge' was not seen as a high priority for gaining entrance to the Political Department. In a native state, rulers preferred a Political who understood their traditions of sportsmanship and hunting and respected their modes of dress and custom over one endowed with excessive intellectual learning. Indeed, an Indian ruler was 'less impressed by a taciturn scholar from Oxford than by an ebullient officer, who was, like them, a sportsman'.[107]

Sir Kenneth Fitze, a one time Resident, is a typical example and his dealings with zenana succession disputes, as will be discussed later, are illustrative of the period. Fitze was drawn to the Indian Civil Service because his father had commercial interests in India.[108] Trained in the classics, he first attended the public school Marlborough and subsequently Oxford, where he neglected his studies and performed poorly. As he writes of himself at the time, 'I was anything but a success and indeed within measurable distance of making a humble addition to the catalogue of lost causes'.[109] Life at Oxford in the late Edwardian period was one of relative ease and comfort. He describes that period nostalgically:

> Ablutionary and sanitary arrangements, it is true, were somewhat primitive, but the *cuisine* and the wine list were beyond criticism. The only communal meal was dinner in Hall, but if my memory serves me right, it was permissible to resort instead to the 'Clarendon' or to substitute a *recherché* supper in the dignified seclusion of one's private suite. The service was admirable, luxurious breakfasts being obtainable by the simple process of writing one's requirements before going to bed.[110]

Subsequent training for the ICS degree was similarly leisurely. Refusing to allow his son an additional wasted year at Oxford, Fitze's father enrolled him in a one-year programme at the University of London, which later became the School of Oriental and African Studies. The syllabus mainly consisted of lectures on the Indian codes of penal and civil law and the study of Urdu and Hindi scripts. As Fitze admits, 'our attendance was desultory and our attention regrettably languid'.[111] Education for officers was weak as few received any special administrative training. While armed with 'a bevy of manuals, grammars and legal texts', the young ICS officers were pushed into the work by 'experience' rather than instruction.[112] While the formal training was minimal, recruits to the Political Department were given *A Manual of Instructions to Officers of the Political Department of the Government of India*.[113]

Malcolm Darling, a close friend of the novelist E. M. Forster, also served in the ICS as a secretary to the Maharaja of Dewas Senior, Tukoji Rao Puar II. Like Fitze, he had been groomed at an early age for a career in India. He was schooled at Eton and then later King's, Cambridge and his family, part of the intellectual and cultured bourgeoisie, was associated with the Bloomsbury group. His schoolboy and university days filled him with a love for friendship; a homoerotic urge, according to Dewey, that was inculcated by his schoolmasters and college tutors and later affected his feelings of intense affinity towards the Indian ruler, whom he termed his 'Indian brother'.[114] Darling's emphasis on the more epicurean and aesthetic delights of intellectual friendship found little satisfaction among the Anglo-Indians he met, whom he and his wife Josie found decidedly dull with their interest in service gossip and shikar.[115] In contrast, Darling observed that the environment of the native states was far more akin to the world of King's, which he had treasured as a student. When the Political Department sent him to Dewas Senior, he described it as the 'oddest corner of the world outside Alice in Wonderland' and in that way was perfected. The princely states were free of the political unrest, which had 'poisoned' race relations in British India.[116]

Motivations for joining the Indian Civil Service or Political Department were multifarious. Some like Kenneth Fitze were drawn to India out of a sense of adventure or imperial mission. The tantalizing prospects of a 'diplomatic life', replete with 'parties, shikar expeditions, and ostentatious ritual' were highly attractive.[117] Anglo-Indian fiction, by writers such as Rudyard Kipling, G. A. Henty and Flora Annie Steel, contributed to this construction of India as a place of exotic colour for the young man in search of a quest.[118] In 1905, Lord Curzon in an attempt to make the work of life in the Residencies sound diverse and exciting to potential appointees wrote:

> The public at large hardly realizes what the Political may be called to do. At one moment he may be grinding in the Foreign Office, at another he may be required to stiffen the administration of a backward Native State, at a third he may be presiding over a *jirga* [assembly] of unruly tribesmen on the frontier, at a fourth he may be demarcating a boundary amid the wilds of Tibet or the sands of Seistan. There is no more varied or responsible service in the world than the Political Department of the Government of India. I commend [it] ... to all who like to know the splendid work of which Englishmen are capable.[119]

In addition to the glamour of living in the princely states, many joined for financial remuneration. Recruits to the Political Department holding the Army rank of Lieutenant immediately received a raise, which allowed some of them to marry more easily.[120] Others had family connections, with several generations serving in India.[121]

Life in a Residency or Agency was one of diplomatic manoeuvring. Perspicacious political agents juggled office work and socializing with the key personages of the state. The main purposes for a Political Agent or Resident was to 'overcome the natural suspicion of a ruler and his court that the foreign interloper was merely the Government's spy'.[122] Hence, an afternoon game of tennis or a shikar in the Raja's jungle was not without a 'solid political' motivation.[123] For some, this focus on etiquette, pandering and socializing was less than appealing. One former Resident described working in the princely states as a 'poodle-faking job, spending a great deal of time being obsequious ... counting exactly how many steps you would take when you met the Rajah ... all this stuff ... it would be a waste of anyone's life'.[124] By the 1930s and 1940s, there were strong urges to reform the Political Office in India. However, when the war began, it would serve as more than an interruption.

The princely states of Rajputana were among the most coveted destinations for hopeful Politicals. They embodied the romanticism of Anglo-India in incomparable ways. Visitors were tantalized by the thought of living in a world of 'medieval ... castles, courts, minstrels and dancing girls' where the 'age of chivalry was not gone'.[125] Politicals in Rajputana often led a leisurely life in picturesque environs. Those who worked in the frontier provinces described the Rajputana Agency as the Great Sloth Belt.[126]

The Indian Civil Service and the Political Department were quite separate from each other. Although ICS officers, such as Malcolm Darling, did enter the Political Department, once they were in princely states they served much more ambassadorial roles. Generally, the two cadres disliked each other. Just as Darling found the Anglo-Indians in British India to be without character and preferred his role as a political officer in the native states where he had close proximity to an Indian prince, members of the Indian Civil Service were similarly not enamoured by their colleagues in the Political Department, whose jobs they believed were neither intellectually nor administratively challenging.

In a sense, the princes and the colonial officers who came in contact with them were in a halfway house. Manu Bhagavan suggests that the princes were themselves transgressors between boundaries, connecting and separating British India from indigenous populations and definitions of government:

> As Indian emissaries of the British overlords, and armed with more power and wealth than any other 'natives', the princes were able to bridge the gap between the colonial and the colonized. Donning one hat, they could claim to be loyal representatives of the empire, then, donning the other, the last line of defence protecting the 'Indian' people from the full onslaught of English evil.[127]

While British Political Agents were first and foremost representatives of the Crown, they simultaneously represented the princes in relation to the Government of India. Some were too partial, such as John Malcolm and James Tod, who retired in 1822 from his post in Rajputana because of his pro-Rajput stance. Others such as Colonel Phayre in Baroda were considered too harsh.[128]

Queens as Regents

For the British political officer, the world of the princely states appeared plagued with outmoded conventions, irregular sexual practices and bizarre royal ritual. In this environment, he was perhaps most intrigued and perplexed by the power of women rulers behind seclusion. Because of the hierarchical and politicized nature of the zenana, with each queen vying for her son to succeed, the environment often could be deadly. In the pre-colonial period, there were several examples of Ranis, eunuchs and servant maids who murdered or poisoned heirs and others in the line of succession and who governed the state with Machiavellian strategies.[129]

The colonial zenana was similarly characterized as a place of intrigue, black magic, murder and dangerous jealousies, where feuding factions battled out dubious succession claims. As Resident Fitze noted:

> ... the zenana, dominated only too often by ignorant, obstinate and superstitious mothers and grandmothers, was apt to counteract the efforts of the most efficient and conscientious of tutors and guardians.[130]

The British were particularly worried by the influence of zenana politics on the upbringing of young princes. In 1844, a British observer noted 'there are no universities or public schools in which young men might escape, as they do in Europe, from the enervating and stultifying influence of the zenana'.[131]

Despite having an Empress as their monarch, British officials were averse to female heirs, encouraging and often enforcing Indian princely states to practice primogeniture.[132] However, in cases where a prince was a minor when he ascended the *gaddi* (throne), it was not unusual for his mother, one of the widowed queens of the deceased ruler, to serve as a regent in the intervening period until his majority, if she was 'capable of it'.[133] British officials generally denigrated local regencies, held by royal females (often the mother or grandmother of the minor ruler), as 'motivated by self interest'.[134] Nonetheless, these dowager queen-rulers or regents proved to be formidable adversaries to the political officer.

It is important to note that the institutions of zenana life, such as the private, hidden geography of the palace and *pardah* dress, allowed women greater mobility along with the advantage of secrecy. They were able to promote policies and nurture political units within the court often without the public knowledge of the crown officials stationed in their own states or the men of the royal family. Male rulers in contrast had to display themselves in a public venue and make their affairs more transparent. In this manner, *pardah* not only served to protect women from the obtrusive gaze and panopticon surveillance of the colonial warden, but also allowed them to use the sanctity of tradition to subvert the very limitations of their secluded state.

The sequestered nature of zenana life, reinforced by custom and palace architecture which shut British administrators out, could elude the direct observation of the colonial government. Such lack of access caused frustration and a general distrust of Zenana politics and the motivations of princely women, even more than that of indigenous male rulers. The zenana thus became a locus for resistance. Barbara Ramusack observes:

> Since the British did not have direct access to the zenana or women's quarters, they were particularly anxious to reduce the influence of Indian women, whom they stereotyped as superstitious and of doubtful morality. Here the British conflated their Oriental concepts of the exoticism of Asian women, especially an uncontrolled sexuality and lack of intelligence, with British disdain for alternative sources of identity for young princes.[135]

In many ways, *pardah* did not prevent Zenana women from augmenting and maintaining political power. It engendered an elaborate system of covert communication. For matters of state, slates (*pattis*) were sent by serving ladies, (*davris*), through which Rajput royal women communicated with their administrative officers (*kamdars*), ministers and heads of state departments. The messages on *patti* could be easily rubbed out and for this reason there was less danger of them falling into enemy hands unlike communications written on paper. Zenana women also had sophisticated channels of information from 'personal servants and officials' as well as through women from the town who came to visit them with news of the outer community.[136] Indigenous rulers had a sophisticated system of local intelligence gathering, often through the use of *wakils*, or courtiers, who provided them access to courts outside their own kingdoms. Indian rulers, as did Zenana women, often avoided, discredited and rejected the intervention of Residents and Political Agents, as will be seen in the following accounts, by writing directly to regional governors, the Governor-General or Viceroy and English monarchs, thereby overstepping local British officers.[137]

Sometimes, curtains were also erected through which the ladies could speak with outside men who were not members of the immediate family, such as state ministers and British officials.[138] Val C. Prinsep, whose father was a member of the East India Company's Civil Service, was an avid traveller in the princely states of Rajputana, often painting portraits of the Maharajas. He describes an audience between the Hindu Jat Maharani of Dholpur and her Political Agent, Major Dennehy:

> We were taken to a small verandah, opening into which were two pierced windows, and a door on which hung a thick wadded silk *purdah* or hanging. On each side of one of the windows were placed chairs; inside the window was quite dark; probably there, too, was a *purdah*. Major Dennehy talked through the window and presently a voice answered.[139]

In this manner, the queen could reveal as much of herself as she wished in conversation, maintaining the ability to observe the British officer (through the curtain or the windows), while he was unable to see her. Ironically for the paramount power, in such dialogues, it was the woman who had the upper hand for she could have access to two worlds through the gaze: her own and that of the Englishman before her, while his visual knowledge was one-sided.

The Internal Hierarchy of the Zenana

The zenana, itself, had a complex hierarchy. The royal household could hold as many as thirty or more wives as well as *pardayats* (concubines), which could exceed the number of wives. Their serving ladies and attendants all lived within the zenana as well.[140] In 1940, when Maharani Gayatri Devi of Jaipur first arrived in the Jaipur Zenana she was amazed by the sheer number of women:

> In the year of my marriage, there were still 400 women living in the zenana. Among them were widowed relatives and their daughters as well as their servants and attendants; the Dowager Maharani and her retinue of ladies-in-waiting, maids, cooks, and other servants; comparable retinues for each of [my husband's] three wives and all the retainers of the late Maharaja's other wives. Presiding over them was the only one of the late Maharaja's wives who were still alive. She was known to us as Maji Sahiba and we treated her with the utmost deference. As one of Jai's wives, I could almost never uncover my face in her presence and always had to be seated a few places to her left.[141]

In the social order of the zenana, the first tier consisted of the *Rajmata*, the mother of the ruler, followed by the *Patrani*, the mother of the heir apparent, and thereafter the other *Ranis*, or wives of the ruler. Then followed the *Maji Sahibas*, or other wives of the former ruler. The second tier consisted of the *Pardayats* and *Paswans*; concubines who were not often of the same caste background and thus not formally married to the king. The third tier was an extended circle of female relatives and the retinues of the royal ladies.[142]

The Rajmata by far had the pre-eminent position in the zenana. As the mother of the ruler, she was given the greatest honour and obeisance.[143] After her, came the Patrani. Traditionally, a Rani acquired the status of Patrani after she gave birth to a male heir. In some Hindu Rajput royal families, when a Rani became a Patrani she had a special religious ceremony and the ruler gave her a *poshak* or ceremonial dress.[144] The Patrani's cash allowance was then doubled over that of the other queens and during birthdays and holidays she distributed gifts.[145] Before the Mughal period and the adoption of *pardah,* some Hindu Rajput *patranis* sat beside the ruler in formal durbars.[146]

Concubines were also treated in a ceremonial manner. Traditionally, they came from castes that provided servants, dancers and singers. In certain Rajput royal households, during the confirmation ceremony for the mistress, the ruler gave her the right to wear gold on her feet and ivory bangles. Gold on the feet was a sign of royal favour. Once a woman acquired the status of concubine, she became a member of the zenana and, like the Ranis, was given her own jagir (land with its own revenue), but a much smaller one, which was often confiscated after the ruler's death.

Other than concubines, there were also *daroghas*, or women in service. In Rajput Zenanas, the unmarried daughters of *daroghas, davris*, were often given in dowry with the Ranis when they left their father's homes. In addition, there would have been a female head of staff and other families from different caste groups, including the wet nurse, tailor, dyer, cook, female priest, washerwoman and genealogist.[147] The servants who accompanied a new Rani were presented a house (*nohra*) close to their Rani's apartment. They were provided cash and grain and were a strong component of support for a young queen far from her familiar community in the foreign environment of her married home.[148]

While the Patrani and Rajmata were atop the social ladder of the zenana, the Ranis and concubines were also vying with each other. There was the wife most favoured by the ruler, the *manetan*, who had her own faction, and the queen least favoured, the *kumetan*. The hierarchically most senior wife was often the first one married until the mother of the heir replaced her. Senior women rarely liked the entrance of a new co-wife nor did the fathers of daughters like to marry their girls into large polygamous households. The medieval bardic literature of Rajasthan is rich with the jibes and petty insults of competitive wives in the zenana. The following are two passages from Rajasthani story literature:

On Co-wives:

This water is salty
May my co-wife drink this water.[149]

One song of a Younger Co-Wife to the Older:

Why are you so proud of yourself?
If your husband gets a brick made for your house
He gets a palace constructed for me.
... If he cleans his teeth in your house
He prepares for it in my house

If he eats in your house
He gargles in my house

Don't think he is your husband
I have just lent him to you for 10 days.[150]

Many women did not admire their co-wives, but there are instances of some women who asked their husbands to marry again to provide them with companionship. Sometimes, co-wives were able to impose restrictions on each other. One Hindu Rajput Rani, in the medieval period, only allowed her husband to remarry on the condition that after the marriage ceremony, he would not visit his new bride's apartments.[151]

In coming into contact with Zenana women, the British encountered the intricate hierarchy of the institution. Not only were Zenana women vying against each other, particularly in succession disputes and regency claims, but they were also intriguing against indigenous males and British intervention.

Regency Cases

As regents, Zenana women were artful strategists, wielding political, religious and military influence in their kingdoms. Rani Kalindi, the wife of the Buddhist Chakma Raja of the Chittagong Hill Tracts, a territory on the borders of east Bengal and Burma, is a particularly fascinating example of a *pardah* regent. Although ordinarily observing primogeniture, the nineteenth-century Buddhist Chakma ruler, Dharam Bux, was succeeded by the senior-most of his three Ranis, the daughter of a Dewan in his state. His two other wives were her cousins. Her descendent, the Chakma Raja Tridiv Roy, writes this description:

> Rani Kalindi, the Queen Regnant, was renowned for her wisdom, statesmanship and generosity to all her subjects that belonged to different religions. The Chakmas then were evidently practitioners of the Mahayana form of Buddhism. Their religious literature comprising the various Taras, are still extant. In Mahayana cosmology Tara is the female counterpart of the Buddha and denotes wisdom.[152]

Under her patronage, she reformed the Chakma Buddhist clergy and supported the publication of the first book on Buddhism ever published in Bengali, the *Bauddharanjika*, after it was translated from the Burmese. In 1856, she invited a Buddhist Theravada monk from Arakon to revise the Chakma Buddhist liturgy, particularly in regards to animistic or tantric practice.[153]

Rani Kalindi's strong administrative arm and her popularity with her subjects made her a difficult opponent for the British superintendent in the region, T. H. Lewin. Lewin was confirmed as Deputy Commissioner in 1867. A year later, he moved the district headquarters to the capital of the kingdom, Rangamati, appropriating the site of earlier Chakma royal property.[154] It was a crowning success for the young Englishman. In a letter home, Lewin pompously assured, 'I am King in everything save in name'. He claimed to his mother that he was almost an absolute monarch over thousands, his influence growing daily.[155]

Rani Kalindi, who observed *pardah,* refused to 'personally meet Lewin who was reputedly power drunk and arrogant, and professedly antagonistic to her. When he tried to force his way into the palace at Rajanagar he was forcibly barred from doing so'.[156] To protect herself from Lewin's grandiose ambitions, Rani Kalindi fostered a more centralized government, by sending her own ministers (dewans) to peripheral regions of her state and creating more districts directly under her control. In addition, she protected her southern borders from Lewin's encroachment by entering into a written treaty with her neighbouring ruler, the Bohmong Raja, in 1869.

In a later episode, British officials were compelled to seek her guidance in a case of kidnapping, infamously commemorated as the 'Lushai expedition'. In this incident, a regional tribal group, the Lushais, burnt a British settlement, killing twenty-five people and taking captive thirty-seven. One of these was a young girl by the name of Mary Winchester, daughter of a doctor. Lewin, who was now promoted to Political Officer of the Chittagong column, was put in charge of the rescue expedition.

At his wit's end, he called upon the assistance of the Chakma Raj, led by Rani Kalindi and her grandson Harish Chandra Roy. However, the five hundred Chakma volunteers withdrew their cooperation. In desperation, the government appealed again to Rani Kalindi, despite her feud with Lewin. On the Rani's direction, Harish Chandra interceded and persuaded the Chakmas to assist with the rescue mission. Lewin, believing Harish Chandra to be 'malleable', urged him to depose his grandmother. However, 'Harish Chandra's respect and veneration for the old Rani ... was too great to permit such action'.[157] In this example, the British political officer's judgement misfired. He underestimated the influence of a female ruler and the allegiance of her grandson. The popularity of this queen subsumed the potential authority of a dynastic male. Thus, Rani Kalindi used political intelligence to curb the influence of the local British officer and strengthen her hold on her family and subjects.

Queens also, though infrequently, engaged in battle, emerging from *pardah* to do so. In western India, the Rajmata of Wudwan, a Hindu Jhala Rajput state in Saurashtra, went into battle to fight a succession dispute. George Le Grand Jacob, then Special Political Commissioner to the Southern Mahratta Country, provides a fascinating description of a succession dispute between two Zenana women: Maharani Goelwao of Wudwan and Rajmata Raj Baee of Wudwan, a state in the Gujarat Peninsular. After the Rajmata returned from an annual pilgrimage, she discovered that her daughter-in-law had usurped the throne of the heir, who was still a minor. Raj Baee then assiduously cultivated the support of the Political Agent, Sir John Pollard Willoughby, who resided in the administrative centre of Rajkot. Although attempts were made to solve the dispute by arbitration between the two belligerent parties, they ultimately failed. Returning to Wudwan with an army of mercenaries, she led her charge into battle. In a startling exchange, which resulted in the old dowager queen taking to the field of war, Le Grand Jacob writes:

> ... mounted on horseback at the head of her troops, and attended by some of the chiefs, she once more presented herself at the gateway of Wudwan, this time in full hope of admittance. But some of the garrison, not let into the secret, or not sufficiently

bribed, opened fire upon her, and a chief fell dead at her side. Nothing daunted the plucky old lady rushed on, trusting to her star ... and not in vain, for the guard opened the gates to her, and she effected a triumphant entrance into the town.[158]

While such incidents were not typical, they have been celebrated in the histories of royal India. Queens, like Raj Baee or the better-known Rani of Jhansi, are valorized for taking to the field of battle and throwing aside the constraints of *pardah*. They are indicative of a martial spirit of resistance, which informed the worldview of courtly Indian women.

Succession Disputes

While female regents had overt ruling powers, those who manipulated successions had as much or more influence. For the political officers and the western travellers who visited India, the zenana became synonymous with battling feuds. Being a polygamous, multi-tiered, hierarchical institution, various factions of women vied with each other to place their favoured son or cadet on the *gaddi* not only to protect their places in the courtly hierarchy, but also to indirectly govern through the male appointee they had chosen. Robert Stern paints the colonial polygamous zenana as a world of artful diplomacy and strategy, where the real life of the court was centred. In his history of the Rajput princely state of Jaipur in Rajasthan, he writes:

> the zenana was often a hub in Rajput palace politics. Ranis (queens) and Thakuranis (noblewomen) – the wives of rajas and thakurs – particularly those with sons, were the head of figure heads of the rival factions composed of their relatives, connections and servants. Through these factions, in part, palace politics were linked to the politics of the Rajput principality and the politics of Rajputana. Concubines who were the favourites of their masters or the protégés of powerful courtiers were also women to be reckoned with in Rajput palaces ... [the zenana] ... also brought political considerations with virtually all of the personal relationships.[159] [Italics in original].

To counter the 'zenana's impact in the public sphere', British policy was to 'appoint a local political agent to the council of regency'.[160] In particular, censure of female marital partners was a contentious issue from the dawn of colonial intervention, as such decisions affected the dynastic line. The British were involved in deciding all succession issues and often were instrumental in determining who was the legitimate heir. These debates were particularly heated when the dead ruler had several wives or concubines.

According to British mandate, widowed queens were allowed by the Company and later the Crown to adopt their own successors in cases where the deceased ruler had no legitimate heir. As one political officer noted this became a standard procedure, 'the widows of the deceased chief ought ... to be the best exponents of their husband's intentions and or preferences and they can so far contribute to the material upon which the Viceroy's selection and decision will be taken'.[161] In 1820, when the *gaddi* of the Muslim state of Bhopal fell vacant, the Begum chose the successor.[162] Similarly, in 1843 when the Hindu Maratha ruler, Junkoji Rao Sindhia of Gwalior, died without a male heir, his widow fixed the adoption.[163]

In the 1875 Baroda succession, Maharaja Malhar Rao Gaikwad died without male issue. The widowed Rajmata Jumna Bai, wife of his deceased elder brother, Maharaja Khande Rao Gaikwad, was named the official choice to select the adoption.[164] She declared that her decision had three stipulations:

1. The child must not be lineally descended from Malhar Rao.
2. He must be a member of the House of Gaikwad (hence a part of the blood clan).
3. He must be someone 'who she could with propriety adopt'.[165]

With the help of a British official, Sir Richard Meade, Jumna Bai picked Gopal, the son of a cadet line who had lived most of his young life in an outlying village. According to legend, Jumna Bai selected him from his two brothers because of his sharpness of mind, wit and physical beauty.[166] He became one of the most enlightened and forward looking rulers during the early twentieth century as Sayajirao Gaekwad III of Baroda.

Succession disputes were key sites where the British official came into contact with the sequestered Zenana woman. The two either cleverly out-strategized one another or were compelled to form some sort of working relationship. In the cases of Limree and Kolhapur states, the succession disputes led to numerous political difficulties as different members of the Zenana court took to the field to exploit their own interests. In these examples, the crown representative was far from unchallenged in his authority.

In 1837, the Raja of Limree died, leaving three widows.[167] Limree, located in contemporary Gujarat, was a Jhala Rajput kingdom in Kathiawar. The ruler died without issue and his dowager queens were given the authority to adopt an heir. As Le Grand Jacob, who was then an assistant to the Resident, noted: 'they had hostile interests, each wishing the succession to be in the line where her influence prevailed'.[168] The state minister, Nuthoo Mehta, suggested a young boy 'approved by the majority' for adoption.[169]

To make matters more confusing, the nephew of the lately deceased ruler, Akhabhaee, contended he had the right to the *gaddi*. When the minister of the state, Mehta, extracted some monies from the treasury to send as a gift to the new Political Agent, a native officer by the name of Munguljee became incensed and joined forces with the aggrieved nephew. Le Grand Jacob, at the time, was directed to find Akhabhaee and his supporters and place them in confinement. To add to the political officer's difficulties, his own native assistant became a co-conspirator.

In this situation, the British political officer was co-opted into the world of the court as even his own clerks and assistants worked against his instructions.

In the midst of these tensions, one of the three young widows of the deceased ruler suddenly claimed to be pregnant, to the great alarm and discomfort of three out of four of the older dowager Ranis. Only the Rajmata, the uterine mother of the dead king, who 'held the greatest power in the Durbar', supported the pregnant queen.[170] For the three other dowager Ranis, this development was a direct threat to their potential powers as possible regents or selectors of an adoptive heir, through which they might indirectly have governed. The recognition of the boy's birth would consolidate the authority of the Rajmata and pregnant Rani in the palace zenana during the years when he would be a minor.

Meanwhile, Akhabhaee's forces had increased. Nearly the entire '*bhayad*' or brotherhood of nobles and the three irate dowager Ranis had allied with him. In addition, Le Grand Jacob's native assistant (an elderly Brahmin named Madhow Rao), as well as the dismissed Munguljee and one Deosee, a wealthy merchant from the princely capital, became his supporters. Deosee was a particularly useful ally. He was acquainted with both English and Indian cultures, being on friendly terms with European gentry. In addition, he had great wealth and a 'subtle, plausible and well mannered' demeanour.[171] Meeting in secret, the members of the aggrieved faction believed that a 'spurious' child was being introduced into the zenana and that justice was being undone. In their eyes, the 'British Government had tied [their] hands'.[172]

On learning these developments, Le Grand Jacob hurried to Limree where he sought audience with the dowager Ranis. During his visit, he believed he was being poisoned. As it was customary for the Durbar to send milk, firewood and hay to its guests, Le Grand Jacob drank the milk that was offered him and became ill with 'vomiting and other choleric symptoms'.[173] Later, the Agency doctor informed him that he had barely escaped with his life.

Soon after, the young Ranis requested that the wife of the Resident visit them and validate the condition of the pregnant Rani. This was not an uncommon practice. The wife of Resident Fitze had also been asked to preside over the birth of a young Rani's child. As Fitze noted, 'my wife should come and be present at the delivery, doubtless by way of insurance that any subsequent allegation of the substitution of a male for a female child be summarily dismissed'.[174] With such methods, Zenana women used the legitimizing seal of British approval to bolster their own position among the contending parties of the female court. While the British saw themselves as arbitrating disagreements, the Zenana women were simultaneously utilizing the British to support their own claims. Therefore, it can be argued that the presence of the British gave some Zenana women more leverage within the dynastic family than they might have had in the pre-colonial period. Earlier, these women would have entered diplomatic and military agreements with factions within the court, where their own personal authority would have been subsumed by the presence of belligerent male members of the family. Arguably, politicized groups, such as younger sons, brothers, uncles or nephews of the ruler, like Akhabhaee, might have had more control in such succession disputes.

In addition to the inspection by the Resident's wife, the Limree royal house requested that women in the nearby senior Jhala Rajput kingdom of Dhrangadhra perform two more examinations on the pregnant Rani. While Le Grand Jacob and the Resident believed the pregnancy was legitimate, both the three dowager Ranis and the Dhrangadhra contingent continued to question it. According to Le Grand Jacob, he believed the Dhrangadhra ladies had been bribed to voice such opinions.

In order to protect the young pregnant Rani, she was removed to a distant mansion under the supervision of troops headed by a British soldier. Knowing too intimately the cloak and dagger strategies of zenana life, Le Grand Jacob did not want to encourage any possibility of 'foul play'. In addition, the dowager Ranis were requested to inspect their female assistants, which numbered between thirty and forty, to see if any were pregnant, so as to assure the legitimacy of the Rani's child.

Two months later, the Rani was in labour. Le Grand Jacob summoned the dowager Ranis and Akhabhaee's attendants to bear witness. The dowager Ranis, however, hesitated in coming. The Agency doctor arrived in time for the birth and claimed the baby was in good health. Despite such assurances, the dowager Ranis disputed the birth. They argued that the young Rani had not given birth to the child and that it was not newly born nor of noble blood. They claimed that Le Grand Jacob had brought 'dishonour … by smuggling in some coolie's child' to sit on the *gaddi*.[175]

The dowager Ranis' arguments were not without foundation. They had to rely upon the statements of the young Ranis and their female attendants, despite the presence of the Agency doctor. Traditionally, the *pardah* ladies did not meet males who were not related to the courtly family. It would have been highly unlikely that the doctor was present in the delivery room at the time of birth or that he ever saw the young pregnant Rani, but rather he would have been given accounts of her health from her attendants or at most spoken to her behind a curtain. In all likelihood he did hold a new born, male child in his arms, for he would have been permitted to see the boy and heir to authorize the birth, but as the dowager mothers might argue, there was no guarantee it was the Rani's child.

Le Grand Jacob deemed the arguments of the dowager Ranis irrational and coloured by their alliances with Akhabhaee and his party: 'How, thought I, could these ladies disbelieve the evidence of their senses when their idea of magic could no longer delude them, and how was it likely that they would have dared to outface the truth unless prompted and supported by powerful parties.'[176]

Prevented earlier from speaking with them, he was finally granted an interview from behind 'curtains stretched across the tent'.[177] Le Grand Jacob transcribed the following conversation with the older queens:

> *Ranees.* 'We have come to ascertain what steps you intend to pursue relative to our throne'.
>
> *Self.* 'Nothing but what is customary on the birth of an heir'.
>
> *Ranees.* 'You do not really mean to tell us that you consider the thing you showed us this morning to be our heir'.
>
> *Self.* 'I am at a loss to know what you mean; do you doubt the evidence of your senses?'
>
> *Ranees.* 'Not at all; the child you showed us was at least two or three days old. We thought that you merely wanted to avoid a scandal, and let off the guilty parties as easily as possible consistent with the rights of our family; but we wish positively to know what you are going to do, that we may take care that those rights should be maintained'.
>
> *Self.* 'The British Government will uphold those rights; and I am here, as its agent, to see that they are not sacrificed either by fraud on one side or by lying and conspiracy on the other'.[178]

The dowager Ranis would not accept any of his arguments. They continued to believe, even after they had examined the premises, that the child had been 'smuggled in'.[179] He suspected that they hoped the pregnant Rani had given birth to a girl child, which would have allowed them to continue to play a role in the adoption process. The Ranis further charged Le Grand Jacob with being party to the younger Ranis' 'Durbar intrigue'.

To articulate their grievances more effectively to the British officials, they acquired the assistance of a native lawyer from Ahmedabad. He wrote good English and was related to a prominent functionary in Kathiawar.[180] Even though the Dowager Ranis did not accept Le Grand Jacob's choice and several local chiefs appealed to the Bombay government, the boy was placed on the *gaddi*. In the end, the wife and mother of the deceased ruler prevailed in having their candidate succeed to the Limree throne.

As Le Grand Jacob noted at the end of this chronicle, he was often a pawn between the varying forces of the women in the zenana. Their actions directly curbed his ability to arbitrate disputes. Had the dowager Ranis infiltrated the protected quarters of the young Rani, he would have been 'an innocent accomplice in the crime of murder, while simply executing my duty'.[181] He saw himself as a tool, and at times powerless, when confronted by the tactics of Zenana women. As he observed. 'the mother of each adheres to the cause of her own child as a hunted tigress to her cubs, and it is often no easy matter to the Political Agent to decide between them'.[182]

Not unlike the quandary in Limree, the later succession dispute in Kolhapur state during the mid-twentieth century was similarly complex. In this instance, the Kolhapur Maharaja died without male issue or ensuring the rules for adoption of his successor.[183] His nearest relations were the Maharaja of Dewas and his son, for the previous Maharaja of Dewas had married a princess of Kolhapur. However, it was not a happy marriage and the young queen of Dewas had returned to her parents' home, where she acquired great power over her brother.

The novelist E. M. Forster, who had served earlier as the private secretary to the Maharaja of Dewas Senior in 1922, was acquainted with the Maharani and the politics of Zenana women. As he recounts in his memoir, *The Hill of Devi*, the Kolhapur princess in her younger years seemed quiet and unassuming, the mute woman of orientalized imaginings:

> She was extraordinarily beautiful, with dark 'gazelle' eyes. Having shaken hands all round, she lent against the doorpost and said nothing. There was an awkward, if respectful, pause, and after Malcolm had talked a little Urdu and received no answer, we went. Her dress was on the negligee side, but she had not been intending to receive.[184]

According to Forster, the Dewas Zenana was full of intrigues. In addition to the ruler's 'mother and his aunt, there were all the grievances of the zenana over jewelry and precedence, connecting with the grievances of males outside, there were marriage connections with other courts ... [and] there was always the possibility of poison'.[185] Forster further noted that the Maharanis employed spies to keep track of the ruler's actions, who were ordinarily strangers, sometimes a 'dignified courtier, sometimes a buffoon'.[186]

Unlike Le Grand Jacob, he believed that only the strong hand of the British official could control the turbulent environment within the zenana. In particular, he highlighted the role of Malcolm Darling, an ICS officer appointed as personal tutor to the Maharaja. Darling was miraculously able to smooth over contentious relations between the Maharaja and the Dowager Maharani, who adopted him. Where there had been animosity, there was 'no trouble in visiting her Dowager Highness now' through the wise intercession of the political officer.[187]

However, the record reveals that the succession dispute in Kolhapur was not so easily smoothed over. At the time of the Maharaja's death, his mother favoured her grandson and great-grandson from Dewas, while the Kolhapur widow was averse to supporting her sister-in-law and so prevented this decision. In contrast, she wanted her daughter to become Maharani of Kolhapur, either in her own right or as the wife of any boy to succeed.

The British government officials responded that the successor had to come from a collateral branch of the family and could not be a female descendent. They rejected the Kolhapur princess' choice for it was 'at variance with history and practice'.[188] They argued that the heir must come from the Kolhapur family directly, the Bhonsle clan, not from Dewas, whose mother ceased to be a Bhonsle on her marriage. The Maharani was then given the opportunity to select a near collateral of the Kolhapur family, which she did. A few years later, the adopted child fell ill and died. The Maharani then performed a surprising *volte-face*, and adopted the Maharaja of Dewas, who simultaneously became the heir of Kolhapur.[189]

Like the Limree dowager Ranis, the Kolhapur Maharani sought legal aid for her defence. Through the manipulation of legal rhetoric, both Hindu law and British precedent, she secured a strong position in her dealings with the Crown government. In this case, 'the Maharani and her lawyers, in genuine or diplomatic oblivion of 'political practice', took their stand on ordinary Hindu law and eventually succeeded, by virtue of circumstances never previously encountered, in securing a substantial deviation from departmental orthodoxy'.[190]

These late colonial European accounts of succession disputes and female regencies reveal the hesitations, contradictions and ambivalence inherent in British perceptions of zenana politics. While the female courts were painted as dangerous worlds where women practised Sapphic love and were ruled by polygamy, *pardah* and outmoded religious practices based on the hegemony of an Eastern prince, several of these histories and travelogues provided a more dynamic account of female leadership and resistance. British political officers, such as Kenneth Fitze, Malcolm Darling, George Le Grand Jacob and T. H. Lewin, were unnerved by the tactics of Zenana women, and at times overwhelmed by them, even if their praise was given grudgingly.

During this period, female members of the princely court served as influential regents, regnant queens and significant players in male succession disputes. The Rajmata of Baroda, the Ranis of Limree and the Maharani of Kolhapur adroitly tried to manipulate 'domestic politics' to chart succession outcomes in their favour. Zenana women, despite being in seclusion behind *pardah*, thus manipulated the politics of the women's court, the larger male arena within the kingdom as well as the outer boundaries of the princely state and beyond. At various moments, *pardah* worked in their favour as it prevented the prying eyes of others – members of the larger indigenous male court or British officials – from intervening or being cognizant of their affairs.

Zenana queens headed armies, confronted imperial authority through strategy, appointed male heirs when the succession was in question and thereby implicitly governed the state. They affected the internal flow of power within the court and challenged the reigning authority of male members of the dynastic family. In contrast to the conventional portrait of *pardah* females, these women were not the silent, passive, constructed objects of an occidental fantasy. In their own right, they were assertive, politically astute, wise and sometimes autocratic leaders, who despite their seemingly cloistered existence, were informed about matters of *realpolitik*.

During the late nineteenth and early twentieth centuries, Zenana women came in contact with the agents of British imperial power. British political officers who were trained for posts in Indian princely states were expected to be skilled in diplomacy, knowledgeable about local, princely history and ceremony, accomplished on the playfield and imbued with a robust character – qualities that were particularly favoured by indigenous princes but which did not always prepare them for the workings of the zenana.

These observations reveal layered histories, which do not yield one mono-lithic definition of the indigenous courtly woman. Such divergent views reflect British imperialists' lack of consensus when interpreting the zenana and their simultaneous frustration at being unable to penetrate the walls of the palace. While T. H. Lewin saw royal women as obstacles towards European expansion-ist visions of territorial gain, Kenneth Fitze believed they were uneducated and irrational and thereby a hindrance to the proper education of young princes. George Le Grand Jacob in contrast expressed eulogistic praise, noting that courtly women often ruled in the place of native men and with greater skill and success than their male contemporaries. By virtue of these different accounts, these women come across as either the libidinous sexual objects of a polygamous male household; the *pardahnashin* shyly reclining behind opaque drapes and curtains; powerful queens and matriarchs who incorporate the tactics of war-fare, espionage, intrigue, law and political intelligence for their own ends or as implacable and unyielding resisters to colonial intervention. Such a multiplicity of portraits lies in what might be termed the 'colonial confusion' over the identi-ties and roles of both Indian princely families and native women.

This confusion emerged out of the larger colonial project of the 'civiliz-ing mission', which sought to purge the princely state of odious, backward and degenerate influences in a larger process of 'enlightened' reform. This colonial ambivalence was based both on ignorance of local normative behaviour and an ideological orthodoxy which did not enable the viewer to interpret an alternate circumstance except in a pejorative light. This imperial agenda permitted colo-nialists to remove children from parents and indigenous boys from traditional learning systems as part of the larger goals of empire: that of spreading European moral education, the rule of law and progress upon its colonized peoples. Wom-en's assertion and agency is interpreted as marginal and exceptional, individual and aberrant. This colonial confusion, which expressed itself in forms of praise or denigration, reflects both imperial and nationalist readings of the zenana, not that of their subjects – the princely woman within the walls of the palace itself. Thus the encounter, while certainly lopsided, was not entirely one of hegemonic domination by the British Raj upon its Indian subjects, but a dialogue between the two. Zenana women proved to be formidable and clever adversaries to their foreign occupiers, using both indigenous and European methods to obstruct the powers of the Political Agents and Residents in their states.

2 READING THE ROLE OF WOMEN IN SUCCESSION DISPUTES: KENNETH FITZE'S *A REVIEW OF MODERN PRACTICE IN REGARD TO SUCCESSIONS IN INDIAN STATES*

The late nineteenth and mid-twentieth century bore witness to dynamic forces of change affecting the succession policies for royal dynasties. As a consequence new systems relating to succession were adopted, which in certain cases questioned earlier precedent or reinterpreted customary practices by revisiting pre-colonial patterns that had been largely forgotten, and in other instances paved the way for novel ideas. In 1947, Sir Kenneth Fitze wrote an official, concise history of succession in princely India on the eve of Independence for use within the Political Department. Fitze, who figured in the last chapter, had been a one time Resident, trained in the classics.[1] This document was classified as confidential and provided a review of 'modern practice in regard to successions.' In particular, it highlighted the role of colonial intervention within princely India in regards to succession law.

Fitze's report is valuable as it brings out of the archive some of the primary succession cases in late colonial princely India. In particular, it reveals the crucial role of royal women – both as symbols and players – in the 'dynastic politics' of these kingdoms. This chapter probes into the way that marriage choices and attitudes towards miscegenation contributed to the succession disputes within the states of Idar, Bijawar, Phaltan and, most significantly, Pudukkottai, which receives an in-depth analysis by Fitze. In addition, it will critique those instances where female rulers directly altered succession law, particularly the examples of the Maharani of Bastar in 1922 and the Begum of Bhopal in 1926. The aim of this chapter is to provide an outline for exploring how regal dynasties were changed by the introduction of western attitudes relating to inheritance and succession law and how they simultaneously opposed exogamous influences. In certain cases, there was sharp discontinuity with pre-colonial practice and in others an upholding of earlier traditions.

The nature of colonial intervention was often undefined and ambiguous. It was in a constant process of change and redefinition. Political officers maintained the authority of paramountcy while celebrating and endorsing indigenous forms of kingship. The hoary and ancient lineages of Indian rulers were lauded and eulogized, even as the British incorporated them under the mantle of the Crown's rule in India.[2]

Kenneth Fitze's report on succession in the princely states demonstrates that there were no consistent or comprehensive rules regarding succession in Indian princely states or the protocol for colonial intervention in local disputes. As he highlighted:

> the principles by which the Paramount Power has been guided in the matter of what Indian States are pleased to called their 'dynastic affairs' are themselves involved in a continuous process of change and development and that, for that reason if no other, it would be gravely embarrassing to give authority to them in any form which could be regarded as authoritative.[3]

His record however is a kaleidoscopic window into the ways in which Zenana women were involved in succession disputes.

Irregular Passions, Dangerous Women

Near the start of his report, Fitze illuminated the importance of religion in affecting marriage law. Muslim and Hindu private law were widely divergent, as they related to succession. Islamic law in regard to marriage is 'expansive and accommodating,' incorporating broad definitions of 'nuptial ceremonies' and appropriate 'social status' for Muslim brides. With regard to Hindu law, he observed that while Hindu marriage practice had long been stratified and particularistic, it too had allowed for unorthodox alliances by the mid-twentieth century. As he outlined: 'In Hindu society, and particularly in conservative Rajput circles, conditions are very different, but in modern times there has been a clearly observable drift towards unorthodoxy, both upwards as well as downwards.' In particular, he cited the then recent marriages of Indore, Mysore, Kashmir and Patiala, who 'would ordinarily have looked askance at the bridegroom's caste' before giving their daughters. Such unusual unions, while 'repugnant' to 'orthodox Rajput sentiments,' were not frowned upon by the paramount power 'as long as there is reason to believe that full recognition would be favoured by any influential body of opinion in the State itself or among brother Princes of the Ruler concerned.'[4] Fitze pointed to the importance of local consent and traditional practice in legitimating marriages and thereby possible successions. In particular, he referred to the marriage of Gayatri Devi from the eastern Kshatriya state of Cooch Behar to the Jaipur Rajput Maharaja, Man Singh II, which allegedly was morganatic.[5]

Nonetheless, certain women were 'dangerous' and their progeny would be excluded from inheritance. The Maharao of Sirohi in 1944 attempted unsuccessfully to secure the recognition of his son by a marriage to a woman 'of dubious social status.'[6] The Rajput Maharaja of Idar had a long association with a Zoroastrian woman, alluded to as the 'Parsee Lady,' who had been given the honorific of royal courtesan, 'Shri Paswanji Saheba of Idar.' In addition, she had been well received in Bombay society. Fitze, however, underlined the distinction between her social position and that of a legitimate Maharani within the Hindu social hierarchy. He provided this example to emphasize the difference between Muslim and Hindu marital law, where religious conversion overrode social or ranked difference: 'This case is only cited in illustrating how utterly a high caste Hindu Ruler is debarred from what is easily permissible to a Nawab, who is free to marry any woman who is prepared to profess herself a Muhammadan.'[7]

In the following Bijawar/Orchha succession, Fitze examined the effect of caste in illegitimate alliances. Maharaja Sir Sawant Singh of Bijawar was adopted from the House of Orccha when there were no near relatives of the previous Maharaja. A Bundela Rajput, he took as his mistress a woman of the Ahir caste, a tribal community traditionally of cow herders and shepherds who are classified as Sudras, whose previous Ahir husband was still alive. By 1911, he had a son named Aman Singh by her. Yet he did not notify the authorities of his son's birth until 1925. As the Maharaja had other sons from his existing Rajput wives, he did not seriously see Aman Singh as a successor at the time. However, when he later pressed for Aman Singh's recognition as heir, the request was denied on the grounds that it would be 'greatly resented by Rulers not merely in Bundelkhand but in Rajputana and Kathiawar, where Bundela Rajput Rulers have in recent years contracted marriages.'[8] It appears here that the Maharaja was not concerned that the status of his lineage might be weakened with such a disputed heir or the possible ostracism he might face when choosing a bride for his son later on among the normative pool of partners from eligible families. In contrast, maintaining local tradition was a key principle of colonial intervention. Furthermore, Fitze noted that divorce was prohibited in Hindu practice, and Aman Singh's mother could not have contracted a legitimate marriage with the ruler. Disregarding this advice, the Maharaja adopted Aman Singh as his successor when he died in 1940. Nonetheless, the Government of India did not legitimate Aman Singh as his heir but chose the son of a collateral relative, who had been overlooked in the earlier adoption by the Maharaja of Orchha in 1897.

The most modern and relevant case, Fitze suggested, was that of the young Heir Apparent of Phaltan, a Hindu Maratha Deccan state, in 1943. The Marathas have often been seen by non-Maratha ruling families as of Shudra stock. While in university, the Yuvaraj fell in love with a fellow female student, a young Hindu Rajput kshatriya woman, from the Prabhu community. In 1943, they eloped to

British India without informing his parents. Lawyers pronounced the marriage valid and the prince's parents, the Raja and Rani of Phaltan, 'a singularly kindly and liberal-minded couple,' willingly accepted their new daughter-in-law. Such tolerance reflects the gradual acceptance by certain states and dynastic families for unions crossing caste, religious and racial boundaries.

Based on these incidences, Fitze concluded with broad statements regarding the differences between Hindu and Muslim marriage contracts:

> From the above review it appears legitimate to conclude that *the Muhammedan Ruler's choice of a consort is almost unlimited, provided only that the lady is of Asiatic origin and professes Islam, and that even for Hindus and Sikhs there is a fairly wide margin of permissible departure from traditions hallowed by custom and tradition. The width of this margin depends, however, very largely upon whether the Ruler is of high, low or intermediate caste and upon the degree to which modern and progressive ideas have developed in the State or community concerned, as well as upon individual factors.* For instance what would be permissible in Phaltan or Cooch-Behar would be anathema in Mewar or Cutch. And *for Hindu Rulers, however liberal and enlightened the local atmosphere may be, the fact that the Hindu religion does not admit of divorce must always*, as in the Bijawar case and despite what has recently happened in Baroda, *be a limiting factor.* The one exception is Manipur where divorce is well established by custom. The present Ruler as Maharajkumar divorced his first wife in 1941.[9]

Through such assertions, Fitze stipulated that religion defined the distinctions within marriage practice. He delineated certain key presuppositions of marital law for Muslims and Hindus as well as for varying castes with the Hindu system. It seems, however, that he is most concerned with Hindu marriage. Muslim rulers had a greater variety of prospective spouses and more flexibility in cementing unions. Hindu and Sikh rulers, premised on their position within caste groupings or other tradition-based hierarchies, were bound by convention to more specialized and particularistic matches. He conceded, however, that no generalities existed across regional or caste affiliations, noting that the unusual 'love' matches by the states of Phaltan or Cooch Behar would be an 'anathema' to the traditional Rajput states of Mewar and Cutch, which had a proud history of 'pure' marriages, maintaining a legacy of non-intermarriage with foreigners dating from the Mughal period. Furthermore, Fitze relayed that the practice of divorce, unauthorized by Hindus, excluded certain types of women from ever legitimately being recognized as queens or Maharanis. This case is particularly resonant with European succession law. The dispute behind the succession of English queen Elizabeth I to her father, Henry the VIII's throne, was largely enflamed by the definition of her mother's marriage. Catholic contingencies objected that, as Ann Boleyn had been tried for treason and adultery (based on the assertion she had taken lovers, including her own brother), she was seen to have been a morally blemished wife and therefore 'illegitimate.' Hence Elizabeth, as her daughter, was a bastard and exempt from inheriting the throne.[10] The type of marriage was as much coloured and defined by the type of woman married.

Such an analysis into Muslim and Hindu marriage law revealed the commonplace fact that British colonial officials from the late eighteenth-century onwards did not intend to 'invent' or 'import' new laws to the lands they governed. In India, this became more pronounced after 1857 when the Government of India was even more hesitant to involve itself in legislative intervention.[11] Its objective was to 'discover' and maintain the indigenous legal practices of each different community or people they ruled. As Rosalind O'Hanlon suggested, the British became 'benevolent guardians of local systems of law and justice and neutral arbiters between their diverse and often fractious subjects.'[12]

In addition, Fitze gave attention not only to the distinctly different nature of Hindu and Muslim personal law and its effects on succession, but, in particular, underlined the problems of miscegenation and the progeny of inter-racial marriages. More than any other case in the report, he provided a detailed record surrounding the crisis of the Pudukkottai succession in the early twentieth century.

Martanda Bhairava Tondaiman was adopted at the age of eleven, after his grandfather Raja Ramachandra died in 1886. He had been chosen over his two elder brothers and, at the time of his selection, the British had been 'relieved,' possibly at the thought of having more influence over a younger, minor prince. They had also believed that, as he was such a small boy, he had not yet been exposed to the 'intrigue of the zenana' and they tried, as much as they were able, to keep him away from 'palace politics.'[13] For that reason, they chose a Mr Crossley, a Cambridge graduate, to be his English tutor in 1887. The Maharaja's British advisors hoped their friendship might pave the way for the prince's lifelong appreciation of European ideas and values.[14] Part of this European exposure came through extensive travel to Northern India, Britain and the Continent.

At first, the experiment worked well. Martanda's boyhood appreciation for all things English initially pleased Mr Crossley and his British advisors at the time of his investiture in 1894. However, it was the very anglicized 'qualities so assiduously instilled in him by Crossley [that] were to make his rule highly troublesome' for the British and the people of Pudukkottai.[15] Like other Europeanized princes, Martanda was often absent from his state and engaged in 'amusements', including racing horses, gambling at casinos and amorous pursuits which did not abet either a British or indigenous ideal of kingship or model for good governance. Eventually, his 'fondness for things European' went beyond travel and leisure activities, and influenced his choice in a wife.[16]

Maharaja Martanda was still unmarried at a late age, leading many to the conclusion that he was a 'confirmed bachelor.'[17] In 1915, the Raja '(having been brought up on European lines and finding no suitable consort among the low caste and backward community to which he belonged) married an Australian lady of good social status.'[18] At first, the British tried to dissuade him by encouraging Martanda to choose a Europeanized North Indian woman of high class, not unlike the daughters of Keshub Chandra Sen who married the Maharajas of Cooch Behar and Mayurbhanj (as will be discussed later). But he remained adamant in his decision and would not take into consideration either his role as the ruler of his state or his caste duties as the head of temple ceremonies in choosing his bride.[19] He had earlier been warned against relations with European women, but had nonetheless had affairs with them and was once engaged to an American.[20]

He met his bride Molly Fink in Sydney in 1915. Fink was described as a fun-loving, attractive young woman who enjoyed going to the theatre and whose family had come upon hard times. Her mother, in a last attempt to have her daughters meet eligible bachelors, rented an apartment in the elegant Hotel Majestic Mansions. Martanda, who was a frequent visitor to the races, soon became part of Sydney's social elite. During a dinner at the Australia Hotel, he met Molly and was immediately smitten by her, pursuing her from one hotel to another. The time had come: he was forty and had 'waited long enough.' Within five months of their first meeting, he proposed to her.[21]

The marriage was contracted against the advice of the British government who gave 'a formal warning that a Ruler ought to marry according to the custom of his race and that the offspring of a mixed marriage could not be regarded as eligible for succession.'[22] King George V in a letter to the Viceroy Lord Hardinge expressed official outrage: 'Miss Molly Fink! What a name!'[23] Most of her family were also aghast at the fact that she was marrying a dark skinned man.[24] Here we see two opposing reasons for disapproval of the marriage. On the one hand, British official discomfort with the choice of working class Caucasian women as brides for Indian princes; on the other hand, the displeasure by an Australian family for the introduction of a racial 'other' as a son-in-law. Within weeks of the marriage, Molly and her sister were being described in the language of the exoticized east in the Australian press:

> ... two big-eyed darlings with oval, ivory skinned faces and pouting, pomegranate lips. They looked as if they could be dressed in Persian 'bags' and veils.[25]

In due course, it was concluded that any child from the union would not succeed to the *gaddi* based on his race and religion. A 'Eurasian boy' would cause 'widespread apprehension among Hindu states' and would be unpopular in Pudukkottai. As Dr K. Nagarajan, an English-trained doctor who was then serving in Pudukkottai, described: 'to be ruled by one who was half-a-Hindu would be against law, tradition and sentiment, but the people of the State, being timid by nature, did not raise any serious protest.'[26]

After a 'fairytale wedding' they returned to Pudukkottai. Molly Fink would not last more than five months in the princely state. In India, she became pregnant, but feared she was being poisoned by someone within the Maharaja's personal court with a concoction made of oleander leaves. As the shipping lines were closed to Europe due to the First World War, Martanda and his wife decided to return to Sydney rather than remain in India. There, in 1918, they had a son, who was named Martanda Sydney.[27] The Maharaja later tried several times unsuccessfully to have Molly Fink officially recognized and his son made his heir. By 1920, he decided to abdicate in exchange for a comfortable pension.[28]

The cost of the abdication was a heavy burden for the state, in addition to the insecurity caused regarding the line of succession. As Dr Nagarajan observed, the abdication cost the state twenty lakhs of rupees, nearly fifteen thousand British pounds of the day. Sidney Burn, a member of the ICS who was administering the state, protested against the size of the compensation, stating that the state could ill-afford to provide it. But ultimately Lord Willingdon overruled the objection, maintaining that twenty lakhs was not overly generous as compensation for the upkeep of a former ruler.[29]

The Maharaja abandoned Pudukkottai and took up his permanent residence in Europe. In 1922, he and Molly settled in Cannes and purchased a grand villa by the name of La Favourite. They took up horse racing and a glamorous social life, becoming intimate with high society.[30] In the meantime, the Maharaja's brother was installed as regent. Nicholas Dirks has highlighted this 'ultimate irony' in the Pudukkottai succession for the British had striven so hard to remove the influence of the zenana on the prince only to see the reverse. 'It was British success in wresting young Martanda away from the seething intrigue of the zenana and state,' he notes, 'that led to his premature retirement, indeed total withdrawal' from governing his own kingdom.[31]

Nearly ten years later, the Government of India decided to re-evaluate the succession in 1927. There were several reasons for this volte-face:

1. The next possible heir was surrounded by intrigue and was considered unsuitable.
2. The worrying possibility, as the Maharaja had no other male issue, that he would make an (inappropriate) adoption.
3. Evidence that the local population had changed their opinion of Martanda Sydney and favoured his succession.
4. A more tolerant attitude from other princes, particularly high ranked Rajput rulers, such as the Maharajas of Bikanir and Nawanagar who were in favour 'provided that it does not form a precedent in the case of non-Sudra Princes and that it would be popular with the State.'
5. Support provided by a law-maker that 'marriage between the Raja and the Australian lady is valid in India' and that, even if Hindu law was applied

to the case, 'the marriage being one between a Sudra and a non-Hindu is a valid marriage and the son by such a marriage is legitimate and a Sudra.'

6. Even if the marriage were invalid and the son illegitimate, Martanda Sydney would still be allowed to inherit, according to the practice for Sudras.[32]

The Government of India suggested that the boy come to India to pass a 'test.' If successful, he would be recognized as Yuvaraj. Martanda Sydney had never visited Pudukkottai before.[33] However, the response proved to be negative. The paramount power disregarded the validity of public support, noting that it was, by nature, 'fickle' and often moulded according to the wishes of the ruler.[34] Furthermore, they negated the value of the opinions expressed by the Kshatriya Rajput princes who had approved of the succession, in favour of the Southern, and more important Sudra ruler, the Maharaja of Mysore, who was in definite opposition.[35] In addition, according to precedent, it was seen as unseemly for a European woman to be fully recognized as a princely consort based on the earlier King's proclamation of 1916. Should her son succeed, Molly Fink would ultimately have received the full title of Her Highness the Rani, which was considered inadmissible. Lastly, and most indicative of both western and Indian restrictions against miscegenation, the Raj feared that approval of such unions would only enhance the western fascination for an Indian prince. As Fitze warned: 'the precedent would tend to enhance for European women the glamour of a connection with an Indian Ruler, with the result that the number of such undesirable relationships would tend to increase.'[36] Viceroy Curzon, himself, had earlier observed this undesirable sentiment with regard to Indian soldiers:

> ... 'the 'woman' aspect of the question is rather a difficulty, since, strange as it may seem, Englishwomen of the housemaid class, and even higher, do offer themselves to these Indian soldiers, attracted by their uniform, enamoured by their physique, and with a sort of idea that the warrior is also an Oriental prince.'[37]

Miscegenation was disparaged in official discourse and literature during the nineteenth and twentieth centuries.[38] As Barbara Ramusack suggested, 'British society in India viewed white women who were sexually attracted to Indian men, and thus subverting the colonial hierarchy, as overtly betraying the imperial mission and covertly undermining claims of British masculinity and Indian male effeminacy.'[39]

Despite such objections, Lord Birkenhead in the India Office in London did give the Pudukkottai Raja some hope of his son's potential succession. He suggested a concession might be made that at some point 'Martanda Sydney may appear to be not merely the most suitable but indeed the only suitable candidate.'[40]

In May 1928, the Maharaja died while in Paris. As the succession was being debated, it was clear that Birkenhead would not be able to follow through on his promise to the deceased ruler. On 6 September 1928, the Government of India sent a dispatch, expressing that 'it is best to adhere to the original decision and exclude Martanda Sydney from succession.' They then examined other possible heirs and advocated the selection of Rajagopala Tondaiman, a seven-year-old boy who was descended from the royal family established in 1720. The proposal was accepted and on 17 November, the Resident wrote: 'the selection has given complete satisfaction to the people except to a small minority who advocated the cause of B.R. Ramachandra Tondaiman.' At the end, no one raised a voice in support of Martanda Sydney.

Martanda Sydney went on to study at Le Rosey School in Switzerland, where he was very unhappy, and Clare College, Cambridge. In his youth, he suffered a leg injury, which gave him a lifelong limp. Eventually, he married a spirited woman, who became an alcoholic, and later left him for another man. According to Coralie Younger, Martanda Sydney was not nonplussed by her departure as he was a practising homosexual and his own mother was the chief object of his affections. In 1945, he was arrested in New York City for a series of robberies that he had perpetrated upon his own circle of affluent friends, which led British officials, who still kept an eye on him, to claim that the offspring of mixed marriages inherited the worst traits of both races.[41]

Fitze stipulated the conclusion that '*the case thus became a strong precedent for the exclusion of progeny of mixed marriages.*'[42] Ten years later, when the Maharaja Holkar of Indore married an American lady, the Government of India from the onset precluded any possibility of his progeny rising to the *gaddi*. Holkar, 'without difficulty' was persuaded to announce his intentions in a public proclamation. This particular history will be explored in greater depth in Chapter 5.

The above instances relating to the suitability of certain females as royal brides or consorts show the symbolic significance of royal women within the broader arena of state politics. In these instances, those partners who were not determined 'legitimate', by virtue of tradition, precedent or popular consent, seriously endangered the ruler's attempts to provide heirs and hence the security of his throne. It is clear that these women were not entirely innocent and knew how to manipulate the prince in favour of their own offspring. Whether the married Ahir woman, the Muslim Paswanji who lived like a Rani or the Australian wife of Pudukkottai, debarred from full recognition by virtue of her race and uncomfortable proximity to the colonial dominators of India, these women had significant influence over the highest authority in the kingdom, the king, and, through him, the state and, ultimately, the kingdom's relationship with the paramount power.

Women Rulers and Succession

Not only did women play symbolic roles in affecting succession by nature of their questionable status or race in relation to the princes who wed them, but royal females also, in their own right, were directly involved in succession matters; some as inheritors, others as arbiters in disputes. The most fascinating case of female succession in an Indian state ordinarily practising primogeniture was that of Bastar. In 1921, Maharaja Rudra Pratap died. The village and pargana headmen, zamindars and local noblemen chose not a male collateral heir, but his daughter, Prafulla Kumari, to succeed. The Government of India considered it a 'question of expediency over right,' but reluctantly agreed. The succession was in due course recognized.[43]

In the memoirs of his years in India, Edgar Hyde, who served in the ICS in Bastar from 1928 to 1947, wrote admiringly of the young Maharani. Having been sent to the state while she was living in England, Hyde recalled the celebrations at her return: 'Her arrival was a festival for everyone; she was tremendously revered by the people being regarded as almost as a deity.'[44] He noted that she was 'shrewd and had a sense of humour.' In his diary, he recorded an anecdote, describing a letter about him which she had sent her comptroller, Pundit Gauri Dutt Joshi, in Hindi: 'Hyde Sahib's letter has arrived; from this he seems to be agreeable enough. Later how it will be <u>kaun jane</u>,' a favourite local expression, 'who knows.'[45]

The peculiarities of her succession did create marital problems, leading the Maharani to discuss the position of her husband with the Viceroy. She had married Profulla Chandra Singh BhanjDeo, a cousin of the Maharaja of Mayurbhanj, when she was fourteen years old, against her own inclinations and those of her stepmother, the Patrani of Bastar. At the time of her marriage in 1927, the earlier Patrani had been exiled from the state, and the young Maharani Prafulla Kumari had been put under surveillance until she was finally 'persuaded' to marry Profulla Chandra. At the time, the marriage dispute had caught local attention in the newspapers as well as the British House of Commons.[46] Despite the fact that the British had advocated the marriage alliance, her husband was barred from having ruling powers. For various reasons, the Mayurbhanj prince 'could not reconcile himself to this position which led to great difficulties.'[47] According to Hyde, as a 'Hindu husband,' he could not resign himself to a secondary position to that of his wife. Nonetheless, the Viceroy could or would do nothing to change the circumstances.

On 28 February 1936, the Maharani of Bastar died after several months of illness in England. Her young son of six years, Pravir Chandra Deo, was installed on the *gaddi* by 24 April when her children returned to Bastar. The proper *abhishek* ceremonies were performed and *nazrana* (tribute) paid by the neighbouring states and vassals of the state.

Hyde played an unusual role in the funeral rites before the coronation of the young prince. The Maharani had been cremated in London and her husband brought her ashes back to Bastar. Before the ashes were scattered in the Ganges, the husband, ordinarily, performed a ceremony which involved placing them in a nearby pavilion. Claiming to be ill and bed-ridden, Sri Profulla passed over the honours to Hyde who was compelled to perform the ritual. Later, Hyde was told that the princely consort had not been ill in reality, but was merely chagrined at his exemption from the succession. As Hyde concluded: 'His character was devious and his actions unpredictable; so much so that the Political authorities feared for the safety of his son, of whom he was intensely jealous.'[48] Other British officials had described him as a 'coward' and a 'vicious rake,' in a curious form of character assassination, claiming among other things that he had given his wife syphilis and made her repeatedly pregnant despite medical warnings regarding her delicate state of health.[49] Such observations are in marked contrast to Hyde's views on the Maharani. Sri Profulla also had nationalist leanings, and had written a newspaper article about the weakness of Indian princes under British paramountcy.[50]

Ultimately, Sri Profulla returned to Cambridge, where he became Secretary of the Cambridge Union, and received a first in Anthropology;[51] a performance that Hyde attested was 'an unusually good degree for a member of a princely family,' furthering an imperialist observation that Indian princes were generally untalented scholars. In due time, Profulla remarried in England, never returning to serve in Bastar. In the meantime, the young heir and his royal siblings were placed under the care of a Colonel of the Indian Cavalry and his wife who had been in charge earlier of a minor prince from Gwalior. [52] Prince Pravir grew up to be a 'high strung child, very difficult to handle ... subject to violent fits of hysterical weeping and screaming,'[53] allegedly caused by the cruelty of his father, Profulla Kumar.[54]

The frustration of the princely male consort emphasizes how unusual female succession was in Hindu states like Bastar. As is clear, it upturned traditional notions of gender roles in a Hindu context and created shifting paradigms of kingship, undermining earlier conceptions of exclusive male power. As Fitze notes such examples of women rulers were rare: 'In other words a female may occasionally be marked out by local circumstances as the "natural heir in the direct line"'. Female successions were few and far between in northern India, except in the Muslim kingdom of Bhopal, which leads us to the second extraordinary case.

Bhopal, situated in Malwa in Central India, was known for its rich arable land as a crossroads of trade between India's east and west coasts. It was the second largest Muslim princely state, after Hyderabad, and it had a population that was 90 per cent Hindu. In the nineteenth century, it was ruled by four successive Muslim women rulers, Begum Qudsia (1819–37), Sikandar (1844–68), Shahjehan (1868–1901) and Sultan Jahan (1901–26).[55] This dynasty of remarkable female rulers was much admired in both Indian and British circles for building projects, educational reform, women's rights, literary achievements and strong administrative and economic leadership.[56] Sultan Jahan Begum, the last of this quartet of powerful sovereign queens, wrote strongly in favour of female rulership:

... from a study of the histories of the world and from my knowledge of my own dynasty, I have come to the conclusion that administrative capacity is more inherent in women than in men, and that nature specially intended them for rulers. Men are given bodily strength to earn their living and to enable them to fight in battles. Women have been granted the qualities of mercy, sympathy, toleration, fidelity and firmness. These render them specially suitable as rulers of kingdoms, though, no doubt, education and careful upbringing are necessary for both sexes. Given these, women are superior to men.[57]

She had ascended the throne of Bhopal at the age of 43 with her mother's death in 1901. The two women had not had a close relationship, and for the last fourteen years of Shahjehan's reign they seldom, if ever, met. Sultan Jahan was a devout, stoical woman, deeply religious, frugal and ascetic. Realizing that the state coffers were empty shortly after her investiture, she became involved in a process of debt relief, and took monies from her personal account to pay for the salaries of state officials. She was a 'caring, meticulous and conscientious' ruler who personally examined the state records, inspected the treasury and appointed each state employee herself.[58] She engaged her three sons, Nasrullah, Obeidullah and Hamidullah in the hard work of running the state and did not allow them to indulge in the pleasures of princely life, such as shikar, polo-playing or midnight orgies as had been the wont of her predecessor.[59]

The education and marriage choices of her sons would later become important causes for a contentious succession crisis in the mid-1920s, which would be felt throughout princely India. In 1902, she celebrated the double marriage of her eldest two sons to the daughters of the Jalalabadis, an important aristocratic family in Bhopal, to which her husband was related. The Jalalabadi women were known for their beauty and their political acumen, and in due course much of the nobility of Bhopal, in addition to the two princely scions, were allied to the family through marriage.[60]

Aware of the growing influence of her attractive young daughters-in-law, who gave birth to progeny soon after, Sultan Jahan Begum brought up her youngest son, Hamidullah, in a markedly different manner from Nasrullah and Obeidullah. Afraid of a potential Jalalabadi 'takeover,' she groomed her favourite son according to her own inclinations. She realized that his security and fame could not come through jagirs and financial resources, which his brothers had in greater amount, but through education and political skills. To this end, 'Little Hamid' did not receive a 'traditional upbringing' 'surrounded by flatterers, courtesans, personal tutors, shikar, polo and the wildlife on their estates.'[61] By contrast, he was sent to an Anglo-Indian boarding school, later university at Aligarh Muslim College and received an apprenticeship in politics that protected him from 'feudal influences.' She also arranged his marriage to a non-Jalalabadi woman,

Maimoona Sultan, whose great-grandfather, Shah Shuja, was the deposed King of Afghanistan in 1812.

As a female complement to Hamidullah, Maimoona was an educated, progressive royal Muslim woman. In Bhopal, she learnt to read the Koran and Hadith, studied Urdu and Persian, and was not expected to practice *pardah*. She rode and shot as did most Bhopali royal ladies. She was taught English by a British governess, Miss Oliver, studied French, learnt to play the piano and violin, enjoyed chess and mah-jong and was instructed in western social etiquette. For Sultan Jahan Begum, this married couple of her own creation represented the best amalgamation of Bhopali culture, including indigenous practices and western progressive reform.[62]

As a ruler, Sultan Jahan Begum was known for her highly progressive sensibilities. She revised the parliament in Bhopal state and pushed for the uplift of women, presiding over the All-India Women's Conference on Educational Reform in 1928. She was also the founding President of the All-India Muslim Ladies Conference in 1914, which supported the education of girls, raised the age of consent for marriage, questioned the practice of *pardah* and suggested the potential banning of polygamy.[63]

Her feelings regarding the future of her family came to a head at the time of her abdication in 1924. Her eldest two sons had died prematurely. In some quarters, there was suspicion that they had been poisoned. Obeidullah, who was then a General, had died of cancer in March 1924. Allegedly, he became psychologically troubled and was extremely cruel to his grown-up children; in one incidence propelling his son to commit suicide through verbal and physical abuse and causing his daughter-in-law to die six months after their marriage from neglect and ill treatment. Nasrullah, who had an advanced state of diabetes, died a few months later in September.

It was a deadly political climate, leading Reginald Glancy, the British Resident, to warn the Viceroy in Delhi that the succession would be a battle to the end.[64] This succession dispute became one of the most notorious cases of any Indian princely state. It represented 'a complicated legal conundrum, a murderous family feud and a political thriller all rolled in one' with far reaching consequences felt in India, the Viceroy's council in Delhi, the British Cabinet and ultimately by King George V himself.[65]

In 1925, Sultan Jahan Begum faced a quandary: her two eldest sons were dead, but Hamidullah, her youngest and favourite, remained alive. As Chief Secretary to the Bhopal Government, Hamidullah had begun to see himself as the de facto Ruler of the state, when in 1925 his mother gave a 'long and reasoned' request for his recognition as her heir in place of Habibullah Khan, the eldest son of her first born, Nasrullah.[66] Habibullah, supported by the Jalalabadi contingent, wrote to announce his legitimacy as the rightful heir based on the convention of primogeniture which had been adopted by many states, both Hindu and Muslim, particularly after 1857.

To bolster her position, Sultan Jahan Begum provided five reasons for her son's succession over that of her grandson:

1. As the ruler, she claimed the right to nominate her successor.
2. Hamidullah's local popularity, personal resources and skills made him a favoured heir.
3. Article IX of the Bhopal Treaty of 1818 barred British intervention in internal state affairs.
4. The Canning Adoption sanad and the Government of India's Resolution of 29 October 1920 noted that the paramount power had itself recognized the application of Muslim states.
5. Islamic law articulated that 'the nearer in degree excludes the more remote in the order of succession in the same class of heirs. Consequently, a surviving son excludes all the descendents in the second degree, who had no locus standi in the eyes of Mohammedan law.'[67]

The British administration only took seriously the fifth and last objection. In the process of reviewing her case, they delved into an elaborate study on Islamic inheritance laws among Muslim rulers. Clearly, they favoured primogeniture. In Delhi, the Viceroy's legal and political advisors, J. P. Thompson, K. S. Fitze and G. D. Ogilvie examined the ramifications of the case. They rejected the Begum's argument in favour of Hamidullah as being 'more capable and more popular' in Bhopal than Habibullah.[68] In addition, the Viceroy's office believed that Islamic succession law had not prevailed over the practice of primogeniture in the dynastic line of Bhopal. If it had, the Begums themselves would not have been rulers. Thus it did not appear applicable that the precedent of Muslim law outweighed primogeniture. On 21 May, they ruled that the Begum could not choose her successor.

However, Sultan Jahan Begum was a fighter and did not lose hope. As a concession to her long-standing loyalty to the British and friendship with the English royal family, the Viceroy conceded to send the ruling out from his office to England, where it would be referred to the British Government, which would make the final decision. Immediately, Sultan Jahan Begum set out to England to cultivate support for her succession nominee.[69]

In London, she was vociferous in pleading her case to all who would listen. Slowly, but surely, her support began building. She was well liked by those who met her, and her educated, debonair son, also an acclaimed polo player, cut an appealing figure in the British public eye. In particular, she pushed her case with English royalty. While King George V assured her that he was only a constitutional monarch, unlike herself who still had ruling powers, the Begum believed it possible for him to help her case. As Shaharyar Khan, her great-grandson acknowledges, it is often in the 'corridors of power, in the cigar-filled libraries of London clubs, at country-house fox hunts and at polo matches' that political decisions were made in Britain, for soon after her audience with George V the succession dispute was re-examined.[70] Lord Birkenhead in the India Office in London renewed the investigation. In particular, the India Office believed that the Viceroy's department had not examined pre-Mutiny cases of Islamic succession in enough depth.[71]

In this moment, just as the Government of India had claimed that the weight of precedent was against her interpretation of Islamic law, a book was found in the India Office, which referred to an earlier Mughal case of succession. In 1765 in Murshidabad, sons of the ruler were preferred to the nephew and this relationship was the determining factor in the succession of Akbar Shah to the throne of Delhi in 1804. A similar case was identified with the succession of the King of Oudh in 1832. The importance of Muslim law in the Delhi case of 1804 arose from Warren Hastings's earlier decree in 1772, attesting that civil rights for Muslims be made according to the Koran. Based on such precepts, the Viceroy's office ultimately accepted the Sultan Jahan Begum's case for the preference of a son over a grandson.

The Begum, whose trip to London had not been in vain, advertised her victory in the case publicly. On 29 April 1926, she abdicated.[72] It was thereafter proven that the right of nomination had existed in Muslim kingdoms in Egypt, Turkey, Persia, and in Mughal and Muslim India.[73] The process of this 'rediscovery' of indigenous law by the British in many ways fostered innovation. Colonial officials were thereby able to manufacture quite 'novel interpretations of law' and simultaneously 'unwittingly aligned themselves with one side or another in what were often pre-existing contests for legitimacy and power.'[74]

As Sultan Jahan said at her abdication, when the time came for her to relinquish her duties as a ruler:

> The last few years were the most tragic of my life, and they tested my endurance and my spirit of resignation of the Will of God to the utmost limit ... Nevertheless these sad misfortunes have affected my heart and mind, and I feared lest they might affect State affairs also, hence I decided to transfer the burden of my responsibility to the shoulders of my successor, so that free from all duties of rule and government, I might devote myself to my prayers, and to the service of humanity, especially my own sex.[75]

However, the issue of later successions was not entirely resolved. On 7 May, the Viceroy sent a telegram that he and his council wished to safeguard the rights of her grandsons should Hamidullah, her son, predecease her. As Fitze noted, the Begum was warned that 'she should be distinctly informed before she makes up her mind finally that on the analogy of the private Mahommedan law, if Hamidullah dies before she does, the succession will go to the senior surviving grandson

... in preference to Hamidullah's own children.' The Begum subsequently abdicated on 14 May.

To safeguard his own legacy and protect himself from the intrigues of his nephew Habibullah, for there had been several earlier assassination attempts, the new Nawab tried to ensure the rightful place of his eldest daughter as heir. He assured the paramount power that 'she will of course go out of the succession if a son is born to me, but otherwise she is entitled to succeed me as a matter of course.'[76]

The Government of India was impressed by the new Nawab's arguments that abdication was synonymous with death of a ruler. For this reason, the heirs to his line had to be protected. Nor were the British officials comfortable with the possibility of the 'almost certain prospect of disorder in Bhopal if [Hamidullah] were to die suddenly before his mother with the succession still undecided.'[77] The Viceroy, at a dinner in Bhopal, made public his support of Hamidullah's succession and the rights of his female heir.

The effects of such squabbles within the courtly family could be egregious. In many instances, soured succession disputes engendered a legacy of sadly unfulfilled dreams and intergenerational jealousies and conflicts. In an age where warring was no longer possible, such frustrations were less often played out in 'cloak and dagger' ambushes or on the battlefield, but found expression in the modern malaises of ennui and excess. In the case of Bhopal, Habibullah, the heir presumptive, died of drink and debauchery by the age of 27, while his younger brother Rafiqullah became an epileptic. So, in the end, the daughter of Hamidullah Nawab succeeded.

Concluding Remarks

The Bastar and Bhopal cases illuminate the significant impact of female rulers as active agents in succession, both as inheritors or arbiters, in Hindu and Muslim princely states. In the case of Bastar, a dying Maharaja chose his daughter as his heir. The daughter proved to be a formidable ruler, receiving the praise of the crown's representative in her state. The unusual occasion of a female succeeding, nonetheless, fostered rifts within the private world of her marriage, where her Hindu husband, the scion of a neighbouring state, could not relegate himself to the subordinate and 'feminized' role of princely consort. Though succession law and state governance placed the woman as ruler, Hindu precepts of gender-defined roles and earlier presuppositions of kingship premised as being male, enabled the young husband to take up cause with his wife. Despite the Viceroy's non-interference and his own inability to change succession, Sri Profulla still believed himself wronged as an emasculated man and prince. Ultimately, when he could not secure the Regency for himself or protect his place in the succession, the princely consort left for English pastures and scholarly domesticity.

The Begum of Bhopal, like the Maharani of Bastar, had directly succeeded to the *gaddi*. In her case, there was a long shadow of female heads of state, going back several generations. With her own old age and death fast approaching, she chose to reinterpret Muslim succession law to establish her favoured son as heir. Upturning notions of primogeniture, the Begum successfully argued and won her case in placing her youngest son, Hamidullah Khan, on the throne.

Fitze concludes *A Review of Modern Practice in Regard to Successions in Indian States* by admitting the limitations of both legislators and political authorities from protecting the interests of rightful heirs. It is an important admission, just as the British are leaving India: 'Even the most eminent lawyers have not full access to the necessary material and the Political authorities themselves, who are both the custodians and interpreters of it, would readily admit the difficulty of ensuring that the right precedents and principles shall invariably receive timely consideration and accurate application.'[78] As he observed, almost all the incidences he described fail to be categorized or compared for they 'illustrate the dangers of attempting to formulate a categorical and comprehensive role.'[79] Through observing local contingencies and customs, each case has its own rationality and logic. Nonetheless, while dynastic politics cannot be classified, being in a constant process of adaptation, Fitze does suggest that such investigative studies and compilations have the possibility of making useful conclusions. What is clearly revealing in this broad canvas of unusual succession patterns in late nineteenth- and twentieth-century princely India is the vital role that women played in affecting the most significant transfer of power in monarchical hierarchies: the succession of the next ruler. Either as arbiters of disputes or the mothers of disputed heirs, they played an important role in affecting the outcomes of successions within Indian princely states. Furthermore, female rulers were often aided by the intervention of British administrators and manipulated Anglo-Indian law to rewrite succession practice successfully towards their own ends.

3 A DISCOURSE ON DESIRE: THE POLITICS OF MARRIAGE ALLIANCE IN THE HINDU ZENANA

Then I was taken to the drawing-room, where Mr. Dalton and the Bengali officials awaited me. Mr. Dalton looked kind but critical.

'Won't you play for me?' He asked.

I obediently sat myself at the piano and played a simple piece of music. Dalton scrutinized me as I went up to the piano and back to my seat and as I talked to him; and wrote a descriptive letter to the Maharajah afterwards.

'Very nice', he said, in such a charming way that I did not think he was examining me. He seemed favourably impressed, and so it proved, for in one of his letters to my father he wrote: 'I thought your daughter a very charming young lady, and in every way a suitable bride for the Maharajah'.[1]

Thus Maharani Sunity Devi of Cooch Behar recollected meeting her husband's British advisor for the first time in a Calcutta sitting room. This favourable interview would serve as the prelude to her initial meeting, eventual engagement and later marriage to the Maharaja in 1878. The encounter, however brief, reveals the growing presence of colonial officials in arranging the political marriages of courtly Indian families during the nineteenth and twentieth centuries as part of a larger expansionist project of 'civilizing', reforming and 'anglicizing' Indian princes. In such a manner, late Victorian, imperial attitudes redefined ideals of conjugality, love and sexuality within the colonial zenana. Sunity Devi's marriage was heralded as a novel alliance between two dynastic elites connected for the first time under the unifying *chatri* (umbrella) of the Crown Raj: an eastern Hindu prince of the indirectly-governed 'native states' and a leading family of the Calcutta intelligentsia situated within the culturally cosmopolitan and politically ascendant British India. Theirs was certainly a marriage which would not have taken place earlier without the intervention of the British.

Here, the Maharaja's British advisor served as matchmaker, overruling the position ordinarily taken by family members, such as the mothers of the ruler or indigenous state advisors. Only after Dalton had found the girl to be 'a suitable bride' did the young Maharaja proceed to meet his bride-to-be. In many ways, both the Cooch Behar and Sen families were products of a late colonial psychology of mind in terms of taste, manners, religious observation and education, and this was not the first nor the last state marriage arranged by British political officers.[2]

The young Nripendra Narayan Bhup Bahadur of Cooch Behar had been brought up as a ward of the British Indian government from his infancy until his adolescence. Like other minor rulers of the time, he was being modeled into the ideal, cosmopolitan prince: educated, progressive and modern. In an attempt to separate him from what was perceived to be the nefarious influences of the palace zenana, his English tutors recommended that the young ruler attend public school in England. His mothers and female relations would not agree, however, to Nripendra's voyage across 'the black waters', where he might lose caste, unless he was first married in India. In part, this proposed marriage to the eldest daughter of Keshub Chandra Sen was arranged to appease the palace ladies in exchange for the Maharaja's journey abroad. As Shruti Kapila has argued in the case of Maharaja Shivaji IV of Kolhapur who had a similar, British-arranged marriage in 1878: 'while British political representatives sought his transformation in education, his family members sought to recognize the [prince's] coming of age by entrenching him in the routine and pleasures of family life'.[3] As ever, colonial officials were engaged in a political tug-o-war of compromise with the matriarchs of the zenana.

The prince's proposed father-in-law, Keshub Chandra Sen, was considered to be the Martin Luther of Hinduism. He advocated a dynamic policy of social reform and a 'superstition free' version of Hindu spirituality, which appealed to Occidental, Christian sensibilities. He endorsed monogamy, a theistic view of divinity that emphasized a belief in one God who was omniscient and omnipresent, the eradication of caste distinctions and greater education for women. His philosophy was neatly encapsulated in his lifelong mantra: 'One God, One Life, One Wife'. Sen argued that women who were learned would make better spouses and mothers, and in 1872 urged the British government to pass legislation, known as the Brahmo Marriage Act, which increased the minimum marital age for girls to fourteen and boys to eighteen.[4]

For the British, they could not have envisioned a better prospective father-in-law for an Indian prince they wished to reform. Furthermore, the union reformed religious practice in the kingdom, as Sen would only agree upon the marriage on the condition that Cooch Behar perform Brahmo rites and rituals. Such arrangements demonstrate the emergent role of a 'drawing-room-styled diplomacy' in the politics of royal marriage alliance making as the British became involved in arranging weddings, often with the ambition of 'westernizing' Indian rulers, even as Indian princes and zenana women co-opted Anglo-European attitudes towards companionship and marriage for their own ends.

This chapter traces these broader themes by examining how the intimate institution of marriage was politicized in late imperial and postcolonial India. For royal and courtly women, marriage historically was a function of state. In a world where dynastic families were innately public institutions, rooted in larger cultural, ethnic and religious identities interconnected through tight kinship networks, political marriage was a fundamental way to connect aristocratic lineages, produce royal heirs and brides and cement strategic military, economic and diplomatic compacts between different kingdoms and elite groups.

From medieval times and even earlier, the private, personal arena of marriage had been central to the public domain of power within the royal court. In Kautilya's *Arthasastra*, a Sanskritic *realpolitik* treatise on kingship among other things, marriage was described as sealing political relationships between ruling families over generations. As Daud Ali has argued, the public nature of royal households was deeply interconnected with private family networks such as those built through marriage.[5] In contrast to Partha Chatterjee's argument of a rigid, gender stratified 'ghar' (home) and 'bahir' (world) in *A Nation and Its Fragments*,[6] this chapter argues that the Zenana woman as both a metaphor and lived personality crossed the inner domestic as well as the outer political worlds during the late colonial period. Marriage was not solely a contract between two individuals or families, but an alliance between different kingdoms and vying nationalisms. Thus, while a private rite, marriage was a highly politicized institution, and the bride remained a key repository of power both within and outside the walls of the palace zenana.

During the pre-colonial period, marriage fulfilled the needs for martial alliances and political ties between competing kingdoms, reflecting relationships of fealty between smaller and larger states while serving to provide for blood-based armies, connected through birth and thereby loyalty, to the ruler.[7] This chapter contests that the British imperial presence dramatically altered these pre-colonial definitions of political marriage for under the Pax Britannica, Indian princes no longer had their own internal armies, thus negating the need for marriage alliances based on military relationships. The new geopolitical territory of British India, which linked regions that were distant and distinct, enabled alliances between groups which ordinarily did not intermarry. At the same time, the introduction of occidental attitudes towards conjugality fostered new definitions of appropriate political marriage. English subsequently became an important language of courtship across differing linguistic regions with the introduction of western-styled education in courtly households for both princely males and females. In the post-Independence period, the Hindu Marriage Act of 1956, which prohibited polygamy, engendered more 'deviant', less traditional, 'love' matches across racial, caste, clan, class and religious boundaries, fostering new formulations of power-brokering in an era dominated by republican ideals and business enterprise.

As an architectural structure and a social institution, the zenana has survived in modified versions up through the 1950s, when royal women still lived within its quarters. A 'zenana mentality' regarding marriage still persists to this day within traditional circles, engendering politicized discourse over the appropriateness of marriage practice as recently as 2001.[8] While there is a rich fund of material, the politics of marriage alliance in the zenana has been relatively unexplored by scholars of South Asia.[9] The records available, including the accounts of courtships and marriages from memoirs and biographies of Zenana women as well as their own oral histories, demonstrate how closely linked marriage-making was with household and state politics. Thus, at a broader level, charting marriage politics in courtly families provides a kaleidoscopic window into how the Hindu princely state interacted with external, centralized powers, whether that of Mughal imperialism during the pre-colonial period, British paramountcy at the heydey of empire or postcolonial nationalism.

Bride as Battlefield: Marriage in the Pre-Colonial Period

Until the early nineteenth century, marriage within the zenana served the primary purpose of facilitating military ties between kingdoms. As in early modern Europe, the royal woman often symbolized both the metaphorical and real battlefield between contesting states. Jean Howard and Phyllis Rackin suggest in their history of gender and British nationalism that the body of the royal bride became the locus for patriotic sentiment and national fraternity. The woman, though hidden within the private realm of the family and cloistered geography of the palace, is a potent, if seemingly invisible, player in the public arena of politics and warfare. They argue that, 'in the struggle for power between men of two nations, the sexualized bodies of women become a crucial terrain where this battle is played out'.[10] The royal bride thereby represents the land that is to be courted, seduced, legitimately married, and eventually penetrated by the dominating foreign prince she is gifted to in marriage. Her fertilized womb comes to symbolize the mixed offspring of a new, hybridized nation, and, as a bride, she claims the symbolic battlefield upon which military campaigns were won or lost.

Though ordinarily perceived by British officials and most historians as having limited influence within the public sphere of the princely state, royal Indian women had substantial political powers, even from behind *pardah*. As Frances Taft Plunkett notes, 'their seclusion ... did not prevent [royal] wives from controlling property, notably land grants provided for their maintenance, or from exercising considerable influence on the affairs of state'.[11] The role of the royal bride on the battlefield of marriage alliance was thus threefold: as wife, procreator and mother of the future heir. As the wife traversing the distance between kingdoms, both spatially and culturally, she cemented martial alliances between varying states, and bridged differences based on religion, culture, language or tradition in moving from one family or kingdom to another. In her husband's kingdom, she held an ambassadorial position, representing a foreign kingdom, people and land often distant and different within her husband's court. As pro-creator, she birthed a blood-bound army in her sons, faithful to one ruler who was the head of a clan or lineage. As mother, she provided significant political and military allies for her children through her own kinship networks.

In a time when the sword still ruled the land and Hindu kingdoms, such as the Maratha and Rajput states, fought among themselves and against Mus-lim conquest, marriage alliances were crucial for facilitating military compacts. During the sixteenth and seventeenth centuries, Hindu Rajputs expressed their cooperation with imperial Mughal rule by arranging marriages between their princesses and Mughal emperors. The princely states of Jaipur, Jodhpur, Bikaner and Jaisalmer all gave daughters to Muslim noblemen and monarchs with the exception of Mewar (and for that reason has maintained premier status among the Rajput kingdoms).[12]

The polygamous nature of Hindu royal households historically ensured the dynastic need for male heirs and younger sons who would serve the ruler in blood-bound familial armies. During the medieval period, women thus pro-vided 'the military and political need for male progeny'.[13] Leslie Pierce, in her work on the Ottoman harem, describes this practice as the 'politics of reproduc-tion'.[14] In her findings, 'marital and reproductive choices were one of the means a dynasty utilized in constructing the image it wished to portray publicly'.[15] Thus, as child-bearer, the royal woman engendered an army devoted to a single ruler or regal lineage.

Furthermore, within Hindu Rajput culture, the male relations of wives and mothers served as crucial military allies for rulers. Throughout Rajput history in Gujarat and Rajasthan, particularly during succession disputes, there is evidence of a strong tradition of support provided by the maternal uncle for his nephew. In 1499, the two elder sons of Raja Rajodharji of Halvad, Ajoji and Sajoji accom-panied their father's bier to the cremation ground, and on their return, the doors to the city were locked, by the mother of the third son, Ranoji, who eventually succeeded his father. The army of his mother's brother, his *mama*, in time fought off the two elder sons. Even during the post-Independence period, the *mama* still continued to be an important familial connection in power disputes. For instance, when Maharani Krishna Kumari of Jodhpur was widowed in 1952, her son Maharaja Gajsinhji II of Jodhpur was only four years old. A vulnera-ble child, he was besieged by contesting factions of the erstwhile royal family, including uncles, cousins and his own grandmother, the dowager queen. During this calamitous period, it was his mother's brother or *mama*, the young ruler of Dhrangadhra, who came to Jodhpur to protect his nephew's interests.[16]

With the arrival of the British, marriage politics in the zenana shifted from the arena of wartime allegiances to diplomacy. After the treaties of 1818, which affectively established British paramountcy, interregnal disputes were decided upon through colonial intervention. The tactics of arbitration rather than warfare became dominant in this new political environment. Thereafter the earlier need for clan armies became less essential.[17] From that time on, polygamy remained effective primarily for two reasons: first, to ensure the birth of male heirs, necessary in a system based on primogeniture, and second, to enable daughters to wed families of equal status. During the nineteenth and twentieth centuries, polygamy thereby remained as a system to consolidate political ties between clan and kinship networks while maintaining ranking and status between families.

Until Independence, several Hindu Zenanas continued to uphold polygamy. Rajput Hindu rulers Maharaja Takhat Singhji of Jodhpur (1843–73) had 27 wives, Maharwal Lakshman Singhji of Banswara (1844–1905) had twelve and Maharao Raja Raghubir Singhji of Banswara (1844–1903) had ten wives. In certain instances, rulers in serious need of alliance making would contract several marriages at the same time. In 1870–1, the Jodhpur heir made a tour, during which time he married women from Narsinghgarh (Central India), Jaipur (Rajputana) and Shahpura (Rajputana).[18]

In marrying their women, royal homes generally practised the custom of hypergamy or isogamy, whereby their daughters wed men of similar or higher status. Louis Dumont noted that hypergamy, or marrying up in the hierarchical structure, was an ancient convention in Hindu society and particularly honoured by Rajputs.

> [Hypergamy] is how the *Rajput* caste ... appears in the literature. If these clans are strictly hierarchized in relation to each other, as is theoretically the case, then one could not marry an equal since one must marry outside the clan, and given that one cannot marry a woman of superior status, hypergamy will be obligatory.[19] [Italics in original].

In the *Manusmriti*, the Sanskrit Hindu legal code for dharmic duty, these kinds of marriages were called 'anuloma' or 'with the hair' and were acceptable.[20] Marriages where men of lower caste or status married women of higher rank were called 'pratiloma' or against the hair and seen as an anomaly. During the Mughal period, Hindu rulers, such as the Rajput kings of Mewar, prevented their daughters from marrying Mughal emperors and noblemen which they believed fostered such 'pratiloma' unions. In certain situations they preferred to marry their daughters to lower ranked Hindu Rajputs rather than to Muslim scions. There is the famous instance of the Maharana of Mewar who would not wed his daughters to Rajput rulers who themselves had given brides to the Muslims, and instead married his daughter to his vassal, the subordinate Jhala chief of Sadri. This 'pratiloma' union quickly soon led to marital difficulties. The princess would not condescend, at first, to bring her husband a glass of water, citing the superiority of her status to his, and the Maharana, himself, had to intercede to solve the dispute.[21]

These traditions of polygamy and hypergamy affected the marriage politics of certain princely states.[22] In Rajasthan, there were long standing ties between the hierarchically wealthier kingdoms of Jaipur and Jodhpur, which historically intermarried. In the early twentieth century, the Jaipur ruler, Maharaja Man Singh II, continued to honour this tradition. At the age of twelve, he wed a princess of Jodhpur, twelve years his senior, and subsequently her niece at the age of 21.[23] However, his third and most well-publicized marriage was one of love not traditional alliance. Such newer marital choices reflected influences of love and companionship upon redefining political marriage during the colonial period.

Diplomacy in the Drawing Room: The Marriage of Negotiation Under the Pax Britannica

By the nineteenth and early twentieth centuries, the primary motivation for royal marriages was to maintain tradition and facilitate ties between courtly and ruling dynasties.[24] Marriage politics had ceased to be a war of arms and became a war of words. As Mrs Modi instructed the young Rajput princess Jaya, heroine of Gita Mehta's novel on the British Raj, times had changed: 'The era of warrior kings ended half a century ago. ... This is the era of negotiations, not heroism, darling'.[25] Negotiation entered the private sphere of marriage arrangements, replacing the battlefield with the Victorian drawing room.

The emergent East-West cultural amalgamation influenced the marriage politics of Hindu royal women. For the colonial government, penetrating the inner sanctum of the zenana was an important way to infiltrate the sacred space of the Indian king, whom it wished to dominate, influence and ultimately assimilate. The royal woman by virtue of her privileged status and sex offered the British Raj access to that most privileged and inaccessible site: the private universe of the indigenous ruler.

English officials and royals became instrumental in the politics of marriage alliances. By manipulating unions between dynastic families, the British Indian government believed it could control the lifestyle, customs and attitudes of native princes. The education and travel of Indian princes overseas simultaneously fostered new concepts of eurocentric love and romance as well as the importation of foreign brides. The integration of 'India' under the British Raj, in ways which linked the many sub-autonomous, divergent kingdoms, furthermore, led to intermarrying between states which were distant and distinct in religion, language, geography and clan history.[26] Through this subtle assimilation, the British Raj alienated some Indian rulers from their ancestral traditions towards an embrace of foreign ideals. The polite society of the drawing room, where swords were never drawn nor voices raised, altered the way power was displayed and augmented.

It is useful, however, to begin with instances of more 'conventional' marriage alliances. The weddings between the kingdoms of Dhrangadhra and Jodhpur in 1943 were such unions between Hindu-Rajput kingdoms, which had historically intermarried in the past. While these weddings were arranged within a pre-colonial definition of status building, the education of the prospective partners and their post-marital interactions reflect the growing influence of European attitudes of companionship. In these alliances, royal princesses from both states were wed to the corresponding young ruler or heir apparent. Krishna Kumari, princess of Dhrangadhra was married to the Yuvraj of Jodhpur, Maharajkumar Hanwant Singhji, while her uterine brother, Meghrajji III, Maharaja of Dhrangadhra, married the young Jodhpur heir's adopted sister, Brijraj Kumari. The intermarrying of two brother-sister pairs was not uncommon in Rajput Hindu royal marriages. In fact, the marriage of the Dhrangadhra princess was contingent on the acceptance of the Jodhpur bride; it was an exchange of two women.

While Krishna Kumari was known for her beauty, Brijraj Kumari, although fair complexioned, was not considered a gorgeous woman. In addition, she was adopted by Maharaja Umaid Singh of Jodhpur from his younger brother, Maharaj Kumar Ajitsinhji, who was her biological father. As she was not the full blood daughter of the ruler or sister of the heir apparent, her rank and status were somewhat questionable, and at first caused anxiety for Maharaja Ghanshyam Singhji of Dhrangadhra, who was arranging these dynastic marriages for his eldest son and most beautiful daughter. While Meghrajji was initially hesitant to wed, he agreed in the end to the match once he understood it would be beneficial for his sister and state, by ensuring strong ties between Dhrangadhra and the wealthier kingdom of Jodhpur. In this instance, the issues of beauty and appropriate social status initially engendered problems for settling the marriage.[27]

Beauty has historically played a vital role in aristocratic Indian culture. The high value placed on bodily beauty has classical antecedents, finding reference in the *kavya* verse of Sanskritic court poetry (*c.* 1st–3rd century BC). Sanskrit poets such as Kalidasa correlated physical beauty with moral integrity and virtue, and beauty in the female form was particularly prized.[28] In *Meghaduta* and *Kumbarasava*, Kalidasa's heroines invariably are physically lovely and a feminine stylized atmospheric beauty heightens the natural environments in which the stories take place.[29] The royal bride's beauty was particularly significant in dynastic marriages, not only because of the highly public nature of the marriage ceremony, but also as it projected the kingdom's symbolic economic, political and social power, thus bringing prestige to the ruling House. A beautiful bride reflected the power of her aristocratic husband over other possible rival suitors, symbolized the future health and fertility of the dynastic line and ensured comely and attractive progeny, which was and remains a significant element of regal splendor and visual display. Royal members, both male and female, were meant to be beautiful and hence a mother who provided such genetic surety was much valued. Indeed in Vatsyayana's ancient text on love, the 3rd–4th century AD *Kama Sutra*, the gentlemanly suitor who represented the height of elegance and leisure was the *nayaka*. The *nayaka* balanced physical beauty, aesthetic refinement and nobility in manner and speech, showing 'good health, manliness, friendliness' as well as 'ambition, great energy, firm devotion'. Foremost among *nayakas* was the king, who embodied the ideal of this combination of good breeding, elegant manners, virtuous conduct and sensual beauty. His female counterpart was that of the *nayika*[30] and the most elevated *nayika* was the royal consort. She should 'possess beauty, youth, favourable bodily marks, sweet speech, attraction to virtue (but not to wealth), inclination towards affection and sexual union, firmness of thought, similarity of birth (to the *nayaka*), a desire to achieve distinction, perpetual avoidance of miserliness in conduct, and a fondness of skills performed at gostis'.[31] This description underlines the preoccupation with beauty as correlative with moral integrity and aristocratic conduct. As to physical form, during the classical period, the Hindu ideal for feminine beauty was often represented in the sculpture of the Chandela temples in Khajuraho, where women had rounded legs, thin waists and voluptuous breasts, reflective of forms and shapes found in nature. The Sanskrit court poet Kalidasa described beautiful women as shaped like the *shyam* tree or the ripe *bimba* fruit.[32] Similarly, Mallika Muhammad Jayasi, a celebrated Sufi poet during the time of Akbar, described the medieval Hindu Rajput princess Padmavati, who was desired by the Afghan descended general Sher Shah Suri, as having a torso like a lion, an elephant's forehead for breasts, a peacock's graceful neck for her own, serpents for her locks and a lotus as her face, with the scent of honey bees around her form.[33]

As Gulbadan Begum, sister of Mughal Emperor Humayun, noted in her sixteenth-century memoir, beauty and virtue were prerequisites for any royal bride offered to her brother. Any 'good-looking and nice girl', who was found to be appropriate, was solicited to enter service with the ruler.[34] Such emphasis on beauty as a signifier of royal birth or the status of a royal consort is reflected in the medieval Persian poetry of the time. In his retelling of the Sanskritic tale, *Nal-Dam* from the *Mahabharata* epic, the sixteenth-century Mughal court poet Faizi similarly highlights the beauty of his royal heroine. The Indian Decani princess was at once both sweet and salty, like a 'pistachio nut filled with almonds' and her beauty so great that it must be 'protected from the public gaze' so that 'only her mirror knows her image well'.[35] Her very beauty paralleled her status as heroine and royal princess. Indeed, Humayun's European contemporary, the English king Henry VIII, had similar concerns regarding beauty in royal spousal selection. He famously rejected his betrothed, the unfortunate Anne of Cleves, allegedly on the grounds that she was not as lovely in person as she appeared in her court portrait.[36]

Beauty continued to be prized during the colonial period, although its external markers may have changed. Fair-skinned women were seen as more desirable brides than previously in part because 'whiteness' was an indicator of social class, as it suggested a life of leisure rather than hard labour, as well as through the introduction of European ideals of racial attractiveness.[37] Influenced by the western idealization of the nubile female figure, the beautiful courtly Indian woman increasingly became one who was athletic, appreciated riding, tennis and shooting and was skilled in western forms of entertainment such as European styles of ballroom dance, song and pastimes, including card games or arranging flowers in cut vases. This female body was invariably flexible and slim and had less facial hair, sculpted eyebrows and manicured hands and feet.[38] In addition, modern hairstyles, such as bobs, became all the rage.

Not only was beauty an important factor in marital choice but so was the role of Anglo-European education during the colonial period as a preparation for marriage. In the case of Jodhpur and Dhrangadhra, all four young royals had been informed by English culture, particularly by the presence of British governesses or teachers. The Yuvraj of Jodhpur was schooled at the anglicized palace school in Jodhpur, and the Maharaja of Dhrangadhra was sent abroad to a British public school, Haileybury. While protected from outside influence behind *pardah*, the women were also introduced to western modes of learning. Thus, while the British government had sway over the legal courts and the business boardrooms, European governesses and tutors were direct members of the princely households in affecting the minds, attitudes and tastes of aristocratic members. They were integral in instilling European values from an early age upon young royal Indian women (and men) and imparting Victorian and Edwardian attitudes regarding marriage, domesticity and family upon their young charges.

Governesses were part of a larger courtly staff, which included Indian ayahs, tutors, religious teachers and attendants, who were responsible for teaching young princesses.[39] They brought with them copies of Home education to India and were determined to teach Victorian virtues of 'Regularity, Obedience, Independence, Courage, Precision, Industry and Delicacy, and embroidered mottoes like 'The Key to Pleasure is Hard work' on lace pillow cases'.[40]

In Europeanized Jodhpur, Brijraj Kumari had been brought up under the aegis of a Scottish nanny, Miss Thompson, who would report to her mother on a monthly basis. An arch Victorian, the governess instilled discipline, hygienic cleanliness and moral uprightness in her ward. The young Jodhpur princess imbibed the virtue of tidiness, making her bed in the morning, ironing her clothes and keeping her cupboards tidy. She and her sisters received graded marks for their husbandry.[41] As a student at the Sri Umed Palace School, along with her other sisters and brothers, she was schooled in geography, Indian, European and Empire history, civics, economics, mathematics, English language and literature, Sanskrit scriptures and epics, Hindi, Marwari and Hindu puja. She read novels such as *Black Beauty, Pride and Prejudice* and *Jane Eyre,* wrote out *The Charge of the Light Brigade* in long-hand, sang Scottish ballads and Indian nationalist songs. In her notebooks, she wrote essays on the early inhabitants of Britain, the lives of the Iberians, the Teutonic tribes and the Norman Invasion. Some of her subjects of instruction were less academic as well, such as physical health, hygiene and painting.[42] Brijraj Kumari also had a rigorous schedule of early morning riding, walks and calisthetics as well as, on occasion, *shikar* or shooting.

Krishna Kumari had a similar education as a member of the Dhrangadhra Palace School along with her brothers and male cousins. The Dhrangadhra Rajshala was founded in a wing of the Ajitnivas Palace in 1929, before being moved later to England, when the boys were sent off to school. In England, the school would be renamed Millfield and is today one of the most exclusive boarding schools in England and the only one founded by an Indian prince. Jack Meyer who later became the principal of Millfield supervised the Dhrangadhra Palace School. Meyer's pupils included Krishna Kumari and her siblings as well as her cousins, the Yuvraj of Jhalrapatan, the Thakor Saheb of Wadhwan and his younger brother. It is probable that the girls, in these early years, were schooled in the same subjects, which included British history, English language and literature, classical Greek and Latin mottos, as the boys. They studied the reign of Alexander the Great and memorized glib quotations such as *Veni, Vidi, Vici.* Krishna Kumari was also instructed in English and studied human biology, examining scientific textbooks with pictures of the male anatomy.[43] As Maharaja Meghrajji of Dhrangadhra described a typical classroom scene:

> e.g. the Battle of Agincourt, 1415. (See? I still remember the year, automatic like). We would of course reel off, '*William the Conqueror 1066, William Rufus 1087 ...*' at the drop of a hat. As to non-British dates, such as 'of the French Revolution', pfui! There were no Indian dates either that I remember. When did Babar, the first Moghul, clobber Sultan Ibrahim Lodi at the Battle of Panipat? Who? I think [Jack Meyer's] interest in Indian history began (and perhaps ended) with Clive! I doubt if he'd heard of the Veda or emperor Ashoka or even of yoga.[44] [Italics in original].

Similarly, Sita Devi, Ranisaheb of Kapurthala, received lessons from nine in the morning until two in the afternoon, with athletic games played afterwards, which included riding and tennis. Like Brijraj Kumari, she was instructed in Sanskrit, Hindi and English as well as general studies in literature, history and religion.

Although her father out of 'sheer eccentricity' stopped the girls from learning English, when her brothers were sent for schooling to England, she continued to be educated by tutors.[45] When she married Maharajkumar Karamjit Singh of Francophile Kapurthala, the first thing her father-in-law Maharaja Jagat Singh did was to give her a tutor for French instruction.[46]

In addition, the English governess or tutor was an important companion for young Zenana women in the early twentieth century. As a child, Brijraj Kumari was closer to her governess than her own mothers, biological and adoptive. She remembered that it was Miss Thompson who was the first member of the Jodh-pur household to see her after the many hours of her wedding ceremony in 1943. 'My governess', she reminisced, 'came the next morning. She met [my husband]. She said nice things to me. She told him to look after me and make me happy'.[47] Clearly, her governess' presence during this first day of her marriage remained a stirring memory, even fifty years after the event.

Similarly, when a princess of the Bikaner family had been married, she would not leave her parents' home until she could see her governess, Edith Dent. As the time for her departure drew near, the young bride 'suddenly burst into tears and asked for Nanny. Her husband, the Maharana of Udaipur, was helpless. The train was waiting and guests heaved a sigh of relief when Edith Dent appeared on the platform, bustling along urgently, "smiling, reassuring"'.[48]

Not only were the childhoods of these Zenana women marked by the colonial experience through the presence of the British governess, but so was the intimate exchange of their wedding nights, where English was the primary language of courtship and romance. For Krishna Kumari and Brijaj Kumari, those midnight meetings, after hours of ceremonies, pujas, and dinners with the extended rela-tives and court, were their first conversations with their husbands. As they were marrying across geographic and linguistic divides, English was one way of medi-ating difference. It was the lingua franca throughout the varying principalities of colonial India. As Krishna Kumari recalls, '[my husband] spoke in English because they spoke it in Dhrangadhra; all the children spoke English'.[49] In Brijraj Kumari's experience, the place of education, and particularly British literature, had an even more influential role. As she recalled at the time of her first meeting with her husband, he questioned her on her education: '[My husband] asked me if I was educated. He was well educated'.[50] Her husband subsequently wooed his wife with readings of Shakespeare and lessons in mathematics and history during the early years of their marriage. As women ordinarily did not learn the language of their married homes until after they arrived there, through engaging with their in-laws and attendants in the new home, English served as the language for the intermediary period of transition.[51]

These first meetings between Zenana women and their husbands are power-ful windows into the cultural world of the Indian princely state. When Krishna

Kumari married in 1943, she was alone with her husband for the first time at five in the morning after their wedding rites were completed in the courtyard of the Suraj Mahal Palace in Dhrangadhra. The dawn was lightly washing upon the flat desert and the waters of the Mansar Lake outside the palace walls. She was so nervous that she lost her voice and appetite. The newly weds were both exhausted by the lengthy ceremonies which had lasted several days, but the Maharaj Kumar of Jodhpur was keen to outline the political dynamics within his father's court and his expectations to his new bride. He explained his views on his family, the practice of *pardah*, which he did not endorse (a somewhat radical opinion at the time) although his mother did, and his conception of a royal wife's duty to her husband. The conversation was entirely in English, as the two newly weds could speak no other common language with similar ease, and the concerns raised reflect both an anglicized and indigenous concept of political marriage. He told her that she must embody four different roles as a wife and future queen:

1. She must give counsel like a *mantrin* (minister) in presiding over the palace household
2. She must be a *dasi* (slave woman) in unremittingly looking after her home
3. She must treat her husband and the kingdom of her married home like a *matr* (mother), feeding them love and affection
4. She must be a *rambha* (dancing girl or seductress) in bed with her husband.

This statement clearly delineates the merging of traditional and western ideas and forms of communication. The traditional values for an ideal Rajput wife are expressed in an alien and domesticated language, English, marking the hybridity of private and personal communication among young royals.

As Krishna Kumari believed, the last quality of sexual ability and pleasure fulfillment was as important as the other roles, for it was through the bedroom that she could maintain power over her husband in his affections despite the distractions of a polygamous household, and, thereby more likely guarantee herself the security of becoming pregnant and having a son. As the mother of the future king, her place in the zenana hierarchy would then be ensured as the *patrani*. To prevent her spouse from enjoying other women, particularly courtesans, she argued that a wife has to cultivate the allure of a dancing girl to entice, captivate and retain her own husband.[52]

Such ideals relating to sexual gratification were elemental to ancient Hindu texts on love, such as the *Kama Sutra*. According to the *Kama Sutra*, a high caste or class woman learned about the pleasure of sex from a trusted female, such as a nurse who had brought her up, a sister or a companion. Sexuality, particularly in courtly environs, was intimately tied with aesthetics. In this way, skill in dancing, verbal virtuosity, rhetoric, the gift of song, comeliness in dress, wearing scent and forms of play or entertainment were connected with sexual pleasure.[53] These women incorporated some of these classical conceptions of display, dress, beautification and deportment in their behaviour towards their husbands. At the same time, Victorian concepts of sexual morality had penetrated the zenana. While Krishna Kumari was told by her husband about his expectations of her, both in terms of family politics and in sexual life, neither she nor his sister Brijraj Kumari had ever earlier discussed sex with their female relations, their governesses or instructors. Nonetheless, they would both have been well aware of the presence of their father's and grandfather's courtesans, whom they may have in certain contexts dined, danced and in other ways socialized with, and they understood that marriage and pregnancy were closely linked.

For Brijraj Kumari, whose governess was an old-fashioned Victorian, female sexuality was limited to the world of romantic fantasy, overawed by a disciplined life of routine, personal hygiene, sport and lessons. In many ways, the zenana world Krishna Kumari and Brijaj Kumari grew up in taught them about the broader aesthetics of sexual engagement, such as clothing, etiquette, dance, the wearing of jewelry and scent, cultivating a pleasing temperament and gentility in speech and behaviour, but not perhaps the more explicit elements of sexual intercourse. According to the *Kama Sutra*, courtship before or after marriage should include a period of conversation, where the wife initially refuses her husband until she is wooed by gifts and conversation, in a manner not dissimilar to the way these royal women were wooed by their husbands on their wedding nights and the first few weeks following marriage. In many ways, the early post-marital lifestyles of these women included hybrid elements of both European and indigenous courtship rituals.[54]

Certainly, for the British, the upper class Indian woman's body appeared more sexualized than the non-eroticized femininity of her European counterpart.[55] While her husband focused on the project of empire-building, the British woman in India, often typified by the prudish, self-denying memsahib, was to be a gracious hostess and protector of her husband's physical and psychological health while maintaining the structure and basis for white rule. During the eighteenth century, it had been not been uncommon for Englishmen to maintain households with Indian wives or companions, commonly referred to by Company officials as 'bibis'.[56] Many Britons in India had native women as mistresses and lovers who ran their domestic households and in the process adopted indigenous forms of dress, manners, religious practice and toilette during the early colonial period.[57]

By the time of the Mutiny in 1857 and as the long nineteenth century extended such fluid interracial domestic arrangements became increasingly uncommon, particularly with the introduction of British women to India. The building of new railways, steamships and the Suez Canal in 1869 radically transformed communications between Britain and its prize colony. These new forms of transportation allowed Englishmen to return more frequently to Britain on leave, send their wives home during pregnancy, educate their children in the metropole and enable Englishwomen to travel more regularly to India for the purposes of marriage. Called popularly the 'fishing fleet' these young girls sailed out to India ordinarily at the start of the cold season in search of husbands. European women were often in high demand in British India where there were fewer women than satisfied the demand.[58]

British women were thus integral in creating more rigid racial, class and ethnic boundaries between Europeans and Indians after they began coming out to India in the second half of the nineteenth century and onwards. While the image of the memsahib has become a crudely drawn colonial stereotype, there are elements of truth: the memsahibs did further the colonial project of creating rigid racial boundaries between Britons and Indians, limiting relationships of friendship between the two communities, and fueling fears of Indian male (and female) lascivious sexuality.[59]

India with its exotic sensuality may well have roused the curiosity of British women as well as heightened their anxiety. The Indian woman, who lived within a polygamous household under the stultifying influence of a hot climate, would have appeared to western eyes as more sexually experienced and sophisticated than her western contemporaries. Furthermore, the culture of the Indian dancing girl and courtesan, which had received notoriety through the relationships of British *nabobs* with Indian women during the eighteenth century as well as the explicit erotic imagery of Hindu temple architecture, suggested that both Indian women and men were more libidinous than Europeans.[60] Anglo-Indian novels romanticized the taboo relationship between white women and lascivious Indian men, particularly in the theme of the disputed rape.[61] E. M. Forster's *A Passage to India* and Paul Scott's *The Jewel in the Crown* both deal with the controversial theme of interracial rape and the response of tight-knit Anglo-Indian communities to the threat of violence against their women.[62] When the female heroines of both novels choose not to testify against their alleged (Indian) rapists, their own people turned upon them.[63] At the same time, Indians saw English women, who walked freely in public, danced with men they were not related to or displayed naked décolletage at social functions, as loose and sexually available, synonymous with the prostitutes and dancing girls of their own society.[64] When the ruler of Oudh visited a European ball in the days before the Mutiny, he took the ladies on the dance floor to be dancing girls, and not particularly gifted ones.[65]

The lives of these early twentieth-century Indian royal women reflect aspects both of imperial sexual restraint and companionate conjugality as well as the influence of a pre-colonial indigenous traditions of aesthetics and courtly sexuality. It is hard to argue whether these Hindu women were less bashful about sex than their western contemporaries or vice versa, but certainly their experiences combined aspects of both indigenous and Victorian definitions of female sexuality.

Not only were traditional marriages affected by western attitudes towards conjugality but the creation of an Indian 'whole' under the Raj encouraged inter-marriage between princely homes, which may not have earlier intermarried. Just as Rajput Hindu princely states tended to principally marry other Rajputs, most other royal houses, whether the Sudra descended Marathas, the Sikh kingdoms of Punjab or the east Indian kshatriya principalities, also chose to marry within tra-ditional circles. However, as the 'idea of India' began to shift, so did perceptions of political marriage and desirable partnership. Two such marriages, the marriages of Vijaya Raje Scindia, a Rajput-Rana noblewoman from Nepal married to the Maratha ruler of Gwalior state, and Sita Devi, a Rathor Rajput princess who wed a Sikh prince from Kapurthala, are informative of this trend. The choice of these women demonstrates how the pool for desirable mates widened during the colo-nial period to allow for a greater diversity of possible choices.

In many ways, Vijaya Raje's marital choice reflects her family's upwardly mobile aspirations in political alliance making as well as the decision to go beyond earlier, traditional circles. The Ranas of Nepal claimed descent from the Sesodia Rajputs of Mewar in India. In her case, the Nepalese court had exiled Vijaya Raje's family to India. Generally Ranas living in India inter-married with other Rana families or the Rajput clans with whom they had earlier marital connections.[66] Vijaya Raje, herself, went through several marriage propositions. It is interesting to note how, as time went on, the proposals came successively from higher status men and from farther afield, beyond the pool of eligible Rana and Rajput men. Her first proposal came from a Rajput man who worked in the Indian Civil Serv-ice.[67] Her second marriage proposal arrived from another Rajput nobleman, this time a Lieutenant in the King's Commissioned Officers of the Indian army. This proposal was broken after the young lieutenant was called to serve during the Sec-ond World War in 1940.[68] Her third marital invitation came from the brother of the ruler of Tripura, a kshatriya Hindu state in eastern India. Through an intro-duction to the Tripura royal family, her uncle was able to facilitate an engagement with the higher-ranked, larger Maratha state of Gwalior in Madhya Pradesh.[69] She married Jivajirao Scindia on 21 February 1941.[70] In many ways, the story of her successive proposals demonstrates the aspirations of her family to procure the most advantageous husband, one who might not have been accessible in the ear-lier, pre-colonial period. The idea of a desirable husband here was not limited to a man of an old or illustrious bloodline (e.g. Rajput aristocratic lineages) who the Ranas had earlier intermarried with, but one who reflected the wealth and power of a newer dynastic elite. It is also interesting to note that her meeting with her prospective husband and the final marriage agreement took place within the met-ropolitan city of Bombay in the hub of British India. To her prospective in laws, she was portrayed as a girl of good stock, with both Rajput and Rana parentage, who was religiously devout and yet modern.

The Scindia monarch was one of the most prominent Maratha rulers in mid-twentieth-century India. Except for her mother-in-law, who was a Rajput, Vijaya Raje was the only non-Maratha woman to be married into the Scindia family in 200 years. As she noted in her memoirs, 'Caste and clan considerations made it obligatory for [Maratha rulers] to find their brides from among their own people, and from within a hundred or so families which possessed the proper origins and ancestries'.[71] Indeed, their union represented new expressions of suitable alliance. She wrote so 'was that how marriages arranged themselves, I wondered. At some stage they slipped out of the clutches of the arrangers and took off on their own. For even though no one had said anything definite yet, I had already become convinced that the Maharaja of Gwalior had made up his mind. And so had I'.[72] In post-Independence India, Vijaya Raje was to play a significant role in national politics, serving as vice-president of the Hindu nationalist Bharatiya Janata Party (BJP) in the late twentieth century.[73]

Similarly, Sita Devi's marriage reflected these early twentieth-century aspirations for legitimacy through purity of bloodlines. Born into the small Rathor Rajput state of Kashipur in the United Provinces in 1915, Sita Devi was brought up believing she would marry a nobleman from another Rajput princely state. Kashipur observed the traditions of the zenana, and she grew up in strict *pardah*, after the age of seven-and-a-half. At thirteen, she was married to Maharaj Kumar Karamjitsinh of Kapurthala, a Sikh state in the Punjab.[74] The two states were distant in geography, religion and observance of zenana traditions. In many ways, she was desirable to the Kapurthala family, which although highly westernized wanted to cement ties, as did the Marathas, with the ancient, status-bound Rajput dynasties. For them, a Rajput bride would help connect their younger royal lineages with older feudal lines. At the same time, the Kashipur family recognized the wealth and power of the Sikh royal dynasty in the late colonial environment. Indeed, Sita Devi herself represented a blend of tradition and modernity: she came from an old, Rajput aristocratic background yet was being educated to hold her own in the English language and European subject disciplines.

Rajput-Sikh intermarriages generally were not condoned. The Yuvraj ('heir apparent') of the Jhala Rajput state of Jhalarapatan in Rajasthan had been engaged to the Sikh princess of Patiala. His mother was horrified at the prospective union. As the Maharaja of Dhrangadhra recalls, 'A Rajput marrying a Sikh? Forsooth! Unheard of, unthinkable! She went on a fast. At last, my father [who was the head of the Jhala clan and whose wife was the elder sister of the Jhalarapatan queen] ... intervened. He wrote to my uncle. 'Break the match'. That was that'.[75]

Kapurthala, a westernized, progressive state, was keen to foster ties with the ancient dynasties of Rajputs. Sita Devi's father-in-law, Maharaja Jagatjit Singh, was an avid Francophile and the family spoke French, visited Paris annually and fashioned their palace in the style of Versailles. They did not observe *pardah*. When Sita Devi arrived as a young bride, the first gesture her father-in-law made was to take off her *ghunghat* (a veil worn by married women), and walk her, open faced, through a throng of people who were waiting to greet her at the Kapurthala train station. He told her gently, 'This is your home now, and your people want to see you'.[76] In this manner, Sita Devi, like her European-educated sister-in-law Brinda, was chosen because she was a Rajput bride, who brought added luster to the family while further establishing the Kapurthala dynasty. At the same time, she was fashioned as educated, westernized and in this way thoroughly 'modern' equally at ease within the zenana as well as a Parisian salon.

In other instances, the role of the colonial presence was more acutely felt when British officials were asked to arbitrate marriage alliance disputes. In 1853, Maharaja Ram Singhji of Jaipur in mid-western India was travelling to Rewa in Central India to marry the daughter of the ruler. Knowledge of this event excited protest from the Maharaja of Jodhpur, whose daughter was also affianced to Ram Singhji. As the Jodhpur engagement had been initiated earlier, the Jodhpur Maharaja demanded his customary right to have his daughter marry first. To press his claim, he 'lost no time appealing to British authority to enforce tradition'. British officials warned Ram Singhji that if he did not honour his first commitment, he would lose his ceremonial honours when passing through British Indian territories. Under this threat, the Maharaja yielded with alacrity and proceeded first to Jodhpur.[77]

Drawing room diplomacy was most strongly apparent, however, when the British became involved in arranging weddings, sometimes, with the ambition towards 'anglicizing' Indian rulers. The marriage of Sunity Devi to the Maharaja of Cooch Behar is indicative of this trend, and the events of her engagement clearly demonstrate the intervention of the British in arranging the affairs of courtly domestic households. Her niece, Benita Sen, a granddaughter of Keshub Chandra Sen, would also marry into princely India – in her case, the Buddhist kingdom of the Chakma Raj in eastern Bengal. Just like the Cooch Behar court, the Chakma Raj was also in favour of selecting a schooled and westernized young woman as their Rani from a leading kshatriya Bengali family. The Sen family had already married several of their daughters into royal homes, including Cooch Behar, as well as Mayurbhanj and later Kapurthala. While it is not clear if British officials were involved in the marriage negotiations, certainly her future father-in-law desired a progressive, westernized girl for his heir. In this regard, Benita Sen's pedigree was excellent. While her father's relatives were educationalists, leaders of religious reform and intellectuals, her mother, Nirmala Sen, was also descended from an erudite, politically powerful kshatriya family. Benita Sen's maternal grandfather, Purna Chandra Sen, served as the Advocate General of Burma and one of her younger brothers, A. K. Sen, was a judge of the Calcutta High Court. The Sens, while not a royal family, were of kshatriya stock and the descendents of the Sena Rajput kingly dynasty of Bengal from the tenth and eleventh centuries.

Benita was born in Surrey, England on 18 August 1907, while her father, Saral Chandra Sen, was studying for the bar. As a product of two intellectual families, she was known as a 'brilliant' student as a girl and won a number of prizes for her scholarship at Bethune College in Calcutta and elsewhere. Her engagement, even if to a Raja, came as a rude awakening to her and she considered marriage a great distraction from her studies. At age eighteen, she left college for the rural environs of Rangamati, the capital of the Chakma Raj kingdom, in the Chittagong Hill Tracts. Similar to Cooch Behar, Rangamati was a place of relative isolation from the hub of metropolitan India, where she lived a countrified existence in a region of great geographical beauty with rivers, lakes and forested hills. For a woman who was used to the urbane circles of cosmopolitan Calcutta, becoming Rani of, in her words, a 'primitive' state, was very difficult. The Chakmas practised a foreign religion, spoke the Tibeto-Burmese language of Sangma rather than the Sanskrit-derived Bengali and wore costumes of indigenous weave, which were different both from traditional Indian saris and the dress of the Europeans and anglicized Indians whom she grew up with.

Despite this fraught transition, she was fortunate in have a doting husband who encouraged her to continue her interests in both western and Indian education and in time she grew to appreciate the Buddhist traditions of her married home.[78] In the 1970s, she would serve as a Minister in the central Bangladesh Government.[79] In this way, the desire for modern, yet connected brides reflected the ambition of various princely lineages – Maratha, Sikh and Buddhist – to display, on the one hand, the public face of modern change through the institution of marriage and the person of their new daughter-in-law, while at the same time cementing bonds with established, old families, which would heighten their prestige according to pre-colonial definitions of status-building.

Not only did British government officials serve as matchmakers or western-leaning, prospective fathers-in-law, but so did English monarchs in these drawing-room negotiations. Their aim was to reshape the Indian princes as ideal indigenous rulers, upholding customary practice by emphasizing lineage purity and ancestral tradition, as well as progressive, westernized dynasts, successfully adopting the more 'enlightened' principles of British education, the English language, and companionship in marriage. In a famous case, Queen Victoria was instrumental in proposing an alliance between the deposed Sikh ruler Duleep Singh of the Punjab and the Hindu princess Victoria Gourrama from the kingdom of Coorg in the South. The young Maharaja Duleep Singh, son of Maharaja Ranjit Singh, the 'Lion of the Punjab', was deposed by Governor-General Dalhousie when the kingdom of Punjab was annexed in 1849. The boy-king was quickly made a ward of the British Empire, converted to Christianity, and taken to England for schooling, where he became a favourite of Queen Victoria. In England, Duleep Singh was given a comfortable allowance, worthy of a nine-teenth-century British gentleman, and kept away as much as possible from the influence of his former Sikh subjects and relatives in India. Although later in his life, Duleep Singh would convert back to Sikhism and long to return to the Pun-jab, his story is a case in point of the 'gentrifying' and 'anglicizing' of the Indian kings by the British. As the Queen, who took a personal interest in Duleep Singh, wrote: 'What he might turn out, if left in the hands of the unscrupulous Indians in his own country, of course, no one can foresee'.[80]

Known as a domineering grandmother among European royals, arranging unions between her younger relations from Russia to France, Queen Victoria showed similar interest in Duleep Singh as her godson. The Queen saw the prospective alliance between Duleep Singh and the princess of Coorg as one of compatibility between personalities, culture and religion for 'they are both religious, both fond of music, both gentle in their natures'.[81] While the Queen suggested the marriage, she did not deny the value of love and choice. In a let-ter from Charles Osborne to Lord Login, Victoria Gourrama's guardian, he describes the Queen's intents:

> I know that the Queen thinks that this would be the best arrangement for their happiness *provided that they were to like each other* – of course, without this no happiness could exist. Of course the Queen takes a great interest in the little prin-cess, as Her Majesty considers Herself as *more* than a Godmother to her. [Italics in original].[82]

Duleep Singh, on his part, was surprised to find himself involved in an arranged marriage and, at that, in the West. He believed such calculated proceedings were 'not the European way' and was determined to remain a bachelor.[83] Later, he cited Victoria Gourrama's indiscreet, flirtatious nature as reason for his rejec-tion, noting she would make an inappropriate wife.[84] However, when Duleep Singh expressed passionate interest in a young English aristocrat, the Queen and her advisors adamantly opposed that liaison.[85] Obviously, she did not favour miscegenation.

Duleep Singh was not the only Indian royal or elite the Queen was on close terms with. In 1870, Keshub Chandra Sen visited the Queen at Osborne House, her residence on the Isle of Wight, and presented her with a portrait of his wife. She was 'so pleased' by the gift, as he wrote of their meeting, that she requested his portrait and gave him two inscribed copies of her books, *Early Years of the Prince Consort* and *Highland Journal*.[86] In 1887, the Queen met Maharani Chimna-bai of Baroda, when decorating her husband Maharaja Sayajirao with a G.C.S.I. (Knight Grand Commander of the Order of the Star of India) at the time of the

Golden Jubilee. The Queen was intrigued by the Maharani's clothes and jewels, and her 'gentle ... but very willful' nature.[87] She also encouraged the attentions of the Maharaja of Indore, who was never remiss in sending her a birthday telegram, the Maharaja of Kapurthala, who dined with her in the company of the Tsar and the Kaiser, and Sir Pratap Singh, a leading Rajput nobleman, who was the Raja of Idar and three-time regent of Jodhpur.[88]

The Cooch Behar family in particular had a close relationship with the British royals. They arrived a few months before Chimnabai and Sayajirao Gaekwad for the Golden Jubilee in 1887, and were soon caught up in the functions of the social season. They attended dances, receptions and garden parties, dining with the Prince of Wales and residing in a luxurious gilt bedroom, when they stayed at Windsor Castle.[89] Maharani Sunity Devi was well liked by the English royal family and was on familiar terms with Princess Mary, who later became Queen Mary, the Duchess of Teck and Alix, Princess of Wales.[90] At her formal presentation to the Queen in Buckingham Palace, Sunity Devi was the only woman whom Victoria kissed in greeting that day; a rare sign of favour.[91] A few months later when Sunity Devi became pregnant, the Queen stepped in as the future godmother of her son, Victor, who was born in May 1888.[92] Such close association with the British upper classes would continue when the Maharani returned to India. She and her family feted the leading members of the Victorian and Edwardian aristocracy, who regularly made visits to Cooch Behar for shooting and other recreational activities.[93]

Queen Victoria's partiality towards Indians, both princes and others, was openly criticized. Lord Curzon believed she was too familiar with the Indian rulers, spoiling them through her attentions and 'invest[ing] them with an aura of royalty they ought not to possess'.[94] He wrote that 'almost anyone with a turban and jewels was regarded in Europe as prince and treated as if he was a descendent of Nebuchadnezzar'.[95] Curzon suspected the Queen encouraged these friendships with the princes, in spite of being aware of the true weaknesses of their characters.[96] At the end of her life, she would most famously come under fire for her relationship with her Indian servant, Abdul Karim.

Karim was a Muslim of modest parentage from Agra, who was presented to the Queen two days after her Golden Jubilee. In time, he came to be much more than a servant, rising to the position of the Queen's Indian Secretary and teaching her Hindustani and Urdu.[97] Later, she would unsuccessfully petition to honour him with the highest merits, including a K.C.I.E. (Knight Commander of the Indian Empire), ordinarily reserved only for the most prominent Indian princes, and the Royal Victorian Order, given for personal services rendered to the Sovereign.[98] As she did with the Indian princes, she became involved in Karim's domestic life. She housed his wife and mother in Frogmore Cottage on the grounds of Windsor Castle, and obtained a gynecological doctor, when his wife was having trouble conceiving.[99] Affectionately termed the Munshi by the Queen, it was widely believed that he was influential in affecting Victoria's opinions on India and was privy to her confidential papers, such as the letters of the Viceroy. Members of her royal household, which included the widowed Lady Lytton, wife of the former Viceroy, actively blocked the Queen's attempts to distinguish her favourite. Until her death, his position in the household was highly resented, and Queen Victoria believed that it was an irrational and petty 'race prejudice' which had elicited such fierce jealousy from her staff.[100]

While there were several Indian princes who did not have such intimate relations with the British crown nor were chosen as favourites like Abdul Karim, those that did were deeply influenced by their contact. For much of his youth, Maharaja Duleep Singh viewed the Queen as his mother and she correspondingly shaped his opinions on marriage, religion and family in his early years. His children were even more affected by their proximity to the British court. His son Victor, also a godson of the Queen, would later marry an English aristocrat, Lady Anne Coventry, in 1892.[101]

The Cooch Behar and Baroda royal families, as well as those of Kapurthala and Indore, were also significantly transformed through their close associations with Europeans. These dynasties educated their sons in English or European boarding schools and universities, encouraged their children to cultivate an interest in European pastimes, gave their daughters access to European social venues such as balls, parties and finishing schools, and later, in certain cases, the younger generation fell in love with or married Europeans.[102] Thus, not only did English officials and royals become players in the marriage market, but European perceptions of love and romance also began to create new patterns for royal marriage. As Dipesh Chakrabarty has noted with regard to domesticity in nineteenth-century Bengal:

> The British in India ... promot[ed] the idea that husbands and wives should be friends/companions in marriage ... It reflected the well-known Victorian patriarchal ideals of 'companionate marriage' which the British introduced into India in the nineteenth century and which many Bengali male and female reformers embraced with great zeal.[103]

Two interesting cases are the marriages of Sunity Devi's daughter-in-law, Indira Devi of Baroda, and her granddaughter, Gayatri Devi of Cooch Behar. In both situations, these royal women chose love marriages, which were radical acts for the early twentieth century. They were not only in many ways 'European' in education, having studied and lived abroad, but they would adopt romantic aspirations relating to love and companionship in the choice of political marriage.

Indira Devi, daughter of the progressive Maratha ruler, Maharaja Sayajirao Gaekwad of Baroda, grew up within a strict zenana. Along with Gwalior, Baroda was one of the largest and most influential Maratha princely states. Her father Sayajirao was perceived to be a forward-looking, modern ruler for his efficient and enlightened administration of his state and for supporting the education of Dr Ambedkar, an untouchable and later one of the writers of the Indian Constitution. At a young age, Indira Devi was affianced to the Scindia monarch, Vijaya Raje's father-in-law in an arrangement which was part a 'business engagement as well as romance'. During the negotiations for the ensuing marriage, Scindia sent his aide to inform Indira of their future daily schedule as husband and wife. It was a highly pragmatic proposition. They would ride together on Monday mornings and he would visit her rooms on Thursday nights. The other evenings would be kept reserved for his other wives and mistresses.[104] Indira found this unacceptable and broke off the engagement. Instead, she decided to marry a younger brother of the ruler from the lower-ranked, kshatriya state of Cooch Behar. This was an example of love breaking with conventional marriage trends by engendering a hypogamous union.

The headstrong Indira Devi first met Jitendra Narayan Bhup Bahadur of Cooch Behar (later the Maharaja) at the 1911 Delhi Durbar. She was introduced to him by Pretty and Baby, his sisters, who had studied with her in boarding school at Eastbourne in England. They were immediately taken by each other and contrived to meet clandestinely during the respite periods between the festivities and ceremonies. When Indira broke off her engagement to the Gwalior Maharaja, her parents, Sayajirao and Chimnabai, adamantly opposed her desire to marry the Cooch Behar prince. In a desperate attempt to dissuade their daughter, they embarked upon a tour of Europe only to have Jitendra follow them.[105] Indira subsequently had a covert courtship in Europe, which most likely affected her perceptions of romance and marriage. In 1913, she eloped with Jitendra in England, which created an uproar for both families and was considered inexcusable. As Barbara Ramusack notes, 'Indira had scandalized her parents who were known as social reformers and the princely elite by breaking her betrothal to the ruler of Gwalior, a Maratha state equal in status to Baroda, to enter a love marriage which crossed caste, regional and religious categories'.[106]

It was only several years later that the Baroda family acknowledged their daughter's choice of a husband. They particularly disliked the highly anglophile culture of Cooch Behar; the 'purely 'social' life, mixing with Edwardian society and entertaining streams of Western guests, ranking from royalty down'.[107] In addition, they were uncomfortable with the fact that the Cooch Behar royals were Brahmo, thus not proper 'Hindus', and had intermarried with the women of 'tribal', eastern kingdoms.[108]

Like her mother Indira, Gayatri Devi also married for love. She had been courted by Maharaja Sawai Man Singh II of Jaipur on and off since the age of fourteen and married him on April 17, 1940, a few months before she turned

21.[109] At first, he entered her life as a friend of her mother's, when she was twelve. When she was fourteen, he began inviting her to dinners with him in Calcutta (which she attended under great supervision).[110] Later, in her mid-teens, she was sent to Europe for further study, briefly attending the Monkey Club in London, Brilliantmont in Switzerland and the London College of Secretaries, where she was briefly exposed to the life of a working woman. During her time in Europe, she was courted by the Rajput ruler. As she remembered their romance:

> It was so important to be able to talk to Jai [the maharaja's nickname] without somebody eavesdropping each time. I used to go to this small cubicle where I would try to conceal myself while making my phone calls! Very often he would ask me out and I would happily agree. In order to hide the fact that we were meeting regularly, Jai would park his Bentley in Wilton Crescent. I would walk to that place, get into the waiting car and we would drive off!
>
> Those times were much more fun than an ordinary approved courtship would have been. We were constantly trying to outsmart our elders, arranging clandestine meetings and finding a system of posting letters to each other without our ADCs and other staff getting any wiser. Once in a while we also managed to go boating and on long drives in the country and have dinner at Bray. We formalized our relationship by buying gold rings with our names engraved on the inner surface. I, of course, had to save my pocket money to be able to buy one for Jai. It was a lovely and intoxicating time.[111]

The Jaipur Maharaja, as was noted earlier, had already had two traditional marriages of alliance with princesses, an aunt and a niece, from Jodhpur. In marrying her, he was breaking from earlier precedent in choosing a union of love. In addition, theirs was an unusual companionship between two dynasties, which conventionally did not intermarry: the eastern kshatriya kingdom of Cooch Behar in Bengal and the western Rajput princely state of Jaipur in Rajasthan. Nonetheless, there had been an earlier precedence of a Jaipur-Cooch Behar marriage during the reign of the last Maharaja Man Singh I who had served as a general to the Mughal emperor in the sixteenth century. There was no formal objection from the traditional Jaipur nobility to Gayatri Devi's paternal family. However, they were hesitant of her suitability as a bride due to her Maratha connections.[112] Rajput-Maratha couplings were as unusual at this time as Rajput-Sikh alliances. However, according to some sources, they agreed to the marriage on condition that it would remain morganatic.[113]

Gayatri Devi's mother, Indira, was initially as apprehensive about the marriage as the Rajput nobility in Rajasthan, but for different reasons. She was concerned that her daughter would be entering into a household that still practised *pardah* and polygamy, and, not only that, but as the third and youngest wife.[114] Despite these objections from his own nobility and Indira, the Jaipur

Maharaja was determined to have Gayatri Devi. Having already married conventionally, he now desired a bride and companion who could make the transition to modernity as the public face of modern Jaipur state by his side. As Sher Ali Pataudi observed, Gayatri Devi was an 'attractive modern princess with a most attractive family, well connected and with the kind of upbringing he wanted – modern, European, and yet belonging to the same fraternity'.[115] Ironically, Gayatri Devi in many ways entered a zenana environment of *pardah*, very similar to the one her mother had so obstinately rejected earlier, when breaking off with the Gwalior Maharaja.

'Love', 'romance', 'affection' and 'attraction' were terms fundamental in the emotive vocabulary of western-styled courtship, and their use, by Indian men or women, increasingly reflected a 'civilized' and 'gentile' manner of reorganizing private life as a mirror to the imperial social order. Thus, in this drawingroom style form of negotiation, marriage became a site to recreate a new politicized universe within the princely state. Just as Kapurthala, Cooch Behar or the Chakma Raj introduced educated, but ranked women as brides into their families by virtue of a new definition of desirability, so too did these women and their husbands legitimate, recreate and consolidate their identities through marriage. While Gayatri Devi married ostensibly for affection, hers was simultaneously a political marriage as her husband chose a companion who could help him navigate and negotiate his new social role as a globally connected, modern ruler. Similarly, Indira Devi in rejecting a union based on earlier, pre-colonial markers of appropriate marriage (similar caste, religion, regional background and rank) chose a relationship which gave her prominence in a different political theatre: the global stage of empire. It was this international stage, from the Delhi Durbar of 1911 to British boarding schools in Eastbourne, which was the backdrop to her courtship with Jitendra. By marrying the Cooch Behar prince, she joined a family that was constantly travelling to or hosting guests from Europe, while exiting the closeted interior of strict *pardah*. She entertained a romance, subsequent marriage and lively widowed existence that she would never have had as a traditional Maratha princess or as a Maharani within the Gwalior Zenana. These women actively were engaged in redefining the context and rules of marriage even as they were caught up in larger currents of socio-political change.

At the same time that 'love marriages' were fostering (hitherto) unlikely unions, they were simultaneously introducing foreign, non-aristocratic women into royal Indian families. Both Britons and Indians opposed miscegenation and looked unfavourably upon such relationships. In addition to race, these unions often broke social barriers as Indian rulers invariably married white women from working-class backgrounds.[116] Among the more prominent instances of princes who married non-Indian women were the maharajas of Kapurthala, Indore and Pudukkottai.

In 1910, Sita Devi's father-in-law, Maharaja Jagatjitsingh of Kapurthala wed Anita Delgrada, a Spanish dancer. His heir and European-educated Rajput daughter-in-law, Brinda, would not recognize or meet Delgrada when she arrived in the courtly household.[117] Furthermore, in 1921, a British political officer went to extreme lengths to hide the foreign queen behind potted plants at an official function.[118]

Similarly, the Maratha ruler of Indore, Maharaja Yeshwant Rao Holkar, had two American brides, following a precedent set by his father. The second one, whom he married in 1943, produced one son, Richard Shivaji Rao Holkar, who was not recognized by either the colonial or nationalist governments.[119] He, like other ruling princes who married non-Hindu, non-Indian brides, de-legitimized the rights of his issue at the moment of his marriage, despite warnings from the colonial regime. In 1940, the official letter below was sent from the Political Department in New Delhi to the Resident in Rajputana.

> Dear Mr. Lothian,
> I am desired to say for your information and guidance that early in 1939 His Highness the Maharaja Holkar of Indore announced his marriage with Mrs. Branyon nee Lawler, a United States citizen by birth, at the same time His Highness also made a public statement to the effect that any issue of the marriage would not be eligible for succession to the gaddi. His Majesty the King has now been pleased to direct that this lady should not be officially received or have any official title, but that it is open to any official who may wish to meet and receive her to do so on unofficial occasions. She may be described as the 'Maharani Holkar' without the style of 'Her Highness'.
> 2. I am to add that official occasions should be regarded as including dinner parties at which His Excellency the Viceroy or the head of a Provincial Government is present, and that the inclusion of the Maharani Holkar in invitations to formal dinner parties or private entertainments in public places should be avoided.
> Yours sincerely,
> Sd. D.G. Harington Hawes
> To: The Hon'ble Mr. A. C. Lothian, CSI., CIE., Resident for Rajputana.[120]

Here, the American bride is given an inferior title and none of the power or privilege of being Maharani. She could not be received by the Viceroy or other administrative officials nor were her children eligible to inherit hereditary titles. Such politically impractical, romanticized views of marriage may have emerged in emulation of the act of English Crown Prince Edward VIII, who abdicated his throne to marry American divorcée Mrs Simpson, in December 1936. Furthermore, these liaisons weakened the powers of Indian rulers whose *gaddi* could easily be threatened by the effects of their personal choices. This topic is examined in greater depth in Chapter 5.

At the same time, marriages between high ranked Indian women and Englishmen were not entirely unknown. Englishmen and upper class Indian women had married as early as the late eighteenth century.[121] In 1860, Victoria Gourrama, princess of Coorg, married Colonel John Campbell, 'a dashing widower' some thirty years her senior.[122] Maharaja Duleep Singh had introduced the two prospective partners to each other. The daughters of Maharani Sunity Devi of Cooch Behar, Prativa Devi and Sudhira Devi, also married two English brothers during the nineteen teens: Alan and Lionel Mander, one an English film star and the other a soldier in the British army, despite their family's initial reservations.[123] In the post-Independence period, the daughters of the Chakma Raja, Rajkumari Amiti Roy and Rajkumari Moitri Roy, successively married the British District Commissioner of the region, Angus Hume. The first case will be discussed.

Rajkumari Amiti wed her husband in 1953, two years after the death of her father, Raja Nalinaksha Roy. Sent to a Catholic boarding school in Kurseong in the District of Darjeeling by her mother, Rani Benita, Amiti was attracted to the Christian liturgy and hymnal. When she finished school, she informed her father that she wished to convert to Catholicism. The Chakmas were Buddhists and claimed descent from the Shakhya family of Gautama Buddha. Her family was adamantly opposed to her conversion to a foreign faith. Her conversion created deep rifts with her parents.

With the Raja's premature death in 1951, Amiti suffered an emotional crisis, in part due to the unresolved nature of their relationship at the moment of his death. During the ensuing period of turmoil, when the young successor, Raja Tridiv Roy was still a minor, the family was distracted by various political concerns with the then new government of East Pakistan. While her brother was being installed as the new ruler, Amiti fell in love with District Commissioner Angus Hume, who was on friendly terms with the Chakma Raj family, having been a personal friend of her deceased father and often playing tennis with her brothers, the princes. Hume, who had served as a District Commissioner during the last years of the British Raj, had been retained by the new state of East Pakistan as DC for a brief interim period.

As an extended member of the family circle and due to his own unusual situation as an older bachelor, Amiti sought out the DC during this period of personal upheaval. During her emotional illness, he administered her medications and it is described that, although she was afraid of water, the Chakma princess rowed across the beautiful Karnafuli river that flowed between her family's Rajbari Palace and the DC's official residence at night so she could visit him. Their marriage, like her Catholicism, created initial divides among her family member, but was eventually accepted by them.[124]

These accounts of love marriage, which crossed racial differences, reveals the ways in which imperialism created new contact zones for courtship and marriage between members of Indian royal families and Europeans, in addition to encouraging love marriages which went beyond religious and caste boundaries. Thus, during the era of diplomacy in the drawing room, marriage had become a subtle instrument of assimilation by the colonial subject, even as it was reshaped by the indigenous princes to fit their own purposes. This legacy of imperial rule remained in India long after the Empire was gone. The love marriages of the earlier twentieth century, which crossed race, caste and class boundaries, were no longer anomalies by the 1950s and '60s. With India's Independence from Britain and subsequent construction of a new constitution, laws on marriage, family and gender relations changed. The Fabian socialist agenda of the nascent democratic nation, with Prime Minister Jawaharlal Nehru at its helm, questioned the old order and irrevocably buried it into the past. Where once the tract of the battlefield was exchanged for the Victorian drawing room, the civilized society of the drawing room in turn has been replaced by that of electoral politics and later the boardroom. In postcolonial India, bureaucratic and business elites have altered earlier hierarchies of social division, as the zenana itself is changing with the times.

Deviance and Marriage in the Post-Independent Period

Where once the warring Hindu prince was reconstructed as the anglicized gentleman by the colonial subject, he is now being reshaped as the successful politician, industrialist or business entrepreneur by modern India. It is more and more acceptable for a member of the aristocratic circles to ally with up and coming professional classes, such as doctors, businessmen and lawyers. Former princes themselves are going into a wide array of professional work, including diplomacy, government, academia, business and law.

Furthermore, anti-polygamy laws have yielded a desire for romance in monogamous marriages and women's rights to property inheritance empowers them to choose partnerships of their own preference. When the nation won Independence from foreign rule in 1947, the princely states lost their autonomous identities. Rulers were stripped of their executive rights and their territories merged with the new democracy. In 1971, the princes were derived of their constitutionally guaranteed incomes, the Privy Purse, under Prime Minister Indira Gandhi.

At the same time, women within the zenana evolved with the changing status of royalty. By the 1950s, many who had lived in seclusion behind *pardah* were emerging in public, and some were engaging in discourse within the body politic as members of parliament, heads of charitable organizations and founders of cultural and academic institutions. In a number of instances, traditional patterns of marriage were threatened and negated. In particular, the abolition of polygamy ended the multi-tiered, hierarchical zenana. While Muslims were still allowed to marry at least four wives according to Koranic law, the Hindu Marriage Act of 1956 effectively abolished polygamy within Hindu India. While earlier legislation had been passed during the colonial period, such as the Hindu Widows'

Remarriage Act of 1856 and the inter-religious civil marriages act of 1923, nothing would so dramatically affect marriage alliance within the zenana. According to the new law, two Hindus (the category 'Hindu' also including Buddhists, Jains and Sikhs) can only marry if 'neither party has a spouse living at the time of marriage'. From this time on, the Indian government and society at large only monogamy was a legitimate form of marriage for Hindus.

Young royal Hindu men began to opt for love or 'deviant marriages', which had been uncommon into the mid-twentieth century. According to Jayasinhji Jhala, the postcolonial effects of Independence, such as Partition, democracy and nationalism, led to 'the Revolution of the '50s' which was guided by 'an elite society of persons who shared a common educational, philosophical and occupational vision and experience of the colonizing society they were trying to dismember themselves from'.[125] Traditionally defining perimeters for marriage, such as caste, clan, religion or class, became less critical and the values of 'western secular society' were promoted. Thus the governmental agenda which 'called for a casteless society, promoted the idea of marriage as a union of individuals and not of families, wherein the idea of marriage was conceived to be an undertaking for love and happiness and not for family, clan or lineage continuity'.[126]

Even those royal houses, which had maintained traditional marriage alliance patterns, such as the Rajput states of Dhrangadhra and Jodhpur, began to feel the affects of the new social climate. Maharani Brijraj Kumari of Dhrangadhra's three sons have all married non-Rajput, and sometimes non-Hindu, women. Since the 1950s, the wives of Hindu royal men have included 'English, Swiss, French, American and Thai women. Wives have come from Muslim, Jain, Buddhist, Christian, Sikh, Parsee faiths. Brahmin, Vaisya and Sudra women have become wives'.[127]

The eldest, Sodhsalji, the Yuvraj of Dhrangadhra, married a Muslim noblewoman, Shah Banu, from the nearby kingdom of Palanpur in Gujarat. Earlier unions with Muslim women did not exist in the Dhrangadhra lineage, which historically prided itself on the fact that no Muslim women were brought into the family. The second son, Jayasinhji, married a Buddhist princess from the Chakma Raj kingdom, who is the cousin of Gayatri Devi, Rajmata of Jaipur. The youngest son, Sidhrajsinhji, also married a non-Rajput, Jain woman, Aruna Harprasad, who was not of a princely family although his second wife would come from a Hindu Rajput aristocratic family connected to the kingdom of Jodhpur. Rajmata Gayatri Devi of Jaipur's son, Jagatsingh, married the non-Rajput, non-Hindu princess of Buddhist Thailand, Priyananda Rangsit. Women, too, have chosen non-traditional partners. Yashodaraje, daughter of Vijaya Raje Scindia, Rajmata of Gwalior, broke with tradition by marrying a physician, against her family's wishes.[128] Later, she would divorce him. The princesses of the Jadeja Rajput state of Morvi in Saurashtra also married men of their liking, including an Irish aristocrat and a Parsi businessman.[129] Thus, in independent India, new legal systems and changing political and cultural attitudes relating to marital choice have affected spousal selection for the descendents of zenana women, encouraging the marriage of choice.

The Implications of the Discourse on Desire

During the pre-colonial period of Mughal imperialism, warfare still dominated the relationships between kingdoms and the Hindu royal woman served martial needs as her body, metaphorically and literally, was the battlefield between rival states. As a bride, she cemented military alliances, birthed blood-based armies and provided strategic connections for her sons. With the arrival of British, the battlefield was replaced by the diplomacy of the drawing room where status, acquired through the symbols of etiquette, genealogy and marital connections, became a more significant indicator for maintaining regal distinction.

This shift in marriage alliance policy from one based on military relationships to an emphasis on 'purity' of lineage historically occurs with the decline of feudalism generally. In a similar manner, the British aristocracy emphasized the symbols of 'conspicuous consumption', such as the prestige of ancient bloodlines, when war was no longer common. As Lawrence Stone notes of late medieval England, honour and chivalry were leading considerations within aristocratic circles when it came to marriage.[130] At the same time, the constraints of a new economic order forced some British aristocrats and gentry to wed outside these narrow perimeters.[131]

Marital alliances among Indian royals increasingly were influenced by the concerns of status and prestige during the late colonial period. Blood ties became greater indicators for appropriate partners among royal Indian families and society at large than earlier, military-based compacts. As it had been for the British aristocracy, the circle of appropriate potential spouses thus widened to allow for marrying between princely dynasties, which ordinarily did not intermarry and were distant in geographic space and cultural ancestry, the introduction of non-royal players into the marriage market, such as the daughters of Keshub Chandra Sen's family, and in certain cases, the highlighting of personal motivations, including love or companionship, in spousal selection as occurred in the marital choices of Indira Devi and her daughter.

At a broader level, this chapter demonstrates that these histories show the growing dissemination of occidental attitudes upon marriage alliance making in the late colonial period. The adoption of the English drawing room as an architectural space and social venue was widespread. Marriages were settled within the setting of the drawing room from the late nineteenth-century alliance of Maharani Sunity Devi of Cooch Behar to the early mid-twentieth-century marriages of

Rajmata Krishna Kumari of Jodhpur, Maharani Brijraj Kumari of Dhrangadhra and Rajmata Gayatri Devi of Jaipur. Krishna Kumari and Brijraj Kumari were both 'looked over' by their potential mothers-in-law within drawing room environments prior to the formal engagement of marriage in the city of Bombay[132] just as Sunity Devi had been approved by her husband's British advisor in her father's Calcutta sitting room. Similarly, Gayatri Devi was courted by her husband, Sawai Man Singh of Jaipur, in such anglicized settings as that of Swiss finishing schools, Calcutta restaurants and London house parties. Vijaya Raje Scindia first 'met' her husband at the races in Bombay and much of her future marriage was settled within the social setting of the British-styled Taj Mahal Hotel in the metropolis.[133] In such a manner, marriages became motivated by a political vocabulary of etiquette, prestige and status building, modeled on the social decorum established by the anglicized drawing room.

Long after the British left, western romantic ideals continued to affect marriage politics. Both the socialist, Nehruvian agenda and the emergent capitalist economy of the post Independence period have displaced the erstwhile ruler. The Hindu Marriage Act of 1956 engendered matches across caste, religious and clan boundaries with the prohibition of polygamy for Hindus. New family and inheritance laws allow royal Hindu women to control their marriage choices and secure the destiny of their children. The reduction of former princes into private citizens without the option of polygamy has led a number to marry for convenience and personal choice. This chapter shows how histories of marriage can be used to gauge the political relationships between Indian indigenous elites and the colonial power as well as the role of Indian aristocratic families in the postcolonial republic. In addition, changing definitions of female education, beauty and sexuality, which incorporated both western and eastern characteristics, reflect hybrid attitudes relating to women's identity and domestic politics during the colonial period.

Thus, during the height of empire, the British Raj influenced the personal sphere of marriage, and disseminated westernized attitudes regarding conjugality, love and family relations. From subtle to overt practices, the colonial government helped to reshape the nature of marriage among Indian royals, even while advancing and refashioning certain 'traditional' practices.

4 BREAKING (MALE) HEARTS: THE ROLE OF LOVE, COLONIAL LAW AND MATERNAL AUTHORITY IN TWO DISPUTED ROYAL MARRIAGES IN EARLY TWENTIETH-CENTURY KATHIAWAR

In 1901, Rani Bai Shri Hajuba of Rajkot 'secretly and abruptly' departed her kingdom for a neighbouring state, Dhrangadhra. In a confidential letter sent by the Political Agent of Kathiawar, she was accused of having a 'mischievous advisor' who had misguided her through intrigue (*khatpat)* to leave her kingdom without informing the British management. Seven years later in 1908, the Rani of Palitana, from a kingdom in close geographic proximity, was accused by her Political Agent of similar court intrigue and was questioned for remaining in the home of her brother, the Raja of Bansda, rather than returning to her own state. Both Hindu queens acted in this manner to safeguard the interests of their daughters during disputed marriage alliances.

These two cases, regarding the freedom of movement for Hindu ranis in peninsular Gujarat, relate to the broader theme of British intervention in the internal affairs of Indian princely states during the late colonial period. Colonial intervention in the marriage politics of Rajput princely states was hotly debated, bifurcating opposing groups of royal and aristocratic circles, challenging earlier, pre-colonial dynastic hierarchies and providing new powers and capabilities to Hindu Rajput queens. Expanding upon the earlier chapters, this chapter argues that the British administrative government was often a middle player in the conflicts between Hindu queens and traditional male wielders of power. In certain instances, Zenana women advocated non-intervention in the domestic affairs of their states while local noblemen and ruling princes endorsed and encouraged British influence to bolster indigenous constructs of patriarchy and male rulership.

The interpretation of conjugal happiness was central to this debate. In defiance of earlier Rajput and Hindu precedent, both queens used the language of love, 'choice' in marriage and 'happiness', to legitimate their actions in breaking off their daughter's betrothals. In contrast, male factions argued that such values negated the fundamental principles of Rajput and Hindu family law, and would ultimately lead to a 'revolution' in marriage practice. The introduction of these Occidental values in the language of marriage was problematic. While it should be noted that the Ranis might have used such coloured words in conscious awareness of the attitudes of their colonial audience and to fuel their own agendas, rather than the true desires of their daughters, it was nonetheless a deft political move.

Most strikingly, these marriage alliances suggest that Hindu queens under indirect British colonial rule had perhaps more administrative influence in the governing of Zenana politics and state rule than previously thought. Furthermore, they appear to have been wily negotiators and clever strategists, manoeuvring through the bureaucracy of the British Raj, superseding local officials to supplicate higher-level administrators and maintaining a corpus of legal advisors. Zenana women challenged the status quo, pursued their own powerful interests, galvanized politically expedient support and pushed their platforms of resistance, both in relation to imperial rule and male patriarchy.

The Rajkot Rani, *c.* 1901

> Bai Hajooba dowager Rajkot Rani suddenly and secretly left by today's mail for Dhrangadhra with her daughter who is the ward of the Agency and whose marriage fixed on 10th June next by Assistant Political Agent Halar with intention to marry her elsewhere. She has her own and States valuable ornaments with her. Please detain her at Wadhwan and send her back. Political Agent has been wired at Veraval for instructions in the matter. At any rate do not allow her to proceed further.[1]

On 27 April 1901, Rani Bai Shri Hajuba, the principal queen (*patrani*) of the recently deceased Jadeja Rajput ruler of Rajkot, was detained with her daughter at Wadhwan Junction while en route to the neighbouring Jhala Rajput state of Dhrangadhra in Kathiawar. The Manager of Rajkot State forced her back to Rajkot and her close personal advisor, the state clerk (*kamdar*) Amratlal Premchand, was barred permission from seeing her in the zenana and expelled from her service.[2] It was believed that Amratlal Premchand had caused intrigue (*khatpat*) with his dowager queen, particularly with regard to the state marriage of her daughter, the princess.

The antecedents to these precipitous events had taken place several years earlier. The Rani had betrothed her only child and daughter to the son of a neighbouring nobleman, Kumar Samatsinhji, from Palitana. The first ceremony of betrothal had been celebrated in 1897 with great pomp. It was considered a propitious union between two Rajput royal houses and clans, Jadeja and Gohel, which had a history of intermarriage, and whose children were close in age and similarly educated. As the *Kathiawar Times* described the event:

The ceremony of the betrothal of Kumar Shri Vijaysinhji, son of Prince Samatsinhji of Palitana, with the Kunvari Bai Saheba of Rajkote Thakore Saheb was performed with great splendour and pomp to-day at 12 A.M.; among those who were present were noticed the Bhayats of the Rajkote State, Ala Khachar of Jasdan and his two princes and others. The match is, as far as age and education are concerned, what is absolutely desirable. The Kumar Shri is aged 14 and has studied up to the English 5th standard and has been receiving his education under Mr. Barwell, his tutor. The Kunvari is 13 years old, receiving English education made under Miss Corkery, Lady Superintendent of the Barton Female College.[3]

It was a publicly celebrated occasion, with some two thousand Zenana ladies in attendance, including the Rani of Morvi, from another neighbouring Rajput state.[4] The day was officially proclaimed a holiday, Rajkot schools were closed, state prisoners were relieved of work and sweets were distributed in the streets.[5] The *Kathiawar News* lauded the Rani's choice of a groom from a scion of the Palitana family in a time where there was much 'difficulty experienced in getting good husbands for their daughters'.[6] The *Bombay Gazette* surmised that the official wedding 'will probably take place about twelve months hence'.[7]

More than a year later in May 1898, the two players were again united to perform the 'coconut ceremony', in expectation of the formal wedding in Bombay. Jewels and gifts were exchanged to cement the tie between the two families and states. As the *Bombay Gazette* heralded the occasion: 'A deputation of upwards of thirty State officials, priests and servants, came from Rajkote, bringing the gifts of the parents of the prospective bride, these included a valuable horse whose trapping work were entirely of silver, a handsome gold necklace set with jewels, a number of costly clothes, articles of Cutch silver and the various small presents that are customarily given on such occasions'.[8] A year later in May 1899, Kumar Samatsinhji sent equally auspicious gifts in value of Rs. 60,000 to the Zenana ladies in Rajkot during the 'Samurta' ceremony. The presents were displayed to the Rajkot elite assembled there.[9] On 27 April 1901, the *Kathiawar Times* reported that the wedding had been arranged for the 10 June, less than two months later.

Yet on the same day that the *Kathiawar Times* was advertising the certainty of this union between Rajkot and Palitana, Bai Shri Hajuba had other plans for her daughter. Although she had initiated an alliance between her daughter and the Gohel scion, the Rani had set her sights on a more advantageous union, when it began to emerge as a possibility: a marriage between her daughter and the Yuvraj of Dhrangadhra. While Samatsinhji's son was an eligible potential groom, being a leading nobleman from Palitana, he was not comparable to the ruler of a kingdom. As the future Maharaja of Dhrangadhra, the Yuvraj would inherit a sizable and wealthy kingdom in Saurashtra. In addition, he was socially of the same rank as the Rajkot princess for both of them were the children of kings. It would be a more advantageous, hypergamous marriage from the angle of status and wealth for the Rani's daughter. For a widowed queen who had no sons to protect her future stability and security within her married home, it was vital to ally her daughter with the most powerful partner available.

The Rani's unexpected departure from Rajkot to neighbouring Dhrangadhra, where the heir apparent had recently mounted the throne, alarmed the local British administration and aggravated Samatsinhji, whose suspicions were aroused. The flurry of correspondence, official admonishments, aggrieved letters and stridently stubborn replies which followed, bear witness to the ways in which the British tried to intervene in Zenana affairs and how their influence was often manipulated by local rival groups. Bai Shri Hajuba proved to be an intractable adversary to any who came in her way: the Palitana scion, Samatsinhji, as well as a host of British administrators. Although a recently widowed queen with only one child, she proved implacable to external pressure and could not be swayed from her own interests.

In response to his expulsion from the Zenana durbar, Amratlal Premchand stoutly defended his dowager Rani and criticized British involvement in the court's private affairs. On 15 August 1901, he defied Captain Wodehouse and wrote to his superior, the Governor of the Bombay Presidency, Henry Stafford, Baron Northcote of Exeter, that the Government had no right to expel him from the service of the Rajkot Rani. As he noted, 'I draw my pay from her and not from the State. And therefore none but the Bai Saheb has any power to remove me from her service'.[10] He further argued that the British Raj should not be involved in the running of the zenana: 'British officers are not to prevent any person from visiting such ladies in the harem nor are they to interfere with their *domestic affairs*'.[11]

A week later, Rani Bai Shri Hajuba wrote to Colonel W.P. Kennedy, Political Agent of Kathiawar, that her daughter refused to marry Gohel Samatsinhji's son, and that she, herself, had been coerced by the state Manager against her will to sanction the marriage. She refuted the principal charge that she left Rajkot 'secretly' with jewels in her possession. Furthermore, she exonerated her servants, including the Kamdar Amratlal Premchand, and accused the Manager of coercing her, through removing her closest aides, into marrying her daughter to Samatsinghi's son.[12]

In support of her mother, the princess wrote to the Assistant Political Agent decrying his encroachment on her freedom of movement, which she argued was 'unprecedented': 'I humbly submit that no one has any right to place such unprecedented restrictions upon my personal liberty which amount to a sort of confinement', she wrote, ' This is more so after the Government orders in the case of my refusal to marry Samatsinhji's son'.[13] The strong responses of these Zenana women reflects a language of resistance that is self-righteous and even fearless.

In reply, the Assistant Political Agent admonished the princess for her unseemly behaviour, which defied convention. 'I further disapprove', he responded, 'of young princesses of her age travelling about the country except in case of really urgent necessity'.[14] Here, the British official demonstrated his seemingly superior knowledge of customary practice, appearing to celebrate and uphold indigenous mores. The Rani quickly sent off a sharp missive in response to this intervention in their affairs, checking his right to intercede: 'Surely but respectfully I must object to such an interference as being unauthorized, unprecedented and improper and most probably based upon misgivings created by the Manager'.[15]

The Rani's arguments for non-intervention in Zenana domestic affairs found favour, if not with the local British administrators in Kathiawar, then with the Government in Bombay. In a letter to the Kathiawar Political Agent Kennedy, J.L. Jenkins, Acting Secretary to the Government of Bombay, supported the Rani's claims that the Political Agent did not have the same powers and rights as the Hindu ruler in domestic affairs. 'It is impossible', he proclaims, 'for the Political Agent or the Manager of the State to exercise the same control over the proceedings of the ladies of the family as would be exercised by a ruling Chief'.[16] Furthermore, he argued that Zenana ladies should be allowed free rein in their private affairs: 'where ladies of the zenana desire to have greater freedom it is better to allow them, within certain limits, to go their own way, than to have perpetual complaints of harsh treatment and interference in their domestic arrangements'. In conclusion, he stated that 'the zenana guards and the zenana affairs generally should be left under the orders of Bai Shri Hajuba – that carriages should be assigned to the exclusive use of the ladies, and that Bai Shri Hajuba should be permitted to employ Amratlal Premchand as Kamdar if she chooses to do so'.[17]

Jenkins' only caveat and warning was that the zenana ladies, in return for their freedoms, must act with propriety:

> I am desired to request that, in communicating this decision to Bai Shri Hajuba, you will impress upon her that this liberty has been allowed her in confidence that she will do - nothing to bring the good name of the family into dispute – and that if she disregards the restraints imposed by custom upon ladies in her position she must be prepared to forfeit the privileges of that position.[18]

Frustrated by Rani Hajuba's success in breaking off the match, the father of the spurned bridegroom, Samatsinhji, wrote vociferous letters to the Political Agent of Kathiawar and his higher-ups in the British Indian Government, including the representative of the Bombay Presidency and the Viceroy. He argued that Zenana women did not have the power to break off engagements. The breaking of a betrothal was tantamount to sacrilege, tarnishing ancient codes of Hindu and Rajput custom. In a copious and detailed letter to the Viceroy, Lord Curzon in Calcutta, Samatsinhji minutely outlined the history of the match and the precepts of marriage law which the rani had broken. He invoked the Viceroy to intervene on behalf of the dead male ruler of Rajkot to perform the marriage 'in loco parentis'. In this letter, Samatsinhji requested the British colonial official to uphold native laws and rites, and take on the spirit and person of the deceased Maharaja. Where the Zenana women appeared to be revolutionary, rebellious forces rocking the foundation of an ancient patriarchy, he saw the British as agents to protect a pre-colonial social structure.

Samatsinhji first addressed what he believed were the newly founded objections to the alliance by the Rajkot Rani. While the bride and groom were both from noble Rajput houses, the Rani claimed that her daughter, as the child of a king, should marry the heir apparent of a state of greater size and stature. In this matter, she relied upon conventional marriage practice that Rajput women should marry hypergamously or isogamously, thereby wedding men of equal or higher status than themselves and their families. Samatsinhji's son, being from a cadet line of the Palitana family rather than of the immediate royal family, was not 'heir apparent' but rather 'heir-presumptive'. In the instance that both the ruler of Palitana and his heir died before mounting the *gaddi*, Samatsinhji and his son would be third in the line of succession, but not immediate. Samatsinhji forcefully noted that Bai Shri Hajuba had always known his position within the Palitana hierarchy and was not deceived by him prior to the engagement: 'Bai Shri Hajuba had most carefully considered the advantages and disadvantages in the match, and in particular... whether it will be consistent with the dignity of the Rajkot house to give its daughter to a cadet'.[19] He surmised that the Rajkot Rani had subsequently wished to visit Dhrangadhra with the purpose of finding an alternate suitor for her daughter there; a fear not unfounded.

To support his claims, he provided meticulous details of cases where the daughters of ruling princes married sons from cadet lines and described the great merit (*punya*) of his Rajput clan, the Gohels, whose blood had not been tarnished through intermarriage with Muslims. While the Jadejas, the clan which the Rajkot royal family belonged to, had given their daughters to Mohammedans, the Gohel blood 'has remained pure, and there has not been a single instance of a girl descended from a Gohel family having been given to a Mohamedan'.[20]

Citing the references to contemporary journalistic accounts of the betrothal, coconut and samurta ceremonies, he emphasized the fact that the public expected the wedding and that the Rani had long encouraged the match. While the bridegroom was sent to boarding school in Rajkot at Rajkumar College, the Rani had feted him as if he were her son-in-law. Samatsinhji wrote: 'She treated the bridegroom with the courtesy due to her son-in-law, and made to him the customary presents on the principal holidays of each year and on his birthdays, and showed watchful care for him during his residence at the Rajkumar College'.

In her correspondence to her relations, she addressed Samatsinhji's son as 'var' or bridegroom of her daughter.[21]

Her sudden change of heart appeared to him 'inexplicable'. The match had been agreed upon by 'all' parties, including the Political Agent of Kathiawar, the Manager of Rajkot State and Rani Bai Shri Hajuba herself.[22]

In addition, he refuted the Rani's claims that her daughter would not be happy in the union. Samatsinhji believed that the princess was agreeable to the match and was cognizant of the significance of all the ceremonies she performed. A *jiwai* (allowance) was already drawn up for her, and she had asked her maternal aunt, Samatsinhji's second wife, to know the full amount. He cuttingly responded that her mother's fears for her physical danger were trumped-up charges. According to Samatsinhji, the Rajkot princess had only changed her mind because of her mother: 'the alleged unwillingness of the bride to complete the marriage [is] suspiciously coincident with her mother's change of front, and can only be the expression of her mother's wishes'.[23]

He also argued that the Rajkot princess would be happier marrying the son of a cadet line rather than a ruling prince, for she would not be one of many in a polygamous household, where her status in the hierarchy could not be maintained. This was an argument shared by many.[24] Samatsinhji wrote ' … the bride would be far more likely to be happy as the wife of your Petitioner's son than if she were married to a Ruling Chief, who would, in the ordinary course, have already married several wives, among who she, as a junior wife, would hold a subordinate position'.[25] To strengthen his claim, he provided the example of the erstwhile ruler of Palitana who gave his daughter, Kunvar Shri Keshabah, to a cadet rather than a ruling prince as he knew 'there was more likelihood of his daughter being happy as the wife of a cadet than the fifth or tenth wife of a Ruling Chief'.[26]

According to him, breaking off the betrothal defied Hindu and Rajput law for a woman could not arrange her own marriage. Citing western scholarship on Hindu practice, he quoted the Sanskritist Buhler's account of marriage: 'there is not a single instance known in which [the Rajput woman] has objected to the proposed husband, or such objection was listened to or entertained'. In addition, he referred to Forbes' *Ras Mala*: 'where the ceremony of 'Tilluk' (*i.e.* betrothal) is completed, the father of the girl cannot recede from the engagement'.[27] He further suggested that a Rajput woman, if only betrothed to her bridegroom, would still perform *sati* on his deathbed: 'on hearing of Waghoji's death … the daughter of the (Rajput) Solanki of Kalaria, who was betrothed to him, mounted the funeral pile, although the marriage ceremony between them not yet been performed'.[28] Not only was a broken engagement contrary to Hindu marriage law, but it also caused a lasting cloud of dishonour on both parties and families. As he noted, 'his son and family' would be the 'laughing-stock of Rajputs'.[29]

Samatsinhji further concluded that Rajput royal women had no opportunity to make marriages of 'choice'. As he suggested, living in seclusion or *pardah*, precluded them from having access to eligible men before marriage. He wrote that: 'The Rajputs, moreover, observe a strict purdah system, and males and females of eligible ages are kept strictly apart, and have no possibility of selecting each other and forming what in the West are known as love-matches'.[30]

As love matches were impossible, the Rajkot Rani, in making her case, was merely pandering to a western sensibility and thereby culling the favour of the colonial administrators, not with any true aim of implementing her proclaimed aspirations. He wrote that Bai Shri Hajuba acted 'with the object of misleading the Bombay Government; and in the hope that, that Government, in deciding of this question, would be influenced by the notions and practices of the West, and would not base their decision solely and entirely on the laws, customs and usages of the Rajputs'.[31] In a letter to the Bombay Governor, Samatsinhji stated that the Rani was only using the language of western love and romanticism to push her hopes for a grander dynastic marriage to a Ruling Chief rather than a cadet. He noted 'such a desire ... has nothing to do with the principles which recommend a love-match in the West and is in fact nothing ... better than a preference for a marriage of convenience'. He argued that her breaking of the betrothal did not reflect either Hindu or western values: 'thus the pleas put in the mouth of the bride in the petition made in her name, are equally opposed to Western ideas, and to Hindu and Rajput usages'.[32]

In a later correspondence sent to the Political Agent of Kathiawar, he made similar judgements in regards to Rani Hajuba's manipulation of language, drafted by her highly trained legal advisors: 'hoping that Government in deciding on this question would not be able to altogether put out of sight the notions and practices of the West and to be uninfluenced by them or to base their decision solely and entirely on the laws, customs and usages of the Rajputs alone, without importing into them Western ideas'.[33] He suggested that Bai Shri Hajuba manipulated the language of love to make a politically expedient alliance that was governed by earlier non-western, pre-colonial constructs of marriage rather than the romanticism, which she suggested.

To defy the Rani, Samatsinhji made the ultimate appeal. He requested the Viceroy to intervene and take on the symbolic role of the dead Rajkot ruler and force the betrothal to its final conclusion in marriage: 'Your Petitioner humbly submits that your Excellency is in the position of the late Thakore Saheb of Rajkot, and requests your Excellency to take the same view of the match as he would have taken and to act as he would have done'.[34] He further argued that the Rajkot princess should be removed from the pernicious influence of her mother and placed in the company of her British governess, Miss Corkery, Lady Superintendent of the Barton Female Training College, Rajkot.[35] Here, a contesting local male power hoped to use British involvement in order to reinforce an earlier hierarchical patriarchy.

In appealing to the British, Samatsinhji simultaneously revealed that colonial rule had empowered Zenana women in new ways. He noted that the Rani had more authority in arranging her daughter's marriage as a widow than during her husband's lifetime, for the late Rajkot Thakore Saheb would surely have 'been completing the marriage in according with the marriage-contract'. In his letter to the Bombay Governor, he further concluded that such a situation in pre-colonial times would have resulted in 'inter-tribal war' rather than the diplomatic strategies, which were being used.[36] In such instances, Hindu Ranis did not have access to the influence of external players (i.e. the British) to arbitrate contested issues. The end of martial rule in princely India allowed Ranis greater control in their domestic affairs as individuals, which simultaneously reflected larger political and economic interests.

In part, Samatsinhji's arguments failed to succeed for they were outdated and revealed an uninformed knowledge of his audience. Prior to the Mutiny of 1857, his references to Sanskrit literature and European Orientalist scholarship to support Rajput customary practice might have been successful. During the eighteenth century, Warren Hastings, the East India Company's first governor-general strengthened indigenous Indian legal systems, by referring to classical literary texts in Arabic, Persian and Sanskrit, which were perceived by the English administrators as the 'visible embodiment of Indian law'.[37] However the effects of the Mutiny in the mid-nineteenth century led British administrators to put greater emphasis on customary practice and the complexity of local tradition rather than the Sanskritization of Hindu law. In addition, they relied upon Western juridical principles, which emphasized individual rights over group identities. As the Rudolphs note, 'For traditional Hindu law, the "natural" associations of family, caste, and locality were the units of the moral and social universe, whereas for the British law, the individual was valued over the "artificial" groups in which he might find himself'.[38] It is also worthwhile to note, while Samatsinhji's arguments on *sati* would support customary practice, it would have been frowned upon by British officials who perceived *sati* as a social 'crime', having outlawed it in British India in 1829.

In July of 1901, he additionally wrote a letter to Lord Northcote of Exeter, the Governor and President in Council of the Bombay Presidency. As he had mentioned in his letter to the Viceroy, he reiterated the fact that women's involvement in marriage brokering would lead inevitably to a revolution in all aspects of social life. As brides had no ability to choose partners, because of the nature of gender segregation through *pardah*, it would destroy the delicate balance of marriage politics and gender relations among Rajputs. As he wrote in strong terms, 'the institution of marriage would be threatened with extinction, and the religious, moral and social duties which depend upon marriage would be neglected'. This would lead to the a destruction of the earlier system and to a 'completely revolutionizing Hindu society'. In many ways, Samatsinhji was not off the mark in such perspicacious comments.

He concluded this letter by arguing that Zenana women would ultimately make marriage 'impossible' for any prospective bridegroom would be in constant fear of being publicly rejected 'in the eyes of his fellows by her refusal to marry, and as to mutual selection in the shape of a love-match that is altogether out of the question'.[39] Samatsinhji, in particular, mentioned the psychological trauma his son would suffer, and what a blow it would be to his masculinity should the engagement be nulled. He suggested that he 'will be seriously affected and may indeed be irretrievably injured if his early manhood is to be permitted to be shocked and embittered by the rupture of his betrothal'.[40]

Regardless of his numerous letters and lengthy arguments relying on custom and tradition, by February 1902 the Rani of Rajkot had prevailed. She had chosen the young ruler of Dhrangadhra as the groom for her daughter. The princess wrote to the Assistant Political Agent, Prant Halar, that during the eight months since her betrothal was broken off, she has looked for a 'suitable alliance' and 'Dhrangadhra has been found to be suitable'.[41] The Dhrangadhra Raj showed willingness to marry, if the costs of the wedding ceremony and dowry were similar to those made during the wedding of Bai Shri Hajuba's stepdaughter's marriage to a smaller Jhala Rajput ruler in Vankaner. Thus, the Rani had succeeded in fending off the British from 'meddling' in her affairs, had broken off an earlier engagement despite aggressive moves made by the offended male party and would marry her daughter in a more prosperous union with a higher status man and king of an important regional power.

The Palitana Rani, *c.* 1908

> It was my sacred right as her mother to consider where my daughter would be happy, and to what family I should entrust her fate; and I had every confidence that the Sarkar in its justice and mercy would not interfere in it.
>   – The Rani of Palitana to the Governor of Bombay

Seven years after Rani Hajuba of Rajkot broke her daughter's engagement to Samatsinhji's son, her contemporary, the dowager Rani of Palitana, was attempting the same for her daughter affianced to the Dhrangadhra heir apparent. In many ways, these two cases are interrelated by the players involved. Samatsinhji, as a cadet of the Palitana royal family, was the queen's kinsman through marriage, and the Dhrangadhra Maharaja Ajit Singhji, had earlier 'stolen' the Rajkot princess from his own son. The Political Agent to the Governor of Kathiawar, P.S.V.

Fitzgerald, believed that there was intrigue going on between the Palitana Rani and Samatsinhji.[42] The enmity between Samatsinhji and the Dhrangadhra court had wounds only a few years old, which were unlikely to have healed. As Maharaja Ajit Singhji of Dhrangadhra noted to the Agent to Kathiawar, Samatsinhji 'whose grudge to this family is of too well-known an origin to bear narration here is actively interfering in this matter'.[43] Interestingly, here the Palitana dowager queen used very similar language to the Rajkot Rani, who had earlier broken off the alliance with Samatsinhji's son.

Similar to the Rajkot Rani, the Palitana Rajmata was admonished for travelling outside the perimeters of her state. According to her, she left for her brother's kingdom, Bansda, with her daughter because of her health and in order to distance herself from the internal intrigues within her state. The state administrator, a Mr Tudor Owens, questioned why she was absent from Palitana after he returned from a six-month trip to England. He was alarmed and concerned with her departure and requested her to return as it would greatly please his wife: 'I felt it was inauspicious that I ... should return after being absent six months and that Moti Rani Saheb and Hariba Saheb were absent. I know also that Madam Saheb will take it to heart, if you do not return to give her a welcome'.[44] Tudor Owens clearly was using female intimacy and friendly courtesy, for his wife would have been more familiar with the interior of the Zenana than himself, to subtly admonish the Rani.

In a letter written to the Palitana Rani while she was stationed at her brother's home in Bansda, he encouraged the marriage with Dhrangadhra. He highlighted, in particular, the love and affection between the prospective marriage partners: 'But in this (marriage) tie both the parties (the bride and bridegroom) love each other. So they are sure to be happy ... How much misery is there in effecting a marriage tie in which the bride and bridegroom do not love each other?'[45] Furthermore, he implored her to ignore the rumours spreading about the Dhrangadhra Raj, most likely from Samatsinhji and others.[46]

Like the Rajkot Rani before her, the Palitana Rajmata provided detailed and explicit rationale why she wished to break off the match, and why the colonial Government should not be involved in her private affairs. In a letter to the Governor of Bombay, Sir George Sydenham Clarke, written to bypass the intervention of her local British officers, she wrote that that her daughter's best interests were closest to her heart in taking such action. Like the Rajkot Rani, she used the vocabulary of western romantic love, conjugal happiness and friendship between child and parent, to strengthen the legitimacy of her choice.[47] She described herself as a loving and devoted mother, the 'sole parent and guardian and best friend' of her daughter, Kunvari Shri Hariba. As a dutiful and loving mother, she had 'the determining right in the disposal of her [daughter's] future'.[48] She then meticulously provided the facts and history behind the broken engagement.

When her husband died in 1905, he left behind his own mother (the Ma Saheb), three widows (of which she was the *patrani*), one daughter (her own), and the young heir who was still in his minority. With the consent of her mother-in-law and the Palitana Political Agent, Mr Tudor Owens, she sent a delegation to visit Dhrangadhra, which comprised of the Revenue Commissioner, Jivabhai Pitambar, and the Dewan of the state, Mr Dolatram. She was told by her Dewan that the marriage with Dhrangadhra had been broken off and that she should look elsewhere for marriage partners. After consultation with her Political Agent Tudor Owens, she began a correspondence with the Barwanee Raj. The Maharani of Barwanee was favourable to allying her son with the Palitana princess.[49] As was normal procedure, she inquired about the prospective groom from his tutors. She received favourable news from the Principal of Mayo College in Ajmer, where the boy was a student.[50] And with the consent of the Barwanee Maharani and her own mother-in-law, the Ma Saheb, she cemented the match.

In the meantime, the Agent in Kathiawar and other local British officials were still in favour of the alliance with Dhrangadhra. The Administrator of Palitana State, Major Beale, wrote on 15 September 1907: 'We all think that in not effecting betrothal with Dhrangadhra we are losing for Kunvari Shri Hariba Saheb an opportunity of forming connection with one Patvi Kunwar (i.e. heir-apparent); and in breaking off the betrothal it appears to us that you do not pay any regard to the welfare of your Kunvari'.[51] Despite their political inducements to go through with the marriage, she had come to the conclusion that it was an ill-fated union. In an interview with Fitzgerald, Agent to the Governor of Kathiawar, he expressed her conviction that the 'marriage would mean lifelong unhappiness' for her daughter. Like the Rajkot Rani, she emphasized the importance of contentment and love in marriage, stating that she was not willing to sacrifice her daughter to a family that would treat her poorly.[52] The princess' marriage to Dhrangadhra would 'ensure for her lifelong misery'.[53] The Rani based her decision upon the observations of her two advisers who had visited Dhrangadhra and found the 'customs and manners' of the place to be 'bad'. She underlined the fact that the yuvraj, heir apparent Ghanshyam Singhji, had no observable faults but rather the problems lay in his 'surroundings'.[54]

Not only did she believe the marriage was inauspicious, but the British were urging it on. As she chastised the Government: 'This marriage is formed through the Government Officers. Such a thing had not happened before'.[55] Such involvement in the domestic life of Zenana women had no earlier history, according to her (although there was obvious precedent from only a few years prior to this, as well as several other instances noted in this book). She demanded that the British officials should not interfere: '[Tell the] Agency not to interfere in our private and social functions'.[56] She questioned indignantly: 'Is the Agent to the Governor entitled, and has he just cause for interfering, to compel my daughter's marriage at Dhrangadhra?'[57] She suggested that her own Administrator, Tudor Owens, kept her in the dark during these procedures:

> Your Excellency in Council will observe the state of darkness and perplexity in which I have been thrown and which the Administrator and the Agent have done nothing to relieve. On the contrary when in July I asked for copies of the correspondence relating to the Dhrangadhra negotiations, I was told by Major Beale that he could not give them because he was only the Acting Administrator.[58]

Again and again she reiterated this fundamental point, integral to her cause: Government should not be involved in zenana affairs. Its involvement had lead to a fundamental injustice:

> Your officers told me in March 1907 that the Sirkar would not be responsible if a suitable match was not obtained for my daughter and left me the responsibility. I accepted the position and obtained a suitable match. And in September 1907 your officers told me that they had interfered to prevent the match! Between the individual and individual, such conduct would be open to grave comment. Between the British Sirkar and a widowed Ranee, it ought to be allowed or upheld?[59]

In the above tirade, the Rani made three important assertions. First, she reinforced her claim to a British concept of individual liberties and rights. Second, using the feminine language of a weakened woman, a 'widowed ranee', she placed herself on a higher moral plane as the victim of British cruelty. Third, she enhanced her role as a woman, mother and queen whose powers in all three positions should not be abused. Her tone is regal and excessively confident, as only one who is well aware of her own symbolic and real powers could express. The voice is not of a cowed, dominated queen, but rather explicit in the language of resistance.

Furthermore, she argued that the British Government did not have sufficient knowledge of local customs to be well informed in arbitrating disputes. She exposed her belief in their lack of judicial and moral ascendancy over indigenous groups. As she noted, zenana practices and internal politics were often outside the realm of British penetration, and thereby served as locales for resistance. 'The British Government and its officers cannot have the opportunities, the knowledge, and the experience whereby alone a right determination can be arrived at in matters relating to our families. It is not desirable that they should in such matters espouse the cause of one family against another', she observed.[60] She perceived them as incompetent in working out such family disputes and believed their ignorance would only make further complications: 'To enforce betrothals by official mandates or by official pressure, whether direct or indirect, should be no part of their duties. Otherwise, the only result of such interference must be *assured unhappiness*. Would the British Sirkar undertake such a burden?'[61] As she saw it, the colonial government's intervention only further insulted and weakened Zenana women. As she narrated, 'In the case of the Zenana ladies of a Ruling Family such treatment adds to the helplessness inherent in their circumstances, an absence of courtesy and kindness which should not escape the serious consideration of your Excellency's Government'.[62]

With forceful indignation, she questioned the deviance of the Dhrangadhra Raj in seeking British intervention and thus breaking tradition by placing zenana domestic arrangements within the ambit of British arbitration. She angrily denied the Maharaja's right to press for the marriage: 'The Raj Saheb of Dhrangadhra has no reason and no right to seek the assistance or interference of the Agent to the Governor. He has come to no wedding arrangement with us. He has done nothing according to Rajwada custom. He has, if anything, acted deliberately, to cause humiliation, and to hurt our feelings'.[63] Not only did he break with custom, but he also personally betrayed her faith and good will.

Just like the Rajkot Rani, she squarely rejected indictments of intrigue. As she had earlier suggested that the British were not sufficiently equipped to provide wise rulings in local disputes, she further argued that they had poor intelligence. She noted that British officials were often misled into believing she was involved in *khatpat*:

> I must be pardoned if I am obliged to say in my own defense that such charges and insinuations are much too common in Kathiawar, and that British officers themselves are not seldom duped by designing men into believing too readily the existence of *khatpat* where it may not exist.[64]

In an earlier letter to Tudor Owens, she specifically wrote in Gujarati so he would not suspect any third person was influencing her: 'You write to say that you suspect that letters are written in English through *khatpat* (scheming). For this reason, I want to assure you by writing this letter in Gujarati that I have hitherto communicated to you my own thoughts and that there is no reasonable ground for the suspicion which you have been entertaining about *khatpat* on the part of (my) men'.[65] She also explained that she had left Palitana to prevent becoming involved in intrigues. 'In the difficult position in which I am placed I wish to avoid every occasion for mischief, misunderstanding and misrepresentation which would be likely if I was at Palitana and which is not possible while I am at Bansda'.[66] As is Rajput custom, she sought sanctuary with her *saga*, her brother, the ruling prince of Bansda, where she was able to plead her case more effectively without the close pressure of British agents in her state. The State's Administrator, Tudor-Owens, had advised her to seek her brother's counsel: 'so that the Raj Saheb *should make it his duty to enquire and ascertain* what truth there was in the reports brought by the Dewan and Revenue Commissioner of Palitana about Dhrangadhra'.[67]

This 1908 letter from the Palitana Rani is a significant document of resistance by a Hindu dowager Rani. It illuminates how far Zenana women were from the image of the silent, passive female, shielded and emasculated by *pardah* that was often portrayed in colonial writings. She argues her case for non-intervention into zenana affairs in a manner, which is both lucid and persuasive by virtue of its cool rationality. It is not the letter of a woman who is willing to compromise nor of one daunted by the pressures of the paramount power.

Queen-Mothers Using the Language of Love, Colonial law and Maternal Authority in the Game of Marriage Alliance Making

These two marriage disputes in Kathiawar at the turn of the century suggest that dowager queens and princesses knew how to manipulate the principles of statesmanship and Machiavellian politics in their favour. Here, they are able to combine both occidental attitudes and pre-colonial concepts of courtly strategy, perhaps harking back to the techniques of the ancient, Sanskritic treatise on power and kingship, Kautilya's *Arthasastra*. In both instances, the widowed Ranis of Palitana and Rajkot, when devoid of male guardians in the form of husbands or sons, as neither women were the mothers of men, adroitly counteracted British paramountcy and interference in their affairs while simultaneously keeping at bay local competing forces in the forms of traditional male dynasts. With the support of legal advisors, state administrators and their own intelligence gathering, they combated external constraints upon the simultaneously private, yet public, sphere of dynastic marriage.

Popularly perceived as pawns of the British or princely collaborators and as domesticated females silenced behind *pardah* by men, Zenana women appear not only to have had resisting voices, but also considerable influence to prevail against both patriarchal and colonial forces. As these two cases demonstrate, they were not only used by the British, but effectively used them as well. Skillfully incorporating the language of western law, rights and love, they argued persuasively to extricate British involvement in arranging marriages of state. They advocated that these rites were private ceremonies to enhance their daughters' happiness rather than public events to be managed by the Raj's political officers.

It is also possible, and probable, that they used occidental sensibilities merely to enact, in the end, matches that they believed most politically and economically advantageous. Through an evocation of individual rights, the necessity for love and personal happiness in marriage and the weight of maternal authority, they leveraged British intervention to enhance and advocate their own interests over those of other local aristocratic males. In these instances, as in the accounts regarding regency and succession, certain Zenana women may have had more power under colonial rule than earlier. They claimed their rights as queens, mothers and women and were not afraid to combat both British censure and regionally situated antagonisms. The next chapter examines how princely consorts and brides affected the male ruler's relationship with the paramount power in a different manner: namely, how the 'wrong woman', as symbol or bride, could seriously undermine a prince's sovereign authority.

5 TROUBLES IN INDORE, THE MAHARAJA'S WOMEN: LOVING DANGEROUSLY

In 1926, at the age of thirty-six, HH Maharadhiraja Raja Rajeshwar Sawai Shri Tukojirao III Holkar XIII Bahadur of Indore, GCIE, formally signed his abdication papers. The period preceding it had been a traumatic year for the ruler. In January 1925, a Muslim businessman by the name of Bawla was murdered on a dimly lit street in Bombay's affluent Malabar Hill, and his lover, Mumtaz Begum, who had accompanied him that night, was severely injured with knife wounds to her head. The begum had been at one time a palace dancer at Indore, and a favourite of the Maharaja's. It was soon discovered by eyewitness accounts and police inquiries that their assailants were members of the Indore household, who had been sent under the directions of Tukoji Rao. The murder case dominated national and international headlines when it came to trial in the Bombay High Court and ultimately compelled the ruler to relinquish his sovereign powers.

Thus, from the mid-1920s to the 1940s, the kingdom of Indore in Central India was best known for the romantic trials of its two Holkar princes, the aforementioned Maharaja Tukoji Rao (1890–1978, r. 1903–26) and his son Maharaja Yeshwant Rao Holkar (1908–61, r. 1926–61). Born as sovereigns at the end of empire, these two Hindu Maratha rulers became embroiled in personal crises, which had far reaching political consequences. Their life histories reveal how the private peccadilloes, sexual desires and love unions of the Indian kings were elaborately interwoven with the running of state government and the kingdom's relationship with the colonial regime. In this particular dynastic line, regal consorts and royal wives caused considerable political instability and damage. The Malabar Hill Murder trial cost Tukoji Rao Holkar his *gaddi* when he was compelled to abdicate. Yeshwant Rao's morganatic marriages to two American women forced him to rewrite succession precedence in Indore, making his daughter his heir and precluding the rights of future male issue. Despite the fact that these rulers were aware of the political consequences of their seemingly imprudent romantic liaisons, they still went ahead with them.

Such incidences are not merely accounts of sad, love struck princes caught between the romantic sensibilities of East and West, but examples of how the colonial state regulated Indian princely masculinity in a larger project of cultural assimilation and domination even while colonized subjects resisted and renegotiated such identities. Just as the Indian nationalists were pushing for political freedom in *swaraj*, this chapter explores how these two rulers pursued their personal desires despite the threats of political censure. At the same time, it investigates how the colonial power, and in particular Anglo-Indian legal courts, empowered some Zenana women to contest and undermine the influence of rival princely males.

The story of Mumtaz Begum is that of a young *pardah* woman, poor, illiterate and sexually compromised, who threatened and ultimately dethroned a reigning prince. While most of the accounts provided in this book deal specifically with the power of princely women who were born into dynastic families or married into them, this is an example where a member of the Zenana courtly household, who was not herself a member of the elite, was able to use the intervening authority of colonial judicial courts and administrative officers to counteract the alleged abuses of her regal keeper. Here, colonial courts enabled a low class courtesan to remove herself from the courtly household, while the Maharaja could not resort to traditional measures of patronage and power – his people – as an effective counterbalance. The chapter also exposes the similarities between Hindu and Muslim courtly cultures as well as the overlap between legal provisions for Hindu women and their Muslim contemporaries in late colonial India. In addition, it demonstrates how the introduction of American brides and the rewriting of succession law to favour female heirs emphasized the vital influence of Zenana women in controlling courtly politics and contributing to the contentious debate on imperial definitions of sexuality, gender, class and religion. As symbols and active players, they significantly affected the princely state's relationship with the colonial regime and later the independent republican government of India.

Indore was a nineteen-gun salute state situated in what is today Madhya Pradesh. In 1728, the Maratha Peshwa in Poona granted the territories of what became the Indore state to a cavalry officer in his command, Malhar Rao Holkar of Indore. In 1818, the Indore Raj signed a treaty after the British forces under Sir John Malcolm defeated the Holkars led by Rani Krishnabai Holkar at Mahidpur. The treaty of Mandsaur ceded paramountcy over Indore to the East India Company. By the early twentieth century, its rulers were well known in all-India circles and abroad. As Ian Copland suggests, Yeshwant Rao Holkar was perhaps the Maharaja who 'best epitomised' the 1940s era, both for his vices and his virtues.[1]

The Case for Mumtaz Begum: Law and Religion in Colonial India

It was the British legal principle of upholding the equality of individuals within the courts, which in part allowed Mumtaz Begum's grievances to be heard. In north Indian Hindu law, varying castes of men (and certainly women) were not equal.[2] In contrast, as Pamela Price argues in her research on princely South India, an emphasis on individual rights allowed courtly women to find legal redress from traditional systems of privilege and hierarchy through the British Indian courts. As she narrated in numerous examples, Zenana women, royal and otherwise, found Anglo-Indian courts sympathetic to their views in regards to succession, property and marriage disputes. As individuals before the law, these women used the system of litigation to gain not only voice and symbolic influence, but also tangible successes in the form of property and capital.[3] Hence, in the colonial law courts, a Muslim royal mistress could compromise the authority of the prince while protecting herself.

The legal provisions for Indian women were hotly debated in nineteenth-century India and the 'woman's question' came to symbolize the conflict between British administrators and their Indian subjects over the 'subcontinent's fitness for self-rule'.[4] Both Indian social reformers and Christian missionaries pressured the colonial government to introduce new legislation for women. While this wave of legal reform was not spurred by popular demand, it enabled Indian women to take their grievances to court.[5] British writers such as James Mill in his questionable *The History of British India* had argued that Indian women reflected the 'backwardness' of their own country.[6] Hindu reformers such as Raja Ram Mohun Roy rebutted by noting that before the advent of Muslim rule, women appeared to be 'educated and free' and actively engaged in the socio-political life of pre-Islamic India. He suggested therefore that *sati,* child marriage and polygamy were against 'nature or reason' during this golden age in India's pre-colonial history. Muslim reformers also called for a return to earlier Muslim tradition through the 'restoration of 'pure' Islam free from cultural accretions'.[7]

In large part social reformers focused on the position of disenfranchised Hindu women who did not have legal rights in relationship to property, divorce or customary practices, which forced them to continue to depend on their families, particularly male members.[8] While Muslim women enjoyed stronger legal provisions relating to property inheritance and divorce according to Islamic law, they faced many of the same limitations as their Hindu counterparts in part due to cultural norms based on region and socio-economic class. The social patterns of late colonial Muslim communities in India largely highlight the dominance of familial interests over individual desires and Muslim women bore much in the maintenance of regional customary practices such as early marriage and inflexible inheritance laws. As Shahida Lateef suggests, legal provisions for Muslim women were based less on religious law, at this time, than on local customs and traditions which had similarities with Hindu customary practice.[9] The census of India in 1872 reported that 'indeed, except for the rules of inheritance, in her occupation and mode of life the Mohammedan female does not differ much from the Hindu'.[10] The 1901 Census continued by noting while divorce was permitted for Muslim women, it was rare in Indian provinces. Reform-minded Muslim communities emphasized that the laws and rights of Muslim women had been eroded through their close proximity to non-Islamic Indian communities. Male reformers actively argued for a modernist reinterpretation of Islamic personal law that awarded Indian Muslim women legal entitlements.[11] In 1932, Mrs Hamid Ali, leader of the All India Women's Conference argued for the reinstatement of Muslim law which was 'more equitable' than customary practice.[12] As Lateef notes, 'the status and role of Muslim women in India before Independence could not be significantly differentiated from the status and role of women in other communities; the difference was a matter of region, class and caste, more than religion'.[13]

Earlier Islamic law during the Muslim period in India had been conducted through the intermediary of the Kazi. After 1864, the British Indian government abolished the post and left the organization of Muslim personal law largely to individual members. In 1880, Syed Ahmed Khan argued for the reintroduction of the Kazi in an honorary capacity to regulate religious practice rather than delegating it to would-be self-appointed local kazis.[14]

Muslim women and members of the Women's Movement in India became involved in the discussion over religious law, particularly regarding the practice of *pardah*. The rise of the women's movement in the 1920s particularly heightened the debate against *pardah* and anti-*pardah* movements grew after 1900.[15] As the Maharani of Travancore, President of the AIWC noted 'Under Mohammedan law the property and marital relations are safeguarded, yet seclusion of home (has) led to serious difficulties. Indeed in many regions the strictness of *purdah* is regarded proportionate to the status of the family, and much patient work needs to be done to eradicate such ideas'.[16] The European women's suffrage movement extended the support of British female members of Parliament towards the Indian Women's movement and women gained the right to vote in India. Madras was the first state to give the vote to women in 1921; Travancore was the first princely state to award the vote in 1920 and was followed soon after by Mysore, Jhalawar and Cochin.[17]

Mumtaz Begum's trial evidence in the Malabar Hill Murder case reflects this larger debate. Here colonial legal courts, which privilege individual representation and agency over collective social grouping, enabled an otherwise displaced woman to give evidence against a male political elite. With women gaining suffrage in areas of British India and the princely states by the early 1920s, the lively discussion over women's education, *pardah* and family law by both colonial administrators and indigenous reformers and the colonial regime's tireless efforts to detect 'degeneracy' within princely Indian governments, it is no surprise that this case should have dominated the news media of its day. The story of Mumtaz Begum serves not only to reveal how Anglo-Indian law provided agency to *pardah,* Zenana women, but also how women themselves had become catalysts for recreating their own destinies. Mumtaz's subsequent actions, such as her escape from Indore and her damning critique of Zenana life, reflect her astute awareness of how her testimony related to this larger drama between ruler and ruled, reformer and traditionalist. Her trial evidence not only reinforced the British perception of the degenerate princely household and its sexual excesses, but also served to support reformist critiques of the archaic, outmoded practices of palace life, such as *pardah*, polygamy, child prostitution, early marriage and lack of education for young girls.

Tukoji Rao Holkar: A Ruler Under Fire

Even before the case came to trial, the colonial government was trying to ascertain the political ramifications of the Malabar Hill murder on Tukoji Rao Holkar's reign. The Agent to the Governor-General in Central India, R. I. R. Glancy, on 6 January 1925 wrote 'the time has come to define the political action to be taken by the Government of India in view of the proved connection with the crime of the Indore State and Indore officials'.[18] In addition, he emphasized the seminal role that the courtesan had taken in the palace politics of this central Indian kingdom: 'These [findings] for the most part indicate the predominant importance of Mumtaz in the politics of Indore during the last year and the close connection of the Court party with the conspiracy'.[19]

In addition, it was clear that the Maharaja's governing powers would be circumscribed. There was already talk of the ruler's potential deposition. According to a 1920 Resolution, a Ruling Chief who found himself in such a situation had the right to draw up a Commission of four, which could include two other ruling princes in dealing with his case. Such a Commission, Glancy believed, would be unlikely to rule against another sovereign unless there was 'direct and definite proof of his complicity'. While the Maharaja was charged with 'instigation, connivance or abetment' of the crime, his full culpability in the conspiracy to murder Bawla was not yet ascertained. In an earlier case, where the Maharaja of Baroda was tried for attempting to poison his Resident, a Commission including two other Indian princes, the Maharajas of Jaipur and Gwalior, assessed him. Although declared not guilty by his Indian judges, the Baroda scion was instantly deposed.[20] So even if the commission responded favourably, there was no guarantee that Tukoji Rao's powers would be protected.

If not resulting in the Maharaja's deposition, Glancy argued that the outcomes of the trial could disclose other internal problems in the running of state affairs in Indore, within the state army or police, which 'renders it necessary to deprive the Ruler of his powers'. Thus, he concluded that 'with all the disadvantages, curtailment of powers is preferable to a negative result and deposition being out of the question, it remains to define the powers which His Highness should be asked to surrender'. Glancy did not elucidate the nature of what these powers might be, for he believed it too dangerous to mention in written correspondence. In the end, Tukoji Rao Holkar was not deposed nor was a Commission brought in. But the results are nearly as bad. Due to political pressure, he abdicated rather than be tried in a British Indian court.

The Indore Zenana[21]

The trial began on Monday 27 April 1925 and went on until 7 May. It was Mumtaz's evidence, which opened the proceedings. As she explained in Urdu to the court, long before the fateful night on Malabar Hill, she had been a member of Tukoji's Zenana as a concubine.[22] Although she could not read Urdu, she read some Marathi and her oral evidence was translated into English.[23] She had first arrived in Indore at the age of eleven or twelve from Hyderabad, which was her original home, and had been introduced to the Maharaja as a singing girl at that time. She did not become his mistress until her third visit[24] and thereafter, she lived with him in Indore and travelled to England as part of his entourage along with the Senior Maharani, under the alias of Kamlabai. After living in England for a year, she returned home pregnant with the Maharaja's child.[25]

Mumtaz Begum alleged that Tukoji Rao had used force from the very beginning of their relationship. She recounted that, six years before she ran away, her mother made a complaint that two men had taken her 'forcibly to Indore'; a fact which her grandmother corroborated.[26] In several instances, Mumtaz was compelled to lie about her age on the orders of the palace. When a lady doctor came to examine her, presumably for gynaecological reasons, Mumtaz Begum lied that she was seventeen, when in actuality she was only thirteen years old.[27]

Her relationship with her own relatives in the court deposition appeared to be strained, with insinuations of coercion and psychological abuse. Mumtaz revealed that it was her mother who had facilitated her meeting with the Maharaja as a young girl, and who kept all the jewellery given by Tukoji Rao. When she became the prince's mistress, Mumtaz lived in a bungalow with her family within the palace compound, where they lived for two and a half years with the use of three to four servants.

Later, a senior maid by the name of Shankerrao took her to the Maharaja's old palace where she lived until she finally ran away. She described her life in Indore: 'During those 10 years I was not allowed to go where I liked. I was not allowed to see my relations. I moved about with the Maharaja. My relations were called when my child was born. At first I was not allowed to see them'.[28] She later portrayed this situation as synonymous with being under house arrest: 'I was kept as a prisoner all the time'.[29] Eventually her child from the Maharaja died in unfortunate circumstances.[30]

Tukoji Rao treated her relatively well for the first three years. After that time, however, things began to go very badly: her actions were circumscribed and she was placed in virtual house arrest. She was not allowed free movement or access: 'there were guards round the palaces where the Rani lived. There were watchmen round the house and also inside the house'.[31] As she described to the court, 'he ill-treated me in ordinary manner. He did not allow me to feed or wear whatever I liked. I would have left Indore before I went to England but I did not get an opportunity'.[32] At various times, she wanted to solicit help from the police but was forced to state that she was travelling of her free will when she was not.

Furthermore, the Maharaja was not monetarily generous. He gave her jewels but no money, although her mother received a salary. At the beginning of their affair, she had a car and house, but later these were taken from her and her family. In addition, the jewellery she did wear was never hers, but part of the Indore treasury to be borrowed and then returned.[33]

What was most damning were her allegations against the Indore Zenana. She believed that the Indore nurses had hurt her baby. 'After my child was born', she said, 'I was unwilling to stay at Indore. I was unwilling because the nurses killed the female child that was born'.[34] The death of her baby was the last straw and instigated her decision to leave the Maharaja. While in the train between Bhanpura and Delhi, she hastily wrote off letters to the Police Commissioner in Delhi and the Viceroy seeking assistance on the guidance of her stepfather.[35] The British law courts were presumably favourable to such impressions of the colonial zenana. Here Mumtaz paints the courtly household in the familiar language of social degeneracy and barbarism as an archaic institution where inhumane practices regularly occurred. She adroitly situates herself as the inhabitant of a licentious, deviant household and the victim of a deranged crime: the eastern woman at the mercy of the Oriental oligarch, whose only hope appears in the form of the westernized man, either as physical saviour, legislator or social reformer.

This discussion on the abuse of Mumtaz Begum's child additionally figures into a larger narrative on colonial juridical reform as it relates to Indian women.[36] During the early period of Company rule in the seventeenth century, colonial authorities had relied upon the interpretation of scriptural texts by indigenous interpreters, such as Brahmin *pandits* or *maulvis*, in determining personal or customary law.[37] British Orientalists, under the leadership of Warren Hastings, privileged religious scriptures, whether Hindu or Muslim, when codifying personal law, thereby widening the gulf between textual law and nontextual practice. By 1781, Hastings planned for the adoption of Hindu and Muslim personal law to adjudicate issues such as succession, inheritance, marriage, caste and all religious usages and institutions.[38] This European emphasis on reading Indian society through scripture led to a privileged emphasis on religion, not politics or economics, as defining India's past.[39]

British administrators soon exchanged their reliance on native 'informers' as 'translators' of religious law for a 'codification' of Indian law. William Jones, a British Orientalist who was himself fluent in several classical and medieval Indian languages, was appointed to the Crown Court in 1783. Distrustful of Indian interpreters of sacred texts, he urged for the creation of a digest of Hindu and Muslim law analogous to the British codes.[40] Less then a century later, by 1864, native officials had virtually disappeared as colonial authorities believed they had grasped Indian legal systems sufficiently and there was now an existing body of case law, which future judges could access. Thereafter, colonial judges determined the final outcomes on cases.[41]

By the nineteenth century, the empire had expanded and colonial officials could no longer rely solely upon textual materials.[42] Thus, the codification of laws in the 1830s was premised on the need for a substantive body of law so courts could adjudicate cases accurately in the cause of 'justice, equity and good conscience'.[43] Thomas B. Macaulay, invoking the anxieties of William Jones and Thomas Strange against native informers, argued for immediate codification. Macaulay, heading the First Law Commission, drafted the initial Indian Penal Code which was put into practice by 1860; the second commission instituted the Criminal Procedure Code which was enacted in 1861 and reorganized the court system.[44] Nonetheless, personal law lay outside of the reach of colonial administrators. Thus laws which governed women, were increasingly addressed to their respective religious communities, Hindu and Muslim, for reform measures.[45]

Indian reformers, such as Ram Mohun Roy, who founded the Brahmo Samaj paved the way for legislative acts which were later passed by the colonial government. Roy's discomfort with the practice of *sati* encouraged Governor General William Bentinck's decision to abolish the practice of widow immolation in 1829.[46] Roy and his followers also addressed issues of child marriage, widow remarriage, *pardah* and female seclusion as well as the need for greater education for women. Ishwar Chandra Vidyasagar urged for the better situation of widows, which led to the Widow Remarriage Act of 1856.[47]

Certainly British colonial magistrates and courts, as well as British trained Indian lawyers, sympathetic to the arguments of Indian reformers and the nationalist cause, would have seen Mumtaz's testimony, irrespective of the murder charge, as illustrative of all that was evil in 'feudal' states and domestic households. This is something either she or her legal counsel would have been well aware of. In her indictment, she not only highlights female infanticide and forced under-age sexual relations, but she vividly portrays a zenana governed by the practices of polygamy, concubinage and *pardah*. These were institutions which both indigenous Indian reformers and colonial legislators were feverishly opposed to and keenly attempting to reform as part of a larger mission, on the one hand, for 'resurrecting' India's glorious past of gendered equity or on the other, as a 'civilizing' project whereby the 'rule of law and reason' would govern the day. In this way, Mumtaz's situation could be read by colonial officials to further support an imperial design to recreate Indian society according to Victorian definitions of sexual propriety, good governance and transparency.

The Bombay Businessman

In contrast to Tukoji Rao Holkar, Mumtaz described Abdul Kadir Bawla as a more generous caretaker and lover. Bawla, in contrast to the Maharaja, gave her ornaments and jewels.[48] He also paid her an allowance. As she noted, 'While I was with my mother, Bawla paid me Rs. 1000/ per month. Afterwards he gave me whatever I wanted, i.e. food, clothing and allowance: no money'. She continued: 'I enjoyed more luxuries in Bawla's house than I had at Indore'.[49] Furthermore, she was happy with him, and at the time of the murder was pregnant with his daughter. As she remembered him: 'I had once gone to the Poona Races with Bawla. I was quite happy with Bawla. I never had any intention to leave him'. Her aunt, Nathajan Mahomed Badiud Jamankhan, corroborated that 'He and Mumtaz were inseparable; any warning given to one was given to the other'.[50] Bawla furthermore provided legal support for her when she discovered the Maharaja of Indore was going to issue a warrant for her arrest.[51] It is clear that Mumtaz not only saw Bawla as the object of her affections but also as an instrument towards economic freedom and independence in a manner not achievable within the Indore zenana.

Mumtaz first met the Muslim Bombay businessman in August 1924 through her maternal uncles. At that time, she knew the Indore 'people' were after her. She never travelled or went anywhere alone. The Indore Durbar had issued a warrant for her extradition on the trumped up charge of stealing jewellery from the treasury, which she denied.[52]

She had wanted to leave Indore long before her trip to England.[53] At one point, the Maharaja had told her that she could leave voluntarily if she wished. But Mumtaz believed the Maharaja's avowal of freedom was not sincere:

I made that petition to the Commissioner of Police in spite of the Maharaja having told me to go wherever I liked. I did not get any opportunity to go away before. He made these statements without any meaning in it. I did not make any attempt to go. He was not sincere. I sent this letter to the Commissioner of Police, Bombay, because if I was ordered to go back to Indore I intended to go to Rutlam and from Rutlam to

Bombay. I understood that I was being sent to Mussoorie, but I did not know that the Maharaja would change his mind and order me back to Indore.[54]

As Mumtaz's stepfather Mahomedali Mohamed Yusuf supported, when she left him Tukoji longed to see her. The Maharaja's aid, Zakaulla, visited Mumtaz in Amritsar and mentioned 'that the Maharaja was weeping and he was anxious that she should go to him ... Mumtaz absolutely refused to go to Indore. Then Zakaulla said they would take her any way they liked under the orders of the Maharaja and they left in anger'.[55]

Throughout this period, Mumtaz had maintained strict *pardah*. As she informed the court, 'since I went to Indore I was a Purda Lady. I continued the Purda after I left Indore and after I came to Bombay'.[56] At first her family was ambivalent towards her becoming the mistress of a wealthy man. According to her, she had not met any men in Bombay before Bawla and she had continued to practice *pardah* in Bombay.[57] While her parents ultimately permitted her to see Bawla, she was not allowed to go out late at night. 'In Bombay', she told the court, 'my parents did not prevent me from going about with Bawla, but they asked me not to move about late at night because the Indore people were after me'.[58]

In giving her trial evidence, it is clear that Mumtaz Begum was part of a larger, complicated world. Ever since her childhood she had been bartered between her family and male lovers as a sexual object. Although living as the Maharaja's mistress in Indore, she was also in the company of her mother and stepfather, who had their own house on the palace grounds. It is also apparent that she had been hiding from the Maharaja, and this was in part her motivation for becoming the mistress of her second lover, Bawla. Bawla provided her with a house and enough financial resources to look after her mother and stepfather as well as several other extended relations. She had also met him through her maternal uncles, Allabux and Alladin.[59] Her mother and stepfather were after her jewellery which her grandmother had given her; these pieces were originally gifts from Maharaja Ranjitsinhji, who had been her grandmother's lover, not Tukoji Rao.[60] At one point in their relationship, she requested money from Bawla in order to give it to her aunt, Nathajan Mahomed Badiud Jamankhan.[61] Thus, it is apparent that Mumtaz provided income for the entire family to subsist through her sexual relationships.

What remains ambiguous is whether Mumtaz resented her family's behaviour. At some points, it seemed that she was gently chiding them in her narrative by alluding to the fact that her mother kept her jewels under lock and key or encouraged her into a life of sexual service as a young girl. At the same time, she noted that her parents protected or supported her: for instance, they encouraged her to run away from Indore and write petitions for her safety to the Police Commissioner and the Viceroy. In their oral depositions, her family members deny charges of manipulation. Her stepfather emphasized the fact that the family was getting on well with one another. As he said in court: 'We had no quarrel with Mumtaz. She had no quarrel with her mother, but her mother used to warn her against going out at night and remaining out late at night. There was no other difference between them'.[62] At another moment, her mother's brother Allabux Wazir refuted the fact that he was acting as a pimp or purveyor of sexual partners for Mumtaz.[63] In addition, when Mumtaz contended that Bawla had maintained her well, her stepfather questioned that assertion, suggesting that he only paid her a lump sum of 1,000 rupees once or twice and did not give her any ornaments.[64]

There is a long history regarding princely courtesans in the Indian kingdoms. As the Maharaja of Dhrangadhra remembers the mistresses of his grandfather, there were several gradations of 'kept women'. The *Marzidan*, 'a favourite who could come and go as she pleased and wasn't a kept women' and the *Padadayatji* (Persian) or *Avarodha* (Sanskrit) who 'took the veil and wore gold on her ankles (a distinction once the equivalent of a knighthood for men) ... whose children became charges on the State and the public exchequer'.[65] The *Padadayatji* had her own privileges and the Zenana Maharanis and daughters-in-law of the house would have to curtsy before her in certain circumstances. Lastly, there was the *Paswanji* who wore jewellery and 'sat on equality with the wives'. These ladies were not legitimate wives because they belonged to different castes from the ruler as the Maharaja of Dhrangadhra explains. In the region of Saurashtra, most royal mistresses were Muslim.[66] As these classifications reveal, mistresses had their own jewels, monies and properties given from the state treasury as well as forms of privilege and respectful address. Like the wives of the Maharaja, they shared in the running of the zenana and in some instances indirectly governed the state.

The Saheb Who Rescued Me

On the night of Bawla's murder, they went for a typical evening drive. The car contained Mumtaz, Bawla, the driver Mahomed Sharif and a retainer by the name of Mathews. They drove to Apollo Bunder, then Colaba, Chowpatty, Mahaluxmi Battery, through Walkeshwar and the Hanging Gardens. As they neared the Hanging Gardens, they heard the car horn of a vehicle behind them. They had been driving fast, but the driver slowed down, and the second car drew up to them on one side. It was a quick altercation. She told the court: 'I heard abusive words directed against Mr. Bawla and someone saying "Put down our Bai"'.[67] Both cars stopped, men leapt out of the pursuing vehicle and they were soon surrounded on all sides. She describes the ensuing mayhem: 'I cannot say how many were there. Then someone put his head into the car and fired a pistol. They did that on both sides ... One man dragged me out of the Car, and stabbed me on the forehead. I had three wounds. Someone lifted me up and carried me away towards the other side of the road'.[68]

Three British army officers arrived on the scene. They took quick action, which saved her life, and later allowed Mumtaz to provide evidence, which subsequently endangered the Maharaja's throne. She recalled:

> in the meanwhile the European who rescued us came in a car. As soon as that Car came I shouted out: 'For god's sake, help me' ... Then ... I was made to sit in the Car by the man who struck me with the knife ... I was again struck me on the forehead. Then that Sahib rescued me ... [he] who rescued me bound the man who had struck with the knife hand and foot.[69]

The three English officers had just returned from a round of golf at the Willingdon Club and were heading back to the Taj Mahal Hotel for evening drinks, when they came across the mayhem.[70] Unprepared, they used golf clubs as weapons in the skirmish. John Malcolm Saegert, one of the three, described the scene which they encountered. They had driven down Gibbs Road and then up the Ridge Road:

> I saw two cars draw up to the right side of the road. Just as we came road the corner about 30 yards away we saw some figures getting out of the leading car and then we saw some flashes. Directly after the flashes there were loud screams from the second car. The flashes were the flashes of a pistol. I did not hear the report. When I heard the screams I stopped my car and we all got out ... When I got to the car I saw three men trying to drag a woman out of the car and two men standing level with the chauffeur's seat ... three men were threatening the woman with knives and she had already been cut with the knife. I shouted and ran up when one of the two men near the chauffeur's seat turned round and fired at me with a pistol on the right shoulder and the other man stabbed me with a knife as I ran past. I pulled off two of the men who were attacking the woman and threw them into the road ... As I closed with the man who first fired at me I heard loud screams from the directions of my car. I left the man who was attacking me and turned round and now two men again were attacking the woman. I went back and called out these people and we fought together and as we fought we got round to the front of my car ...
>
> I got up then and saw that somebody had put the woman in my car. She was bleeding sitting on the back seat ...[71]

It was Saegert's co-officer, Francis Batley, who had carried Mumtaz into the back seat of their car. As Batley told the court: 'Next thing I remember clearly is an Indian lady running over to the other car and making to be taken away. She was bleeding profusely and there were three cuts on her forehead. I put her into our own car, put her out of the way of the struggle'.[72] He then also joined the tussle armed with a golf club. These images of protection classically reinforce the imperial fantasy of the white man as saviour of the brown woman from the vices of the native Oriental.[73]

The two Englishmen described in some detail the faces of Mumtaz's assailants and recounted how they had spotted the murderers in a police line-up at Indore.

The culpability of the palace was now established. How close the conspiracy had been to the Maharaja was not spelt out, but the proximity of the murder was near enough to sufficiently damage Tukoji Rao's reputation. There was enough evidence to warrant the Commission that Glancy had prophesized before the trial went to court. Mumtaz, who was then pregnant with Bawla's baby, went off to Hollywood to make her fortune.[74] A film of the story, *Kulin Kanta*, was later produced in Bollywood.[75] Tukoji Rao was left to stand trial or face the Commission, but chose abdication.

The post-trial climate was dangerous for the Maharaja. In a letter from R. I. R. Glancy, Agent to the Governor-General in Central India to the Political Secretary to the Government of India, he pointed out the effects of the trial on the Maharaja's safety. The Bawla family was personally involved in a vendetta against the Maharaja:

> The Prime Minister Indore State informed me that information had been received to the effect that the Bawla family contemplated taking their revenge by assassinating His Highness and had engaged a noted 'badmash' of Bombay named Ali Aliya. He asked that arrivals of suspicious persons, especially Pathans, should be watched and that if such persons entered the Residency bazaars, information should be given to him. The guards on the Palace have been increased and armed guards will in future follow the Durbar motor in another car.[76]

The Maharaja had become a target for all sorts of criminal types. 'Blackmailers' from all over India, including the Rana of Barwani, were requesting money from the Indore ruler. In response, Tukoji Rao had received sympathetic responses from the rulers of Gwalior, Alwar, Bhopal and Dholpur in support of his predicament.

As Glancy suggested, the implications of the crime not only besmirched the reputation of the Holkar ruler, but also affected his physical safety. 'This is purely inference', he wrote, 'but it is obviously thought that the crime has been brought near enough to the Ruler and that to bring it nearer could do him no good. I imagine too that the individuals concerned are too dangerous for the Prime Minister to tackle'.[77] The prince's sexual proclivities and jealousies had gotten him into deep waters.

Above the Law: Maharaja Tukoji Rao's Abdication; a Question of Treaty

In a letter sent to Glancy nearly a year after the murder was committed, Tukoji Rao wrote his official letter of abdication. It is a brief but telling correspondence, and articulates his firm reasons for relinquishing his *gaddi* rather than take the stand at the Bombay High Court. The letter specifically refers back to an earlier 1918 epistle, which he had sent with regard to the Montagu-Chemsford Report. The Report, which formed the basis for the Government of India Act, 1919, gave 'formal recognition to many of the ruler's claims to autonomy'.[78] The Indian princes as a whole had been pushing for greater sovereignty in their own states and the ability to participate in governance around the empire. In 1916, Viceroy Lord Chelmsford had conceded to this demand and organized the first conference of princes in Delhi. By 1921, they had founded their own chamber.

Tukoji Rao's letter outlined the precedent behind the original treaty or sanad between the crown government and his ancestor. Specifically, Tukoji Rao asserted that as a sovereign indigenous prince he was not under the jurisdiction of British Indian law, which was stipulated in the precepts of the original sanad between Indore and the British Crown. As he explained to Glancy, 'Rightly or wrongly, I have all along adhered to the belief that neither on the analogy of International Law nor as a matter resting upon treaty is a Prince of my position liable to be tried'.[79] Citing the earlier reference, which was already eight years old, and hence was not alluded to merely out of convenience, he argued that he must protect the solemnity and authority of his regal dynasty rather than his own personal position as a monarch. As he continued, having the 'status, rights and privileges of a Ruler of my position, I cannot persuade myself to act contrary to my convictions and to accept a commission or Committee of Enquiry. Rather than sacrifice the principle for which I have stood throughout my career as a Ruler, it would be more dignified to sacrifice my own self by abdicating'.[80] The threat of a commission sometimes pushed rulers to give up their powers for a short period or to abdicate completely.[81] During Lord Curzon's viceroyalty, fifteen princes had reacted in such a manner.[82]

Certainly, Tukoji Rao was aware that this action might be translated into an admission of guilt or an expression of cowardice. To many it did appear that he was guilty. He conceded that point: 'I fully realize that the World, from the mere fact of my not facing an Enquiry, may wrongly draw its own conclusion as to my guilt and may never realize that it was not the consciousness of guilt but adherence to principle which had determined my action'.[83]

It is telling how the oral evidence of an illiterate, young courtesan, who had been a member of the prince's household for nearly ten years, could have led a ruler to the final dissolution of his governing powers. This narrative exposes that colonized women had greater agency than earlier perceived and a new changed environment where Mumtaz Begum could astutely remove herself from the princely household, through the intervention of imperial agents, as earlier systems of power were no longer affective. The prince's response, itself, is an interesting aperture into the role of law in princely India, and the relationship between Indian kings and the paramount power. It is important to note that from the Indore ruler's perspective an Indian prince was above trial in a British court.

His Highness as 'an independent ally of the British Government'

While the policy of British indirect rule has sometimes been described as the treaty system, only around forty Indian states signed treaties with the East Indian Company, and its successor, the British Crown. At various times, the treaties referred to specific events, issues or concerns. The 'interpretation of these treaties became arenas of manoeuvre and negotiation among British political officers, Indian rulers and their ministers, and the British and Indian lawyers until the demise of the states in 1948'.[84] Tukoji Rao's detailed reference to the Holkar sanad hence emerges out of a spirited debate on the role of sovereignty and paramountcy between Indian princes and the British Raj. In Holkar's case, British victory at Assaye led by Arthur Wellesley, brother of the governor-general, resulted in the original treaty in 1803.

Indore's treaty sanctioned 'the rights, dignities and privileges secured to [Holkar rulers] by treaties, sanads, and engagements or by established practice'. The British Government would 'observe treaty obligations', 'refrain from interference' and 'protect the States from it'.[85] In addition, the British conceded that each state was different and had its own 'peculiar rights, customs and traditions' which differentiated it from other kingdoms. Hence, the rulers were encouraged to express their perspectives. Due to this 'invitation' to communicate 'his views', Tukoji Rao articulated his particular concerns and those of Indore.[86]

Tukoji Rao, like many of his fellow rulers, was emphatic that he was not in treaty with the representatives of British India but with the Crown itself. This distinction was significant for the native rulers, who did not see themselves as under the jurisdiction of British Indian politicals or civil servants, but rather on par with their fellow monarch, the English sovereign.[87] As he elucidated: 'An autonomous Government of India controlled by the elected or nominated representatives of British India, is not the power with which His Highness' ancestors entered into treaty or political relation'. He did not believe himself under the authority of British India but rather the Crown. In his mind, British India was a 'sister state', like the leading 21 gun salute Indian kingdoms, and was to be treated in a similar fashion. 'With an autonomous Government presided over by a Governor General', he wrote, 'British India can but occupy with regard to Indore, the position of a sister state, like Gwalior or Hyderabad, each absolutely independent from each other and having His Majesty's Government as the connecting link between the two'.[88] Elucidating further the distinctions between British India and the Crown government, Holkar suggested that the Viceroy (while simultaneously Governor General) was only seen as the representative of His Majesty's government by indigenous princes. Since British India was only a 'sister and neighbouring state', Holkar underlined that he had a right to 'deal direct with His Majesty's Representatives in India or his Majesty's Government in London, rather than become a part of, or co-ordinate factor in the machine of any autonomous Government of British India'. His role towards British India was only as an 'independent ally of the British Government'.[89]

In a prescient moment, which he could not have fully foreseen in 1918, he argued against 'being drawn into the whirlpool of British Indian politics where their relations with the autonomous Government would be at the mercy of every political change'. It is this very argument, which he used to support his motivations for not taking the stand in the Malabar Hill Murder trial. Therefore, he concluded that the interests of Indore must remain with 'His Excellency the Viceroy' but not with the 'representatives of British India whose interests may be divergent'.[90]

Tukoji Rao was particularly concerned with how the 'divergent' interests of the British affected their intervention into the internal state affairs of the princely states. He noted that in intervening, the British Indian government broke with the validity of the states' original sanads and treaties. The letter went on to provide a long history for the precedent and legalities of these original treaties, which gave significant internal autonomy to the states, if not external authority. He argued that intervention not only breached the sanctity of the treaty laws but often had further negative results. As he wrote in 1918:

> one of the strongest arguments in my mind against interference is, that it is more apt to work evil than good. There is nothing in our political administration that requires so much circumspection, and caution, and discreet judgment, as interference in the affairs of other States. A single mistake on the part of an agent may cause irreparable mischief; and the power left to agents on such occasions is immense.[91]

He stressed that intervention did not necessarily prevent further calamities but often caused them. As it bears upon the 1925 crisis, Holkar princes were exempt from being tried according to the precepts of their original treaties. A ruler could on no account be put on trial, he wrote. Putting a ruler on trial affected his relationship with his subjects as Tukoji Rao explained:

> the idea of putting a Ruler on trial, though the proceeding of it may not be made public, seems to His Highness to be a of a startling nature. The position of the Rulers of Indian states is unique. Set in authority over millions of their subjects they exercise a power and influence which is a great asset to the Empire. The whole-hearted loyalty of the subjects to their Ruler is entirely a personal loyalty built up on ancient tradition and custom.[92]

Hence he suggested that indicting a prince would weaken his relationship to his *praja* and make it more difficult to govern his state legitimately. In addition, this would threaten the British project of indirect ruler through the legitimacy of traditional leadership. It not only affected just the person of the ruler but the lustre and reputation of his entire dynasty:

What can lower a Prince more than the spectacle of his being dragged like an ordinary criminal before a Court of Enquiry. Even if the verdict is in his favour, his glamour goes forever, thus weakening not only his hold but that of his successors too on the willing respect and obedience of the people that had been paid to the Ruler from generation to generation.[93]

In addition, a trial would render the prince vulnerable to the vices of 'mischief-mongers and busy-bodies' to stir up further 'discontent by exaggerations and inventions'.[94] This is exactly what did happen to Tukoji Rao himself when he became a target for blackmailers after the murder went public. Clearly, this earlier letter created the basis for Tukoji Rao's response to the outcomes of the murder trial and his decision that he would not be tried in a British Indian court.

Provisions for the Succession: A Matter of Allowances

By February 1926, the arrangements for the abdication were complete. As Glancy noted, all other matters would receive the Viceroy's 'sympathetic consideration'.[95] The abdication, itself, involved certain ceremonial, economic and political concerns, particularly regarding the succession and minority administration of the heir, Yeshwant Rao, the personal expenses of Tukoji and members of his royal household, and the celebration of the new ruler's investiture. The issue of family allowances would be a sore one, and arose again during Yeshwant Rao Holkar's own marital troubles several years later. In his official abdication, Tukoji Rao presented a set of terms, which listed the needs of his state, his family and his own personal finances.[96]

As it relates to the state, he proposed that at least one royal family member be in the Cabinet, that no radical changes be made during the minority administration, that the advice of the Agent to the Governor-General would be pursued and followed, and that personnel who were not loyal should be discharged. As to his son's needs, he advocated that Yeshwant Rao should study until 1928 but not longer, when he would have reached his twentieth birthday. In addition, the Maharanis and princesses would maintain their allowances, the marriage of his daughter would take place after he had selected an appropriate groom and his daughter-in-law would remain in his household until his heir reached twenty-one.[97]

In regards to his own affairs, Tukoji Rao favoured retaining his royal residences in Indore, requested no restrictions on his travels, desired sufficient military and police guards for his protection, requested retaining the title of 'His Highness', his gun salute, an allowance not less than Rs. 7 lakhs, customs facilities in and outside of India, and open consultation with the Assistant Governor-General of Central India.[98]

Allowances

As relates to the expenses of the ruler, the government appeared to concede to Tukoji Rao's suggestions. He was informed that he would have a 'liberal allowance'. His father was 'given an allowance of 4 1/2 lakhs when the state revenue was only 60 lakhs against 135 lakhs today and when prices were half what they are now'.[99] In addition they referred to the recent abdication of the Maharaja of Nabha, and noted that in that instance the former ruler received a higher percentage of the state's revenue than Indore would receive; hence there was reason to give Tukoji a liberal sum.

It is significant to note that in dealing with the allowance requirements of the ex-ruler's household, the paramount power was concerned particularly with the upkeep of the women, and did not want to appear miserly. 'I am therefore inclined to maintain the allowances at three lakhs – the figures originally proposed by me rather than give any ground for the suggestions that we are treating the ladies harshly', wrote the British political officer.[100] This literature on the economics of the zenana is important for two reasons. First, it reflects the colonial government's concern with the proper treatment of *pardah* women. Here, it is the Raj's policy that it appear generous and just in its relationship to indigenous females. Second, when originally petitioned by the Holkar Maharaja, these documents reveal the importance of royal women within traditional dynastic politics. Zenana women, married and unmarried, have rights upon the male ruler. Those women were often from other leading royal and aristocratic homes, which would expect their daughters to be maintained in style by the Holkar scion or would be married into neighbouring states. Part of the reason the unmarried Maharajkumari's allowance was projected to be so high was to cover her presumed trousseau and dowry needs. It is also possible that the women may have had strong personalities and bargained for certain financial entitlements, due to their status both within the Indore Zenana and in their father's homes outside, before allowing Tukoji Rao to sign the abdication papers. For a ruler who was often absent from this state, it was the women of the zenana who indirectly governed or had political relationships with his different ministers and their own factions within the kingdom. Having his wives in his good books was crucial just as it was for the British to maintain an image of protecting the women's interests.

The projected allowances for the Indore royal women tallied out to:

	Rs.
Senior Maharani	1,64,900
Junior	86,500
Child wife of present Mah.	17,000
Sister of present Maharaja	74,800
Total	3,43,200

In addition, the widows of the earlier Maharaja Shivaji Rao Holkar had their own allowances of the more modest sum of Rs. 20,000 each, for 'they live in the old fashioned manner and have not the extravagant tastes of the modern ladies'.[101] The Maharaja himself would have a substantial annual private income of Rs. 50,000 per year.[102] In addition, the junior maharani had acquired a great deal of jewellery, which was not on the state's list.

Ceremonial Functions

The Viceroy along with the Agent to the Governor-General Glancy did not believe it would be auspicious if Tukoji Rao was present during the investiture of the minor ruler. As the Political Office informed Glancy, 'it seems inappropriate that he should appear again in public some weeks after his abdication in the role of a Ruler making over the State to his son'. Instead, the Viceroy believed it 'would be much better if the ex-Maharaja did not appear at all at his son's accession Durbar, and in any case he thinks it would be impossible to allow him to make a speech'.[103] Nonetheless, on the actual day of investiture, the Maharaja was described in the programme for the Rajyabhishek as placing his son on the *gaddi*.[104]

The Problem of Another Woman: The American Wife, *c.* 1928

In part due to Tukoji Rao's desire for unlimited travel, and presumably also to get away from the mischief mongers at home as well as the Indian press, he was abroad much of the time after he abdicated. On one such foreign excursion, he met the American Nancy Miller and became embroiled in a further romantic crisis. Seemingly not heeding the consequences of the Mumtaz situation, Tukoji Rao fell in love and married Miss Miller. This would be the first of three generations of Holkar princes who would marry American women and produce mixed offspring who would be excluded from succeeding to the *gaddi*. In Yeshwant Rao's case, he would marry American girls not once but twice.

Several Indian princes were married to non-Indian women from Europe, America and Australia. The Maharaja of Pudukkottai's wedding to Molly Fink in 1916 would serve as the historical precedent in the Raj's handling of Tukoji Rao's impolitic match.[105] Certainly, his vulnerability towards women had become a significant trend in his political life and his private indiscretions had profound public ramifications. These cases highlight the development of a 'Brown Englishman' mentality among Indian princes. By marrying as a European would, Tukoji Rao became an Englishman in psychology and outlook, but his race would make this marital choice appear sexually debased and irregular. In practising polygamy and housing underage mistresses in his zenana, Tukoji Rao appeared a 'barbarous', 'degenerate' Oriental patriarch. In marrying a Caucasian woman, he was painted as touchy, inconstant and morally weak. The case of the American bride also reveals the various tensions among the factions of women within the Indore Zenana.

Nancy Miller was born on 9 September 1907 in Seattle Washington, the daughter of a concert pianist and a prosperous businessman who owned gold mines in Alaska. According to princely historian Coralie Younger, was the exception to the practice of lower class European women marrying Indian rulers, such as actresses and dancing girls. She was convent educated and had been a student at the University of Washington, where she concentrated on Oriental Studies. Her grandfather was French and her grandmother Swiss, and Nancy Miller grew up a frequent traveller: 'both [grandparents] considered it necessary for a girl of good breeding to become familiar with European culture'.[106]

Tukoji Rao met her at the Le Kursali Casino in Lausanne, Switzerland where the young American was staying with her grandparents. At first, he was concerned that the notoriety of the Bawla case would work against him, but in time he brought the family around in his favour. On 26 December 1927, Nancy Miller docked in Bombay on the *S.S. Genoa* accompanied by her grandparents presumably en route to Indore.[107] The American consul received them and tried assiduously to dissuade Nancy from marrying Tukoji Rao. Younger described this meeting:

> It was a delicate situation. Nancy was an American, and the US was a stern critic of Britain's imperial interests. The British were worried about the American press taking up the case. They were not concerned with reading out the riot act to Tukoji but they had to treat Nancy with kid gloves. She was described by the Resident as a woman 'of great charm and goodness amounting to piety. She was a good influence on him'.[108]

Being a foreign woman, Nancy Miller was barred official titles and attendance at ceremonial functions unlike royal consorts of the princely blood. In a 13 March 1928 letter, Glancy wrote to The Hon'ble Mr C. C. Watson, Political Secretary to the Government of India, and asked how she should be addressed: either as 'Her Highness' or as 'Lady Tukoji Rao Holkar'. He preferred to refuse her the title of 'Her Highness' but conceded the address of 'Lady Tukoji Rao Holkar'.[109]

The Tukoji Rao who appeared in the letters of 1928 seemed quite altered from the cool, gracious sovereign who wrote his abdication letter in 1926, with copious notes regarding sanad laws and treaty obligations. He was described as 'very nervous and easily excited'. Glancy, who interviewed him, had the impression of a 'dangerous lunatic keeping himself under control'.[110] In addition, at the time of the succession, his health had appeared on the decline. During the abdication he was 'discredited and subdued', and was believed to be 'tubercular' and not having much time to 'live'.[111] Two years later, he appeared highly excitable and crazed. In British accounts of their foreign marriages, both he and his son are described as distraught and uncontrollable. It is questionable whether this is a historically accurate description or an orientalized construction of princely masculinity. Certainly, colonial officials saw sexual aberrations, whether that of inter-racial marriage, homosexuality, onanism or excessive uxoriousness, as indicative of psychological malaise. They utilized such evidence in undermining the capacity of Indian princes to effectively self-govern. Such arguments further fueled the colonial 'civilizing mission' in its project to provide good laws, government and morality to its colonial subjects. British administrators saw Indian men as lacking sexual 'self-control', which was fueled by their perception of Indian marital practices as governed by 'intrigue'.[112] Nonetheless, it is important to notice Tukoji Rao's apparent transformation in appearance from an ill, sober man to one who seems frenzied and animated.

From the beginning, the British official highlighted the fact that the Maharaja should feel 'grateful' that the government had not interceded and was maintaining a 'neutral' front in light of the marriage. While the paramount power unofficially 'opposed the marriage', official 'opposition would have rendered it impossible'.[113] In addition, he recommended that the Maharaja not bring Miss Miller to Indore as it would give a false impression 'that the marriage had our blessing, whereas our attitude was one of neutrality'. Instead, it was agreed that Tukoji Rao would come alone during his stay in Indore and leave his American wife 'at home'.

In addition, during the course of their meeting, they returned to an earlier sore topic, which had originally been brought up during the writing of the royal household's expenses in the wake of his abdication. The absent jewels, supposedly in the keeping of the junior Maharani, were still missing. Tukoji Rao was asked to return the necklace 'valued at 1, 37,800' taken by the junior Maharani, but appeared loathe to do so.[114] It seems that he either felt high regard or fear towards the junior Maharani and was quite put out, according to Glancy, by her refusal to 'approve the Miller marriage' and did not want to further antagonize her. It seemed that such a stance had 'wounded his feelings beyond words'.[115] Obviously, he was influenced by the opinions of his Indian wives, even if he rarely lived with them. Earlier, he had told Nancy Miller that his Hindu brides would greet her as a sister and include her in all the doings of the zenana. This would have been his hope and wish, and indeed his other wives may have included Nancy in the larger dynastic family and day-to-day functions of the household. But it is also probable that they would have resented her presence as a foreigner, undermined her non-Hindu and non-aristocratic background, tried to prevent her from usurping their power within the Zenana hierarchy and seen her as a rival to their husband's affections. While they were probably well aware that her issue would never succeed to the *gaddi*, they would certainly be anxious that she might oust them from their privileged places within the court and zenana.

This new marriage had further ramifications from the perspective of the British observers. Two years previously, Tukoji Rao had 'shown no tendency to engage in politics and it was considered improbable that he would give serious trouble in the future'. However, as the Resident wrote this no longer appeared to be the case with his 1928 nuptials: 'But this American marriage has quite turned his head and I now have information which shows that he is intriguing in Indore and some check must be placed on his activities'.[116] Similar language had been used for an earlier Maharaja of Indore, who had been declared insane and was stripped of his rights to rule during the turn of the century.[117]

When the Maharaja returned to Indore, he became a magnet for disaffected groups who saw themselves as part of the 'ex-Maharaja's party' in opposition to his son. If he were to move closer to the heart of the capital, 'to either Bijaseni or Sukh Niwas the villas in which he is permitted to reside on the outskirts of the city, he will be come a focus of intrigue'. For this reason the British saw problems for the minority administration of his son, as it would be 'difficult for a young and inexperienced ruler to control his people'.[118]

To counteract this potentially tumultuous situation, the ex-Maharaja was not permitted to visit the environs of Indore during his son's minority administration. If he did not choose to remain in the 'background', his allowances would be cut and 'unpleasant circumstances could follow'.[119] If Tukoji Rao did not respond to these suggestions an official letter would be written, alerting the ex-ruler to the political outcomes of his injudicious alliance:

> to write him a formal letter stating that his recent marriage, which constitutes a departure from all the traditions of his house, renders it necessary for the Government of India to revise the conditions attached to his abdication and to limit his place of residence in Indore state to Barwaha during the period of the minority.[120]

Tukoji Rao appeared to heed this advice and there were no more difficulties. In the end, his marriage to Nancy Miller turned out to be a success and the only Holkar marriage with an American woman which did not end in divorce. A week before her marriage, Nancy Miller converted to Hinduism and took on the name Sharmista Devi. They were married on 17 March 1928, and maintained a lively, social life between India, the United States and Europe. Miller travelled in *pardah* while in Indore and married her daughters to Maratha noblemen. The couple remained together until Tukoji Rao died in 1978 and Nancy stayed in Indore until her death in the 1990s. After her passing, her daughters became involved in a legal feud over her estate.[121]

Yeshwant Rao Holkar, the Sad Unfortunate Prince

In 1926, at the age of eighteen, Yeshwant Rao Holkar succeeded prematurely to the Indore *gaddi*, after his father's abdication. His father's part in the ceremony had been brief. As the Maharawal of Dungarpur noted, Tukoji Rao: 'walked up to the son and put the *Raj Tilak* mark on his forehead, took five steps back, and then turned about and walked out'.[122]

The speech given by the Assistant Governor-General to Central India, R. I. R. Glancy on the 12 March 1926 provides stern, if touching, instructions for a young ruler. These lofty ideals may have been too intimidating for Yeshwant Rao's frail and often sickly temperament. Far from a light-hearted sense of kingship or an exhortation on the glamour of royalty, the AGG portrayed a solemn and ponderous definition of rulership, heavy with gravitas: 'At the same time to succeed to a princely heritage at an early age is not in every respect the height of good fortune. The life of a Ruler is often a lonely life and a life beset with difficulties and disillusion. He has to walk with such circumspection that in some respects he enjoys less personal freedom and liberty than many of his subjects'.[123]

Glancy further advised the young prince to put his heart towards service for his state and its people: 'Your Highness will find by experience that nothing affords such satisfaction as the promotion of the happiness and well being of others and especially of those whom Providence has entrusted to your keeping'.[124] In the midst of all this serious talk Glancy conceded that his words might appear 'discouraging or inappropriate'. In becoming a ruler when in his majority, Glancy gently recommended to Yeshwant Rao: 'I trust without neglecting your more serious studies you may have your full share of the varied interests and enjoyments which are the right and proper perquisites of youth'.[125]

It would be in the area of his private life where these sagacious warnings would seem most prophetic. At the time of his *abhishek,* the minor ruler was already married. As has been noted, the allowance of his child bride had been taken into account in Tukoji Rao's abdication expenses and those of the Zenana ladies. Maharani Sanyogita Bai (b. 1914, d. 1937 in Tarasp, Switzerland) was the daughter of Rajashri Dattajirao, the chief of Kagal (Junior). Yeshwant Rao had been sixteen years old and she was ten when they married. She had been known for her legendary looks, particularly 'the beauty' of her complexion'.[126] According to Rajkumar Martand Singh of Kapurthala, their marriage was happy and her death had a devastating effect on her young husband.[127] After ruling under a Regency Council for four years after his investiture, Yeshwant Rao was given full ruling powers on 9 May 1930. It would be his subsequent marriages to American women in the pattern now established by his father, which would cause the most anxiety.

Yeshwant Rao was a shy youth. In 1923, at fourteen, he was sent to the public school, Charterhouse. His boarding school experience was unhappy and he was not popular with his classmates. The schoolboys described him as the 'black devil' and he did not appreciate the school tradition of fagging. As one contemporary of his remembered, 'I don't think he ever understood fagging ... and understandably he was not very efficient'.[128] Holkar, who was not an athlete, did not shine in an environment which celebrated physical prowess, although he had a fine eye for art, architecture and jewellery. Later, he became well known for his patronage of the Bauhaus architects. As Coralie Younger described him: 'An intelligent but highly strung young man, Yeshwant loved music and the arts'. Being of a 'solitary, inarticulate character', he found 'personal relationships difficult', alternating between 'warm and prickly'.[129] Indeed, English public schools were seen as 'nurseries' in the 'cultivation and pursuit of Victorian ideals – the key ideal being that of manliness, governed as much by the physical vitality of sport as it was the by the moral fibre of personal conduct'.[130] Yeshwant Rao's failure to take to sport appeared to colonial observers to be a premonition for his later character flaws, particularly his sexual aberrations and tendencies towards illness and psychotic behaviour. His un-princely introversion and sensitivity simultaneously conflicted with imperial models for a restrained body and robust mind as integral requirements for sound leadership.

After Charterhouse, he came up to Christ Church, Oxford, where he continued to maintain his solitary lifestyle, encouraged in this behaviour by his English guardians, the Hardys, who were jealous of potential friends. Having succeeded to the *gaddi*, he had an extravagant annual income of 70,000 rupees and tried to buy friendship through lavish parties, but failed. According to Younger, this would fuel his lifelong 'antipathy for the British'.[131] Ian Copland emphasizes Yeshwant Rao's frail health and reclusive nature as being: 'indifferent health and a shyness born of a weedy, unprepossessing physique kept him out of the limelight'.[132] It would be his marriages to American women after his first wife's death, which would change all of that, and bring Glancy's warnings into brilliant relief.

The Question of Succession: A Female Heir

Just as Tukoji Rao had been described when he returned to Indore with Miss Miller on his arm, Yeshwant Rao was similarly portrayed as psychologically vulnerable and in poor health after his hasty wedding to an American nurse. Kenneth Fitze who was then the Resident in Indore sketched him in 1939:

> H.H. was looking extremely emaciated, clad in dressing gown and pyjamas. (He told me that his weight is only 6 st. 11 lbs. and I can well believe it). He was also evidently in a state of extreme nervous tension. I received the impression that in order to fortify himself at the interview, he had been drinking. At any rate his speech was by no means normal and his gestures more profuse than ever.[133]

When Fitze asked him about his health, Yeshwant Rao attributed his 'illness and nervous condition to worry over this marriage and prolonged hesitation as to how and when he should announce it'. In this first meeting, Yeshwant Rao informed his Resident that he had wed a Miss Branyon, an American nurse who had been with him since a debilitating illness in 1936. They had been married earlier that year in Mexico. According to Fitze, the Maharaja was very upset as the marriage had not been recognized in either America or France. Yeshwant Rao stated that he would subsequently inform his Cabinet on the following day and announce the event publicly in a Gazette Extraordinary. He was also aware of the limitations this action would place upon him. Yeshwant Rao agreed to have his daughter from Sanyogita Bai, Usha, succeed to the *gaddi*. Here is an intriguing case of succession breaking from earlier patterns of primogeniture where the ruling prince nominated his female progeny to succeed him.

Yeshwant Rao believed that by nominating his daughter, he would 'revive the traditions of Ahilyabai', a famous and revered earlier regent Maharani of the Indore state. Nonetheless, this case was radically different from the earlier one, as Ahilyabai had been a regent who governed the kingdom during the male prince's minority. She had not been the blood descendent of the regal dynasty, who was subsequently made the royal heir. In effect, Yeshwant Rao was rewriting succession practice and inaugurating a hitherto unobserved tradition in Indore. Should his daughter not be allowed to succeed him, Yeshwant Rao was prepared also to adopt a collateral male heir.

Changing the line of succession in preference for a woman was a highly radical act. While certain dynasties were matrilineal such as the South Indian kingdoms of Travancore and Cochin, most Hindu royal families were patrilineal and practised primogeniture. Even the famous Begums of Bhopal ruled not in preference to male heirs but because there were none for four successive generations. Indeed, when the unbroken chain of four queens was followed by several potential male successors, who were the sons or grandsons of the last Begum, they were immediate players for the succession.[134] Choosing a female heir over a collateral male descendent was a very unusual practice at this time and Yeshwant Rao was going against both historical precedent and customary practice in doing so.

Kenneth Fitze, noting possible problems in the announcement of his marriage, counselled Yeshwant Rao to inform his ministers of his wedding only while simultaneously making a definite pronouncement on the succession. In particular, he argued that his daughter, who was then being schooled in California, return to 'Indore and live more or less permanently here in the future'. Holkar responded that he believed the people would prefer his daughter to a male adoption; the consent of the subjects of Indore being a concern for both men. 'I was fairly certain', Kenneth Fitze recalled, 'that the daughter's position as Heir-Apparent would be recognized unless there were clear indications that such an arrangement would [not] be in accordance with the wishes of H.H.'s subjects. H.H. said that such indications would certainly be forthcoming; but it was not clear how public opinion could be sounded'.[135]

Fitze agreed that the Maharaja's daughter should succeed rather than a collateral male. 'His Highness has already expressed the view that his daughter's claim to succeed him should receive serious consideration'. He wrote, 'I therefore feel that unless and until that alternative has been fully examined and discarded it would be unreasonable to expect him to make an adoption'.[136] In addition, Fitze suggested that the Maharaja might marry again in a more traditional manner, and he did not want to omit the possibility of additional issue. 'In view of the notoriously volatile nature of the Holkars in such matters, it would be rash to assume with confidence that His Highness will never make another orthodox marriage. In that event a premature adoption would be an embarrassment as well as involving unnecessary expense'.[137]

Due to his middling health, Yeshwant Rao intended to return to California, where he had built a new mansion for himself, to recover his strength before returning to Indore. Only with his health strengthened could he carry out his duties towards his State, he argued. In the meantime, he would make over 'all necessary powers' to his Cabinet with the consultation of the Resident. Fitze reproached him for such intentions as his marriage would already have engendered enough worries, which combined with his absence so soon again would 'cause serious indignation'.

A few days later, Yeshwant Rao again stated a desire to leave Indore on the grounds of his health. Fitze further underlined the lack of wisdom in announcing the wedding to the Indore court.[138] 'I think [announcing the wedding] would only introduce an unnecessary complication by further disturbing the Maharaja's officers and subjects, whose patience he has already sufficiently taxed'.[139] In addition, speaking of the marriage would only create animosity directed against the Maharaja's American wife, especially during his periods away from the state.

By the end of March, Yeshwant Rao appeared to be in a calmer state, in Fitze's report.[140] In part, Yeshwant Rao's willingness to accept the advice of his British advisors correlated with his description as less erratic and more reasonable, and thus plays into larger discussions on the linkage between sexuality, madness and politics. The Maharaja was markedly different from the 'hysterical invalid' of 11 March, and was 'quite his old self, clothed and in his right mind, though shockingly emaciated'.[141] Fitze reiterated his earlier comments regarding the princess-heir's return to Indore from California with her French governess. Fitze in consultation with the Indore ministers believed that she should return to the kingdom. In the end, Yeshwant Rao conceded that he would not recognize any potential child of his American bride.[142] But, he simultaneously expressed that he would not mention the succession in his marriage announcements.[143]

In the transcript of his public statement, Yeshwant Rao specified the nature of his marriage and his continued interest in public affairs. Service to the state, he pronounced, was not at odds with happiness in his personal life:

> I know that my first and foremost duty is to serve my people and to take an active interest in the administration. This I can do only if I enjoy sound health and domestic happiness. Therefore I have married Miss Marguerite Lawler, the lady I truly love, so that we both may serve our people whole-heartedly and contribute towards the progress of our State. I am convinced that my marriage will be conducive to our mutual happiness and I know the Maharani Holkar and I shall work for the betterment and well-being of our beloved subjects. I may here tell you that the marriage will not affect the question of succession.[144]

In addition, he promised to work towards rural uplift even if spending from his own pocket: 'For the cultivators we have decided to contribute Rupees one lakh every year from the Privy Purse towards Rural Uplift'.[145] They also planned to create a city park for workers, develop the departments of rural uplift, education and medical relief and enhance inter caste harmony, by protecting and advocating the rights of Harijans.[146] He ended on the note that the 'Maharani Holkar has the true welfare of her people at heart and that we shall together do all that we can for you'.[147]

In light of his new marriage, Yeshwant Rao referred back to the earlier expenses meted out during his father's abdication. As Fitze noted, Yeshwant Rao was keen to cut down the allowances of his father and the two Ma Sahebas. His mother had already agreed to take one lakh rather than 1, 60,000 for her own expenses. Fitze responded somewhat warily: 'I believe that these allowances are guaranteed by the terms of the ex-Maharaja's abdication, but I have promised His Highness to look into the matter and discuss it with him again'.[148]

With the marriage issues out of the way, Fitze believed that the Maharaja would again be interested in state affairs as he had expressed during his marriage announcement. Fitze wrote: 'he has excellent qualities which are again asserting themselves and I do believe his interest in his responsibilities and his enthusiasm for reform and progress to be genuine ... if and when the crisis over the marriage announcement is safely over, I believe that he will begin to make real progress in that direction'.[149]

What to do with Miss Lawler (or was it Mrs Branyon)? Yeshwant Rao's First American Bride

Although the marriage boded well, from the start there were problems and it did not last long. There was a good deal of confusion over the identity of Yeshwant Rao's bride. Was she a Miss Lawler or a Mrs Branyon? This topic of marital status was a discreet reference to the British discomfort with American divorcees.[150]

Perhaps to clarify or legalize issues, she was given an Indian name. In addition, there was confusion as to how the Maharani would be addressed and received by British political servants or the British royalty when they visited Indore. Fitze, himself, asked that no restrictions be placed upon him to visit with the Maharaja in the company of his new bride. He wrote: 'As you are aware, His Highness when in good health, is apt to be very hospitable and to mix freely with local society. Those members of our European community who are in State service will of course have no choice in the matter and I think that it is from all points of view most desirable that no restrictions should be imposed on me or other Government servants in respect of such functions'.[151]

Yeshwant Rao had met Marguerite Branyon née Lawler in Los Angelos in 1937. Weakened by chronic insomnia, alcoholism and drug addiction, he was in an unfortunate physical state when he checked into a local hospital. The *Evening Standard* described Marguerite as a 33-year-old nurse who had once worked as a stewardess for the Pacific Union railroad.[152] She had been married earlier to a Mr Branyon, but had divorced him in April 1938, five months before she married Yeshwant Rao, due to his 'association with another woman'.[153]

According to Coralie Younger, Marguerite nursed Yeshwant Rao back to health, but not away from drug addiction.[154] Kenneth Fitze liked her and gave her a favourable report: 'Information regarding the Maharani's personality is that, far from being a glamorous gold-digger, she is a thoroughly sensible and serious lady, over thirty years of age, with a genuine desire to use her new position for the benefit of the State and people'.[155] One American newspaper of the time similarly emphasized her virtues, and described how Marguerite had aided Yeshwant Rao in his state duties, by helping him to curb his spending: 'known for his lavish tastes, he cut $32,000 from his annual household expenses and declared there "is little justice in maintaining antiquated customs of pomp and pageantry when the pressing needs of poor people are not provided for"'.[156]

Marguerite's true surname and her divorcée status proved to be prickly issues. In the beginning, Yeshwant Rao tried to keep the information quiet from the British authorities. He suggested that American women took up aliases as nurses just as English actresses did when they took to the stage.[157] When Fitze realized that Lawler was a divorced woman, his letters expressed astonishment, displeasure and discomfort. It was nearly a month after Yeshwant Rao's return that he discovered her marital status. Fitze was particularly upset that the Maharaja had hid the information from him:

> I expressed some surprise that he had not told me this during our previous conversations, which would have been preferable to my having to depend upon press information, but he did not seem prepared to vouchsafe any further information except that she had always been known as <u>Miss</u> Branyan since entering the nursing profession.[158]

Yeshwant Rao assured him that the divorce had been completed and was valid, and that the law in the state of Minnesota where it was conducted was amongst the best in America. There was no question of a 'Reno divorce'. Still nonplussed, Fitze asked him why he had denied that the marriage was recognized at their earlier meeting. 'When I asked him why he had previously told me that the marriage was not recognized in the U.S.A. or France', he wrote, '[Yeshwant Rao] said that I must have misunderstood him, as what he had said was that it <u>was</u> so recognized. I find it difficult to accept this, as my recollection is clear and was committed to writing soon after the interview, whereas His Highness was in a very excitable condition.[159] Fitze further expressed urgency that the princess Usha return to Indore 'that at least anxiety about her health may not again become a reason for him to absent himself from his State'.[160]

Marguerite would not be addressed as 'Her Highness' nor appear at formal functions, such as viceregal banquets in Indore, but Yeshwant Rao resisted such enforced restrictions. Clearly disconcerted, Fitze consulted Glancy on the issue. He argued that it would be impossible to limit meetings with the Maharani Holkar only to informal occasions, giving the example of the event of the King's birthday. Fitze's arguments are laced with a peculiarly English sense of civility:

> On the King's birthday a large garden party is invariably given by the Prime Minister on behalf of His Highness's Government. On the forthcoming occasion next month His Highness is likely to be in Indore and may decide to give the party himself. Anyhow he ought to be present and would presumably bring the Maharani with him. Surely on such an occasion I could not refuse to attend unless he leaves her at home? And if I meet her at a garden party given by the State, how could I decently omit to invite her to my own annual garden party which usually takes place in February?[161]

He further queried if the protocol required him to refuse an invitation by the Maharaja. 'Are we to refuse such an invitation, or to stipulate that the Maharani shall not be present? I sincerely hope not'.[162] Fitze argued in favour of the Maharani being given recognition and respect in local venues:

> In all the circumstances I feel strongly that, so far as purely local functions are concerned, there ought to be no invidious treatment of the lady, except to the extent that she should be accorded courtesies which clearly belong only to a fully recognised consort of the Ruler, e.g. the title of Highness, the playing of the State anthem for her at Residency functions, or an invitation to bring a 'lady-in-waiting' with her on such occasions.[163]

Fitze feared the possibility of alienating Yeshwant Rao over the treatment of his wife. As he warned Glancy, they should not 'poison the well of social good will' over protocol.[164] Nonetheless, the Political Office in Delhi remained firm in upholding the precedent. Marguerite should be treated and addressed exactly as Molly Fink, the Maharani of Pudukkottai had earlier been described, with the simple address of 'Maharani Holkar' and not with the title of 'Her Highness'.[165] In addition, Marguerite Lawler could not be treated in any preferable manner to Molly Fink, previously. Hamington-Hawes in the Political office wrote:

> I am to say that it has not been possible to agree that she can appropriately be accorded superior treatment on the ground that the Indore marriage is definitely morganatic, whereas in the Pudukkottai case the position in this respect was not clearly expressed. On the contrary there is one aspect of the Indore case which might merit even stricter limitations on the lady's status, namely the possibility that her position is even more anomalous than it appears to be, since information from America throws some doubts on the legality of her divorce from Mr. Branyon, while details of the precise form of marriage which His Highness went through with her in Mexico are also very incomplete.[166]

Fitze received a similarly inflexible response to his request for a relaxation of the strict policy of when and where the Maharani could be present:

> ... in particular the lady should not be present at any formal or public entertainment which the Resident attends. Any departure from this procedure is likely to compromise the Viceroy's position on occasions when he might be expected to meet the lady in future, while any failure to show clearly that the lady is not a 'fully recognized' Maharani may give rise to rumours that the marriage is not really morganatic, with resultant intrigues against the Maharaja himself.[167]

This correspondence going back and forth between the local representatives of the Raj and the government in Delhi would repeat itself during Yeshwant Rao's third marriage to Euphemia Crane. From the start, Marguerite Lawler was not a strong presence in Indore and their marriage was short lived. By 12 June 1939, the Maharaja was seriously opting to leave Indore again, and Marguerite was feeling unwell.[168] The princess Usha, too, was suffering from a 'serious loss of weight and recurring fever'. Yeshwant Rao himself had lost even more weight, and was 'seriously troubled by insomnia and feels it is essential to take a holiday to recover his health'.[169] In some quarters, there was speculation that Marguerite had miscarried or given birth to a daughter.[170] The Maharani soon lost confidence in local doctors and became determined to return to the U.S. and Yeshwant Rao planned to follow her back to California.[171]

In Santa Ana, he built a monstrous citadel for her and his daughter, Princess Usha. It was celebrated in the American press. An American newspaper ran the headline 'Rifle slots, bullet-proof Glass to Guard Potentate's Daughter' in describing their California residence.[172] As the paper announced, 'the fortress was designed to the be the 'safest place in the world' for the Indian potentate and former Miss Marguerite Lawler to rear the Maharajah's 5 year old daughter'.[173]

It was not just physical ill health which resulted in Marguerite's departure after only five months in Indore, but 'a combination of Yeshwant's erratic behaviour and the machinations of the court had worn her down'.[174] As Younger hypothesized, Marguerite had married a man who turned out to be quite different from the one she had expected:

> When the couple met, it had been Marguerite's robust constitution and no-nonsense attitude that had attracted Yeshwant. In Marguerite, he found the mother he had never had. At first the 'mothering' appealed, but the naughty child behaviour it evoked from him did not appeal to Marguerite. She had thought Yeshwant would meet her half way and that she would be the strong arm that would help him regain an even keel.[175]

After her first visit to Indore, Marguerite rarely returned, while princess Usha remained under her care. Yeshwant Rao would visit them in California, but these visits became less and less frequent when he met Euphemia Crane, who became his third wife.

Maharani 'Fay': A Marriage not only of Class and Race Incompatibility, but Immorality!

In 1942 after being absent for seven years, which led Fitze to describe him in the words of a popular song, 'Some Day My Prince Will Come', Yeshwant Rao returned with Fay Crane by his side and threw himself into the work of the Chamber of Princes as a controversial member of the standing committee. However, Ian Copland notes, 'Yet for all his keenness, idealism and firm political grasp, Yeshwant Rao never lived up to his promise. He remained an impulsive, erratic performer, sometimes working until three in the morning and other days not at all; and the refusal of the government of recognize his new American wife [Fay] gradually took its toll of his highly strung temperament'.[176]

When they met, Euphemia, 'Fay', Crane was married to fellow American, Frank Crane, a senior executive at the Hindustan Aircraft Factory in Bangalore. She was twenty-nine and had been married for seven years. The couple lived in Bangalore, where Frank worked.[177] How she met the Indore ruler was not clear, but, by 1942, Yeshwant Rao and Fay were travelling together to Kashmir, with a Mrs McCarthy as escort. In September that year, they sailed to America, with Fay posing as Yeshwant's secretary while he obtained a divorce from Marguerite.[178] Kenneth Fitze warned that this was not going to be easy: he predicted that Marguerite would be a 'force with which they will have to reckon' with. Yeshwant Rao promised that after the divorce he would give her custody of Usha (of whom she was very fond) and a handsome financial settlement. The Maharaja then charged Marguerite with 'extreme cruelty' and 'making his life a burden' in the divorce proceedings.[179]

In May 1943, Yeshwant Rao married Fay near Reno, Nevada. Fay obtained her divorce from Frank Crane on the basis of 'gross cruelty' in a similar manner to Yeshwant Rao's hasty split with Marguerite Lawler. Fitze observed that this was all 'a monstrous lie' and believed that 'Hollywood standards had governed recent events' in their marital engagements.[180] Despite his earlier promise to Marguerite, Yeshwant did take Usha back to Indore with him.

The British officials did not like any of this and their opinions of Yeshwant Rao, already troubled by his earlier marriage and that of his father, only worsened. They described him a 'lounge lizard' with bad habits and irresolute temperament. In October 1943, it was recorded that

> Nor should it be forgotten that this Prince, behind a smokescreen of lies; neurasthenia; precarious health and all the rest of it, has seduced another man's wife in circumstances which would preclude for life any Englishman who had so behaved from the presence of the Sovereign![181]

In October 1946, F. Wylie, Secretary to the Political Department, further elucidated the British attitude to the marriage in a conversation with the Maharaja of Dewas Senior:

> I was more than sorry that this incident had arisen but after all it was not me but His Highness Holkar who had run away with another man's wife and had married her incontinently in Hollywood or some such exotic place. The man was a Prince whether he liked it or not and noblesse oblige. The English people had thrown out a King Emperor for conduct of that sort. Was it surprising that this lady, after all her adventurous experiences in the matrimonial field, was not allowed straightaway to occupy one of the seniormost places among the matrons of India, viz., as the consort of the Maharaja Holkar?[182]

The trouble with this second American marriage was that it not only broke unspoken taboos regarding race and class but also conjugal morality. While Fay was described by British observers as 'socially better than Marguerite' and was considered 'quiet, charming, an attentive hostess, domestically minded and devoted to her husband, the couple had not only transgressed socially and racially but also morally'.[183] Yeshwant Rao's Indian counsellors also were troubled by his marriage. The Indore diwan, Dinanath, blamed Fay for trying to steal Holkar jewels and making Yeshwant Rao more addicted to morphine. Ultimately, Yeshwant sacked him.[184]

The faults were not all of Fay's doing. As Younger suggests, Yeshwant was difficult: 'he slept all day, not bothering to change out of his night clothes. Always thin, he became positively emaciated and was a bundle of nerves'. In one particularly embarrassing moment, he outraged British women guests at his own New Year's Eve party when he presided over the evening entertainment dressed only in his pyjamas. His ADC excused the prince's eccentricities by noting that addiction to narcotics was the problem.[185]

In 1944, Fay gave birth to a son, Richard. Although he was Yeshwant Rao's only male progeny, he was barred the succession both under the original agreements between the British and Indore, and also later by republican India. At the time of her son's birth, Fay complained to her mother-in-law, Nancy Miller, that she 'was fed up with [her husband] and did not want her baby son to be brought up in this environment'.[186] Fay was never fully accepted by British society in India. 'Disillusioned by life in India', she returned to California in 1947, taking her son Richard with her. Yeshwant travelled back and forth between India and America, rarely staying in his state. They divorced in 1960, one year before Yeshwant Rao's death in 1961.[187] After attending boarding school in America and Stanford University, Richard Holkar returned to India, where he runs a tourist establishment and handicrafts industry in Maheshwar, one of the Indore family's properties. While his sister Usha was crowned Maharani of Indore, Richard remains active in local and Indian public life. He, too, married an American woman, Sally Budd, in 1977 and their marriage also recently ended in divorce.

The Implications of Loving Dangerously: Sexuality, Marriage and Sovereignty

Being 'natural leaders' of the indigenous polity, Indian rulers were promoted as ideal models upon which to graft Anglo-European values. Princes, like Yeshwant Rao Holkar, were sent to Charterhouse and then Christ Church, Oxford to become more 'English' in mentality, which would enable them to be affective Indian sovereigns in the paramount power's larger project of indirect rule. It was in such institutions that they cultivated the attributes of sportsmanship, fairness, anglicized manners and civility, fluency in the English language, the art of diplomacy and, most fundamentally, loyalty to the ambitions and principles of Empire. The ideal Raja was one who was progressive and modern by virtue of his western education, yet at the same time remained committed to his role at home as a living manifestation of tradition and ancestral allegiance to a region and people. From the time of Queen Victoria's inauguration as Empress in 1877, the British hoped the princes would serve as intermediaries between themselves and the Indian masses, taking on the best attributes of East and West, the modern and the traditional.

Nonetheless, by becoming western in education and mannerisms, the princes acquired English mores and attitudes, which alienated them from the very roles that the British had envisioned. In the case of Yeshwant Rao, his British tutors educated the boy-king to psychologically perceive himself as a European in all but race and ancestral history. Looking at the world as an Englishman, he acted like one, courting and wedding Caucasian women, marrying for love rather than political prudence perhaps in emulation of the British monarch Edward VIII, placing marriage above his public duties as a ruler, living for long spells in America or Europe and thus neglecting the needs of his state and cultivating habits, such as alcohol and drug consumption, which he had discovered in his travels abroad.

The 'playboy' attitudes of Tukoji Rao and Yeshwant Rao in maintaining Indian mistresses and courting American women as lovers and brides, with Reno divorces and lavish romances conducted on a global stage, was in marked contrast to Victorian expectations of a robust, but restrained masculinity. The British associated the sentimentality and passion of Indian men, like the Holkars, with degenerate and devious character; one poisoned by the covert intrigues of the palace zenana.[188] Glancy's speech at Yeshwant Rao's *abhishek* in 1926 reflected imperial prerogatives for an ideal, modern, progressive, Indian ruler, who sacrificed his personal desires as a private citizen for service to his state. Yet this very training, which the British had lauded in the Holkars, enabled these princes to challenge the prevailing order by acquiring the agency and entitlements of an Englishman himself. By becoming 'brown Englishmen', through education, marriage and taste, they simultaneously acquired the rights and mien of the colonial subject himself, in being European in all but race. At the same time, they maintained a position as independent sovereigns who were outside and above the jurisdiction of the laws and legalities of British India by virtue of being indigenous, semi-autonomous Indian monarchs.

In choosing women of their own desire, they flaunted their individual agency and resisted colonial regulation of Indian male sexuality. They opposed British prohibitions regarding miscegenation, inter-caste union, class mobility and conjugal morality. Thus the women of the Indore family figure large in the tale of this princely state at the end of empire. The rulers' rejection of British meddling in their choice of sexual partners hints at the development of a social confidence which is at the same time manifesting itself in the nationalist cause for 'self rule' and foreshadows the future Independence of the nation from the colonial yoke.

At the same time, the personal pleasures of these two men had grave results on their capacities to remain sovereign rulers. The women of the zenana, both the courtesan and the wife, were influential in the high stakes game of political manoeuvring between the indigenous prince and the paramount power, both in their corporal, sexualized selves and through their metaphorical, symbolic power. In addition, women such as Mumtaz Begum, used colonial law courts to impugn the practices of abuse within the Indore Zenana at a time when indigenous and colonial reformers were using the courts to critique religiously based practices, both Hindu and Muslim, such as *pardah*, divorce and property rights, while advocating female suffrage. In many ways, this chapter reveals the overlaps in Hindu and Muslim courtly female cultures as well as the similarities over reform issues for both Hindu and Muslim women during the late colonial period. It simultaneously exposes how colonial reform measures introduced female successors into princely states which historically practised primogeniture.

In conclusion, this chapter reveals that the Hindu Maharaja who affiliated with the 'wrong type' of women, either as mistress or foreign bride, compromised and redefined the ambit of his traditional influence. Women like the courtesan Mumtaz or the princess Usha become agents of change; the one forcing the abdication of the princely scion and the other forever shifting the pattern of male succession in the state. In part, these women attained power both because of the weaknesses of male rulers who pursued impolitic sexual or romantic relationships, and by the introduction of colonial legislation, which enabled women to challenge prevailing customary practices.

6 FROM 'PARDAH TO PARLIAMENT':[1] DYNASTIC POLITICS AND THE ROLE OF ROYAL WOMEN IN POSTCOLONIAL INDIA

Democratic South Asian politics has from the first shown a trend towards dynastic rule – whether the Nehru-Gandhi legacy in India, the Bhutto family in Pakistan, the Zia regime in Bangladesh or the Bandranaike government in Sri Lanka. Zenana women, as representatives of traditional leadership, have similarly impacted upon democratic politics in post-Independence India. The postcolonial period witnessed the rise of the princely politician, the 'Rajvanshi', and former Zenana women have emerged as prominent political personalities, such as Rajmata Gayatri Devi of Jaipur and Rajmata Vijaya Raje Scindia of Gwalior. Relying principally on their memoirs as sources, this chapter demonstrates the influence of Zenana women in nationalist India.

From 1947 to 1949, India witnessed the most rapid and peaceful 'republican' revolution of modern history.[2] Within a two-year span, the nearly six hundred semi-autonomous princely states were merged with the new republic.[3] It was a virtually bloodless transition from monarchies to a united democratic nation state.[4] Through the mid-twentieth century, the princes had been far from impotent rulers. Under British paramountcy, they held internal sovereignty, and were denied only control over foreign policy, defence and communications.[5] In 1921, the British inaugurated an entity specifically for the native rulers, The Chamber of Princes. Under the 1935 Government of India Act, which projected a 'future federation', representatives of the Indian princely states would counterpoise elected officials of the British Indian provinces.[6] As David Cannadine notes, their wealth and power was of real significance: they had never been so rich, they spent fortunes on palaces and jewellery, and (in more enlightened cases) on their subjects' welfare: pearls and rubies from Cartier in Paris and London, and hospitals and universities in Hyderabad. Far from being the bearers and wearers of hollow crowns, they were still considered by the British as the 'natural leaders of Indian society'.[7] The period of integration thus was a critical historical moment for princely rule and legitimacy, based on birth, was abruptly replaced by parliamentary government and the authority of democracy.[8]

Most histories of modern India give cursory citations of the princes as mere puppet figures of the British Raj without place in a democratic nation. The nationalist elite warned the former princes that they had no divine right to rule any longer and that power in India now came from the people and its representatives in the Constituent Assembly of the country.[9] Romanticized in the press as hard drinking polo players, hotel entrepreneurs and high society icons, the maharajahs and nobility of yore appear the mere antiquated relics of a bygone era.[10] Although stripped of their privileges and the privy purse since 1971, they are not entirely these crudely drawn caricatures, living in a so-called make believe world of hunting and other pursuits.[11] Former rulers have remained active in the nation's public life, serving as diplomats, governors, patrons of educational and charitable institutions, local magnates, company directors, cabinet ministers and, particularly, as elected politicians.[12] Thirty per cent of former princely families have entered electoral politics since the first general elections in 1952. Of the 284 families, which were granted the Privy Purse and privileges at the merger of the states, more than one third have been candidates for state legislative assemblies or Lok Sabha (the lower house) seats. More than two thirds of these Hindu royal families came from Rajput dynasties.[13]

Region plays a significant role in determining princely involvement in democratic politics. In Rajasthan alone, a state which today is composed of nineteen former Rajput kingdoms and three chiefdoms, several former princely families have entered electoral politics, at the local, state or national level. Since the first general election, seventeen members of royal dynasties have won parliamentary seats in the Lok Sabha (Lower House), six of whom were women.[14] In the Chattisgarh region of Madhya Pradesh and Orissa, nearly fifty per cent of princely families have taken state or national office. In Orissa, the Congress Party exploitation of 'princely political appeal' galvanized former rulers and their families into politics.[15] The former Prime Minister of India, V. P. Singh, was the Rajput Raja of Manda, the present Chief Minister of the Punjab is the son of the Sikh Maharaja of Patiala, the former External Affairs Minister, Jaswant Singh, is a Rajput nobleman from Jodhpur and the current Chief Minister of Rajasthan, Vasundara Raje, is the Maharani of Dholpur and a princess of Gwalior. There are many more such examples.[16] Until his untimely death in 2001, Madhavrao Scindia, erstwhile Maharaja of Gwalior, was seen as a rising star in the Congress party, and a possible future Prime Minster.[17] As political scientist William Richter argues the political vestiges of India's princely state heritage are numerous and generally given short shrift by contemporary social scientists and historians.[18]

The Rajvanshi

Why would such an important leadership from an aristocratic background emerge within a democratic polity, and what motivates the 'princely politician' or Rajvanshi? What distinctive elements does he or she bring to electoral politics? It is important to remember that democratic principles were not foreign to Indic kingship. Although portrayed as despotic or autocratic, most ruling houses did not spend lavishly on personal expenses or court ceremonies. Nor were they 'absolute' monarchs. While in theory, he was born with executive, judicial and legislative powers, the king in practice invariably needed the consent and advice of his noblemen and vassals to legitimate any state decision.[19]

The Rajvanshi, more often than not, was motivated to engage in democratic politics out of dharmic obligation and ancestral duty. For the first generation of princely politicians from 1952 to the 1967 elections, democratic leadership may have been the natural successor to actually ruling.[20] The Maharaja of Dhrangadhra returned to the political fray after several years of absence to oppose the Gujarat Congress, which held a monopoly over the state.[21] The political careers of Gayatri Devi and Vijaya Raje Scindia were similarly motivated by outrage towards Congress-led governments in their own states. In Gayatri Devi's case, she ran for Parliament on a Swatantra ticket to oppose the growing vandalism of Jaipur's historic monuments by the local Congress government. Vijaya Raje, although originally recruited by the Congress, changed parties to the Jan Sangh and Swatantra to support student factions against the local Gwalior police. Both were incarcerated during the Emergency for their anti-Congress stances. Arguably, this was a mere continuation of the traditional *raja-praja* (ruler-subject) relationship, whereby the prince conventionally sacrificed his own personal well-being for the communal welfare.

Among Rajput princes (of the three princely politicians mentioned above, two represented former Rajput princely states and one was the daughter of a Rajput nobleman), this sense of duty might best be expressed through the concept of *sharan*. A fundamental part of Rajputai, or the Rajput dharmic code, *sharan* argues that a ruler give sanctuary to anyone who seeks it, irrespective of any consideration and totally unmindful of the consequences.[22] Under Mughal imperial rule, Rajput princes harboured the exiled sons of emperors Akbar, Jahangir, Shah Jahan and Aurangzeb, despite dire consequences. Thus, it is not surprising that Muslim princes fled to Hindu kingdoms in Rajasthan seeking military protection. Colonel James Tod, political agent to the court of the Maharaja of Gwalior in 1806, eulogized the Rajputs in his *Annals and Antiquities* as heroic symbols of kshatriya honour and potential inheritors of Ram Rajya.[23] The memory of such courageous acts lends the princely politician an inimitable, divine aura. The multiple stormings of Chittor, where whole generations of Rajput princes and noblemen served as cannon fodder to Mughal forces and their women immolated themselves in mass funerals, *jauhars*, rather than be captured by the enemy, is only one example where Rajput princes have been depicted as martyrs.[24] In large part because of this concept of *sharan*, the erstwhile Rajput kings have a broad base of electoral support, crossing lines of caste, class and religious difference, and acquiring the support of minority constituencies. This voter appeal can be extended and applied to the larger concept of the Rajvanshi.

The former king is not merely royal, Hindu or kshatriya, but is the people's king. He or she goes beyond narrow spheres of identity, representing a much more holistic concept of leadership. Rajasthan, which in the decades shortly following Independence was dominated by princely politicians, had some success preventing communal violence and maintained a strong sense of secularization, by appealing to multi-caste communities and Muslim and Hindu voters alike. Even in Gujarat, where recent Hindu-Muslim riots consumed the state in a blood bath in 2002, regions such as Saurashtra, which primarily consist of former Hindu and Muslim kingdoms, have witnessed far less conflict than the urban centres.

Ex-princes have also had a long connection with the scheduled tribes, such as the so-called 'tribals', the Meenas and Bhils, who traditionally have played a significant role in the *rajyabhishek* or coronation ceremony.[25] Rajvanshis and their families easily swept the scheduled tribe constituencies in Rajasthan, which the Congress party had no hold on. As political historians Narain and Mathur note, the massive turn-outs to their election speeches, as well as the high percentage of votes polled by them seems to suggest that [princely politicians] mobilized a multi-caste political base, imparting an element of 'secularization' to the political processes in Rajasthan.[26]

The majority of princely candidates who stand for office are elected and sometimes with as much as seventy or eighty per cent of the vote.[27] These vestiges of feudal privilege may seem anachronistic so long after Independence, but William Richter argues that this is in large part because national leaders have seen the relevance of former princes in politics. Although marginalizing their historical and contemporary role in India, prime ministers from Nehru to Shastri to Indira Gandhi have curried the support of the erstwhile rulers. According to Richter, they are seen more as 'friends and associates than as implacable class enemies and [party politicians] have frequently found princely political support to be valuable for stability, progress or partisan gain'.[28]

Dynastic Rule and the Emergence of the Zenana Woman as Rajvanshi

Unlike earlier models based on patriarchy, the postcolonial dynasties, royal and non, incorporate visible female leadership. The female dynasts may be originally chosen as hollow symbols of the earlier established male head of state. When the Congress leadership chose to make Jawaharlal Nehru's daughter Indira Gandhi chief of the party in 1966, they were 'secure in the belief that they could control her'.[29] What soon emerged was the reverse: a strong female presence with her own political agenda. In time Indira Gandhi eclipsed her own party and on occasion disregarded her father's democratic principles by inaugurating dictatorial rule, most memorably her twenty-two month Emergency. Sunil Khilnani suggests that she offered herself as an individual object of adulation, identification and trust to her electorate.[30]

While Indira Gandhi's cult of personal politics is not representative of all democratic dynasts, it is illustrative of two seminal points: first, the continued significance of dynastic politics in postcolonial South Asia; and second, the development of the female politician as an individuated personality. Once empowered by political agency and public support, she can unmask her own ambitions, distinct from those of her father, husband or party.[31] A similar trend is noticeable among former Zenana women who enter electoral politics. Ordinarily elected as representatives of an earlier patriarchal kingship, being wives, daughters or mothers of former rulers, these women in time became charismatic leaders in their own right, divorced from the family or courtly identity. After Independence, political power was no longer implicit behind the *pardah* walls of the zenana, but explicit through the public spectacle of the campaign process.

The lives of two former Maharanis, Rajmata Gayatri Devi of Jaipur and Rajmata Vijaya Raje Scindia of Gwalior, are particularly relevant. Their personal histories are deeply intertwined with the tapestry of twentieth-century India, following the patterns of the typical Rajvanshi. Both born in 1919, they married the rulers of two large, influential princely states, Rajput Jaipur and Maratha Gwalior. As Maharanis, they lived within multi-tiered, hierarchical zenanas, sometimes housing as many as several hundred women. With Independence and the integration of the princely states into the nascent republic, they began to take on far more politicized roles, emerging out a world dominated by the culture of *pardah* into the body politic. Though wooed by the Congress, both joined opposing parties, the Swatantra Party and the Jan Sangh, respectively.

When they came closer to what Gayatri Devi describes as the evening of life, they chose to write their autobiographies. Their narratives portray an inherently politicized familial world. The post-Independence period put greater emphasis on the role of royal families as families, and less so on their hereditary position as ruling dynasties. Women as members of the new political unit have equal and sometimes more public presence than their male compatriots who conventionally would have held overt authority during the late colonial state. Furthermore, the nature of multi-party politics allows more members of the politicized family to contest electoral power than just the male ruler.

By sharing their views through dialogue within the 'public sphere', such as the publication of memoirs, articles in newspapers or television interviews, these women can now influence external opinion, whether it be their party, constituency, or the larger Indian or international community. Both of them wrote autobiographies although their husbands did not, and remained influential figures long after their husbands had died. Contrary to the perceptions that exist about the condition of widows in Hindu culture, widowhood did not hamper them. Instead, they had their most productive years in politics as widows, and it was this period that cemented them within the consciousness of the new nation. Arguably, their sense of female agency was inherited, since both were born into families where women had long played dominant, and often visible, roles within the state and the courtly family.

The memoirs of Gayatri Devi and Vijaya Raje reveal a world hitherto shielded from the external eye. They 'unveil' a Zenana mentality earlier cloaked behind *pardah*, and the private workings of royal families whose symbolic mystique has often been protected through distance from a reading public. Unlike their male counterparts, it is relevant to note that former Zenana women participated not only in one but two twentieth-century revolutions: peaceful transition from princely state to the republic, and emergence from *pardah* into the political arena.

Gayatri Devi, Rajmata of Jaipur (b. 1919): The Princess as Public Servant

> The woman with the most staggering majority anyone has ever earned in an election.
> – American President John F. Kennedy's words when introducing
> Gayatri Devi during her visit to the White House.[32]

Known as a queen, famed beauty, politician, social reformer, businesswoman and educator, Gayatri Devi has influenced Indian society since her girlhood. Even now, in her eighties, she is cited as one of India's lasting icons alongside dancers, Bollywood stars, and religious gurus. She was described by *Vogue* as one of the world's most gorgeous women and was a favourite for society photographers and columnists.[33] This chapter, however, will deal principally with her life as a Zenana lady and subsequent career as a politician in democratic India. In particular, it will focus on her commitment towards public service.

Gayatri Devi was descended from families with dedicated female public servants. Both her paternal and maternal grandmothers had contributed to the intellectual and cultural life of turn of the century India. Her paternal grandmother, Sunity Devi, Maharani of Cooch Behar, was the first Indian woman to write her autobiography in English[34] and was one of a few to attend university, Bethune College in Calcutta.[35] She promoted female education in Cooch Behar and all over Bengal. Gayatri Devi described her as 'a gentle and affectionate presence throughout my childhood'. Outside of the State, she worked diligently to encourage emancipation of women in Bengal.[36]

Sunity Devi, as mentioned earlier, was the daughter of the kshatriya Bengali Hindu reformer, Keshub Chandra Sen. She grew up in a household which encouraged women's learning and agency and promoted classical Indian culture. Her father advocated the Civil Marriages Act, which increased the average marriageable age for Hindu girls and boys.[37] Intimately connected with the family of Rabindranath Tagore, the Sen home was full of music, song and theatre. Sunity Devi's brother often put on open-air theatricals, such as the *jatra*.[38] In 1878, she married the Maharaja of Cooch Behar. It was a union in large degree endorsed by British Indian officials of the Raj, who saw educated women, like the daughters of Keshub Chandra Sen, as desirable brides for eastern Indian rulers.

The nineteenth century brought changes in perspective to travel beyond the kala pani or black waters. As Siobhan Lambert-Hurley writes, 'Native princes, in particular, began visiting Europe and Great Britain for both personal and political reasons around the turn of the century' and their names were mentioned in major English newspapers.[39] In 1887, Sunity Devi was the first Indian maharani to emerge out of *pardah* and travel to England where she openly entertained within European society.[40] Her third son, Victor, later became the godson of Queen Victoria.[41]

Gayatri Devi's maternal grandmother, Maharani Chimnabai of Baroda, was a similarly impressive female figure. Her husband, Maharaja Sayajirao III of Baroda, was known as a most progressive ruler of his day. Five of his grandchildren and great-grandchildren were engaged in state or national politics by the 1970s.[42] In 1911, Maharani Chimnabai published an influential treatise on the status of women in Indian society, *The Position of Women in Indian life*. While she did not formally attend university, she was a self-taught woman of letters and became an advocate of the women's movement, eventually serving as President of the All India Women's Conference.

She wrote her book after travelling in the Occident, which generated contrasts between women in India and their counterparts in Europe and America. The purpose of her work was to 'awaken [her] Indian sisters from their lethargy of ages, to enable them to take their proper place in Indian public life'.[43] It is an encyclopaedic text and takes on prolific thinkers and ideas. The treatise discusses the role of women all over the world and through time, guiding the reader on a whirlwind tour. She examines women in hunter-gatherer communities, the Arab countries, heroines of the Sanskrit epics and those of ancient Egypt and Greece. She provides an analysis of European women as government leaders, professors, and salon intellectuals. She describes Churchill's views on women; catalogues great women rulers ranging from Maratha princess Ahilya Bai to Queen Victoria and discusses women's education in India.

The chapter headings of the book are themselves illustrative of the Maharani's broad interests. They include sections on professions for women, agriculture and land ownership, the arts, intellectual calling, philanthropy, business, domestic science (husbandry, cooking), women inspectors, money-lending, rescue women and women's interests, such as issues of labour and work, and concludes with a chapter on the position of women in Japan, a country she had visited. Ahead of her time, she emphasized the importance of cultural relativism when comparing societies. As she argues, the West is not paramount to the East and certain Indian customs are inimitable and admirable:

> Some of the projects will no doubt appeal to them, but it would nevertheless be well for them to bear in mind the need to guard against too slavish an imitation of Western notions. Every country by intelligent observation can learn something from other lands, but at the same time each should strive to preserve its own racial characteristics, just as each sex should endeavor, not to ape the other but to make the most of its own peculiar distinctions of character. There should be no hasty adoption of customs essentially foreign to our nations. In the words of Bacon the great English philosopher: It were good that men into their innovations would follow the example of Time itself, which, indeed, innovateth greatly, but quietly, and by degrees scarce to be perceived ...[44]

As a descendent of these women and an inheritor of their social, political and intellectual legacies, it seems only natural that Gayatri Devi would turn to writing her own autobiography, *A Princess Remembers*, in her later years and to commissioning biographies. Nor is it surprising that she would be inspired to commit a substantial part of her own life to public service, first as a Maharani and later as a Swantantra MP and Tourism Minister of Rajasthan.

As a young princess of Cooch Behar, Gayatri Devi led a fairly free and open life, where she did not observe *pardah*. She was one of three sisters and two brothers. They lived mainly under the guidance of female relations, her mother and grandmothers, as her father and grandfather had passed away early in life.

Her own mother, Rajmata Indira Devi of Cooch Behar, born the princess of Baroda, was her principal role model. She described her mother 'as an unparalleled combination of wit, warmth and exquisite looks'.[45] Furthermore, Indira Devi challenged the prevailing social norms in India, which prescribed widows to a life of inner reflection and asceticism. In contrast, she proved 'that a woman, a widow at that, could entertain with confidence, charm and flair without being in the protective shadow of a husband or father'.[46] This example of a spirited widow would return to Gayatri Devi, when she herself took on a new life after her husband's death.

Like her mother, Gayatri Devi chose a 'love marriage'. In 1940, she married Maharaja Sawai Mansingh of Jaipur.[47] The Jaipur Zenana she entered of the early 1940s housed as many as four hundred women including widowed relatives, daughters, ladies in waiting and their staffs, the Rajmata (queen mother) and other wives of the former ruler, as well as two of her husband's own co-wives.[48] At first, she found it difficult to adapt to the strict hierarchy she found herself in, being accustomed to a more informal social environment in Cooch Behar. She writes that she 'used to plead with the ladies in the zenana who spoke English to talk freely with me, to argue with me, even just to call me Ayesha [her nickname] in private, but they would smilingly, deferentially, ignore my request'.[49]

During the war period of the 1940s, she slowly began to emerge out of the zenana and *pardah*. She opened girls' schools in Jaipur and attended meetings of the All India Congress of Women, like her Baroda grandmother before her. She went to Red Cross work-parties where she met women who were teachers, doctors and wives of government officials. Their company was far more stimulating than that of the *pardah*-ridden palace ladies.[50] In 1943, her private school for girls, the Maharani Gayatri Devi School, opened in Jaipur. Her intent was to educate Rajput girls from noble families in Jaipur, who had never been outside of *pardah*, in a western style forum. At first, it was difficult to find families who would enroll their daughters. However, in time it became a pre-eminent institution for girls.

By the mid 1940s, rumours of the nationalist movement had reached Jaipur and in 1947 India proclaimed its Independence from colonial rule. While Independence was a happy occasion, the princes had little realized the impact it would make on them and their ancestral forms of governance. While her husband was stripped of his executive powers, he was briefly given the position of Rajpramukh or 'Head of State' of the new Rajasthan Union whereby he would have the overall supervision of the administration of the entire province during the interim years of integration.[51]

With Independence, Gayatri Devi began more and more to emerge out of the zenana perimeters. In 1952, she attended the meeting of the All-India Congress of Women, which introduced certain rights for Indian women such as legal provisions for divorce. In 1957, she was asked by the Chief Minister of Rajasthan to stand for Parliament on a Congress ticket. She was surprised by the unexpected invitation; 'the request that I – of all people – should start to play a role in Indian politics'.[52] At first, she refused to run and abandoned any thoughts of political activity.[53]

Later, she discovered that Jaipur's medieval city walls and gates were slowly being torn down by the state government. She wrote to then Prime Minister of India, Jawaharlal Nehru, passionately urging him to cease the vandalism in Rajasthan. Around the same time, her husband began to convert the old palaces, such as her first home as a bride, Rambagh, into hotels for visiting tourists. It was part of his strategy to move with the times, for the private incomes of the princes were gradually dwindling in post-Independence India, and it was impossible to maintain ancestral properties. He was the first ex-ruler to make this decisive move.[54]

After twenty years of marriage, she embarked upon a political career. In 1960, speaking out against the growing vandalism of Jaipur medieval architecture, Gayatri Devi was nominated for a seat in Parliament. Adamantly opposed to the Congress party she, like many members of former royal families who were then engaged in Indian politics, chose the independent Swatantra Party. The Swatantra Party was of particular national consequence during the elections of 1962, 1967 and 1972. In 1967, it emerged as the second largest party in the house after Congress, winning forty-four seats in the Lok Sabha.[55] Gayatri Devi joined the Swatantra party for the following reasons:

> There were many like myself, who had never joined a political party before, and even if they had wanted to, couldn't have found one that expressed moderate and liberal views. They rejected the muddle-headed socialism of the Congress Party and the even more impractical schemes of the Socialists and they couldn't subscribe to the extremism of the Communists on the left, or the religiously oriented, orthodox Hindu Jana Sangh Party on the right.[56]

While she had emerged from *pardah* gradually after the war years of the 1940s, it was not until her campaign in Rajasthan that Gayatri Devi was perceived as putting the zenana behind her. She travelled to hundreds of villages, giving public appearances and speeches, visiting homes, schools and hospitals. She moved around without the constraints of *pardah*, neither covering her face, as she would have done earlier when she was first married, or travelling in curtained vehicles.[57] As her husband's representative, she was not seen as foreign, even if her face was.

Her campaign experience, which she described as a campaign of love, revealed that the historic connection between the Jaipur royal family and their constituency had not weakened in the years after Independence. As she recalls:

> It was only when I saw the jubilant, trusting reaction of the crowds – many of whom had walked as much as fifty miles to attend our meetings – that I began to grasp the full extent of the responsibilities we had taken upon ourselves.[58]

In 1962, she won her seat to Parliament with the largest majority in any democratic election at that time recorded in the *Guinness Book of World Records*.[59]

While this achievement was a personal one, it simultaneously reflected the continued influence of her husband's family in Jaipur. She repeatedly reiterates in her memoirs the importance of his presence in her campaign where he often addressed the electorate not as a candidate but as their living ruler.

As a Member of Parliament, Gayatri Devi pushed for several reforms, particularly an amendment to the Constitution regarding the right to property. She supported public service works in Jaipur, advocated environmental conservation in India and encouraged women's education in Rajasthan. She also criticized Pandit Nehru's Congress after the 1962 Indo-China War, which India lost. She bitingly chided him for his careless, poor management of that crisis. In repartee, he replied: 'I will not brandish words with a lady!' At which the Opposition, her party amongst them, called out 'Chivalry!' in equally mocking terms.[60]

Real problems began to emerge when Indira Gandhi became prominent in politics in 1967. This was the first election in which Indira Gandhi herself contested a parliamentary seat, despite having campaigned for her husband and father in the past. She travelled throughout India and when she came to Jaipur a Swatantra group protested. Her relationship with Gayatri Devi had childhood roots for both women had studied at Shantiniketan as schoolgirls.[61]

At the end of the election, the results were 'agonizingly close'. In Rajasthan, the Opposition parties won the majority with 95 seats, with Congress close behind at 89. The Governor was meant to invite the majority party to form state government but delayed the process. Gayatri Devi and her party believed it was due to pressure from the central government in Delhi. In response, violence erupted in Jaipur and a twenty-four hour curfew was placed on the city. She went to Delhi requesting the Home Minister and President to lift the curfew, which they agreed to. However, when the curfew was lifted the security forces, who were not Jaipur police but had been brought from neighbouring regions, began firing upon people whom they claimed had violated the curfew regulations. Nine people were killed. Disheartened by the state of affairs, Gayatri Devi wrote in her diary on 9 January 1967:

> Nepotism and corruption have reached the limit ... and the victims as always are the innocent poor. And this from a party which claims to be socialist! It is ironical, sad and heartbreaking to see what is happening to the wonderful people who are Indians. Proud good people sacrificed for the greed and lust of a few. Justice does not exist. Truth is a thing to laugh at. Honesty is a fool. But hunger and want is real.[62]

Her biggest blow as a politician came in 1975. By this time Gayatri Devi was a widow. However, instead of retiring into a private life, which is the convention for widows in Hindu society, she had continued her commitment to public service as a Member of Parliament. On 12 June, the Allahabad High Court annulled Prime Minister Indira Gandhi's election to the Lok Sabha in a sensational judgment charging her with campaign malpractice. 'Under the parliamentary system', Gayatri Devi writes, 'her choices were to resign and seek redress through the courts. Driven by the misguided perception that "India was Indira" and that without her the nation could not survive, and spurred on by her coterie of self-seeking advisers, she unleashed events that almost destroyed democracy in India, a democracy so carefully nurtured by people like Pandit Nehru, her father'.[63] In response to the accusation of malpractice, Mrs Gandhi declared the Emergency, which was a dark midnight on the promise of Indian democracy. Opposition leaders and members, some thousands of people, were jailed without the right to call legal assistance and newspapers throughout India were censored. Gayatri Devi was also imprisoned with her stepson, the young Maharaja of Jaipur, Bubbles, without due legal process or habeas corpus. She recounted her arrest in the following manner:

> Rather embarrassed they told me they had come with a warrant for my arrest. I asked them what the charges were. They told me C.O.F.E.P.O.S.A (Conservation of Foreign Exchange and Prevention of Smuggling Activities Act). I was quite taken aback and asked if I could ring up my lawyers. I was told I could not use the telephone.[64]

She was sent to the Tihar Jail in New Delhi, where she lived in a small room at the centre of the women's quarters during the Emergency. There, she was soon joined by Rajmata Vijaya Raje Scindia of Gwalior.[65] In jail, she mixed with women of all socio-economic groups – rural workers, prostitutes, mothers, and intellectuals – and describes that period as one of hardship but also of friendship and credits the life of the Zenana tradition as giving her the strength and skill to survive in that imprisoned world with a sense of humour.

After several months, she became ill, fearing possible breast cancer, and was convinced she would die in Tihar jail. She had stayed there for 156 nights, the longest she had lived ever in one place continuously. She was admitted to hospital, both for fear of breast cancer and in need of surgery for gallstones.[66] After the procedure, she received parole and returned to Jaipur. In March 1977, Indira Gandhi lost her campaign for re-election and the Emergency was over. No longer on parole or with an impending trial, Gayatri Devi was exuberant as was much of India. Money was thrown in the streets and free sweets distributed as if a grand festival was being celebrated.[67] Her incarceration did not make a dent on the princely politicians or her own continued political involvement. As Narain and Mathur note, 'the very fact that such "punishment" failed to break Smt Gaytri Devi's political back testifies to the depth of the ex-rulers' grip over the political allegiance of the people of Rajasthan which even a shrewd national politician like Indira Gandhi failed to gauge'.[68]

By the 1990s, Gayatri Devi led a quieter life between India and Europe. Her views regarding contemporary Indian politics are now more complicated by criticism and nostalgia. She notes during an interview in 1999:

> Everybody in India is corrupt and nothing can get done without bribes. It's not a true democracy. What kind of a government have we got? Coalitions are going to happen over and over again. Indian princes, (I'm saying this since I come from that kind of family), ruled far better than India is governed today. When the states went, we had to go too, it's a part of history. Whether it will come back again, who can say.[69]

As Gayatri Devi states, 'when the states went, we had to go too, it's a part of history'. So, too, is the role of a Zenana woman at the end of the twentieth century. She suggests that the remaining work now lies with her children, and through them traditional kingship can survive in a democratic nation. As she notes:

> I would like to tell my grandchildren if I have a chance that their priorities are looking after people who have been looked after by this family. It is their duty even if the states have gone, even though the *jagirs* have gone, the people still look up to you as the head. Even if you don't have the money, lend a sympathetic ear, to be able to give advice, to intervene with the authorities. It's not normally very successful, because of the manner our government functions, this, that, always keeping an eye on the next election and politicians just wanting to amass money. But people like my grandchildren should lend a helping hand.[70]

Gayatri Devi emphasizes here the importance of a familial commitment to public service for the next generations of her family. Although the financial means of the former kings are depleted and their authority unrecognized by the central government, the tie between the people and hereditary rule remains through service. At some level, this is the essential meaning of leadership whether in the new or old order.

The recent history of her family has been a sad one. Her only biological child, Jagat, died in 1997 at the age of forty four, due to alcoholism, a disease which had affected the men in the family for nearly three generations, in the Baroda, Cooch Behar and Jaipur royal lineages.[71] In a more recent autobiography, Gayatri Devi argued that her son's alcoholism was exacerbated by the cruelty of his former wife, the Buddhist Princess of Thailand, Priyananda Rangsit. She noted that

> Unfortunately he had a lot of unhappiness after his marriage broke up. He was not allowed to see or communicate with his children who were the most important part of his life and he missed them terribly. The pain of not being able to meet them is what led to his deterioration. He took to drinking to offset his unhappiness and in the end this caused a liver problem and eventually his death ... I blame myself and wonder about life and death.[72]

Such allegations led to an aggrieved response from the Rangsit family. Priyananda Rangsit contested the book's allegation that Jagat's alcoholism was caused
by her behaviour. She propounded that her former husband had been an alcoholic long before they married, from his school days in a British boarding school,
and that Gayatri Devi's charge was false. In addition, she claimed that Jagat had
not assisted her at all in the financial maintenance of their two children, Devraj
Singh and Lalitya, and that his volatile behaviour had led to the end of the marriage.[73] At present, Gayatri Devi and her former daughter-in-law are engaged
in a troubled dialogue over the future of her grandchildren's relationship with
Jaipur; a legacy she now wishes to fulfil at the end of her life.

Vijaya Raje Scindia, Rajmata of Gwalior (1919–2001): The Maharani as Hindu Fundamentalist

> Rajmata was tender as a flower but also tough like lightening.
> – Prime Minister Atal Bihari Vajpayee on the occasion of
> Vijaya Raje Scindia's death [74]

The above description of Vijaya Raje as politician and individual illuminates
her binary personality: at once gentle, yet unbreakable in her resolve. These
contrasting personas are evident throughout her life, especially in her political
involvement where she is often criticized as putting politics over family. In January
2001, fifty thousand people travelled from all over India to witness the lighting
of her funeral pyre in Gwalior, where she had first come as a young Maharani in
1941. Those who came to her funeral to take darshan envisioned her as a saint
and goddess. As Maharani and Member of Parliament, she successfully bridged
both the arenas of dynastic rule and democratic politics. Her funeral symbolized the meeting of these two worlds: princely India and the nationalist republic.
Several members of the BJP elite arrived to commemorate her passing, including Prime Minister Vajpayee, Vice-President Krishan Kant, Rajasthan Governor
Anshuman Singh, Madhya Pradesh Chief Minister Digvijay Singh who is the
Raja of Raghugadh, Rajasthan Chief Minister Ashok Gelot, UP Chief Minister
Rajnath Singh and Jammu and Kashmir Chief Minister Dr Farooq Abdullah.
Furthermore, a dozen Union ministers, 80 ministers, 100 legislators and over
30 members of Parliament came to pay their respects. Members of royal families
from Jammu and Kashmir, Nepal, Gujarat and Rajasthan were also present.[75]

As a modern day dynast, Vijaya Raje was skilfully able to perpetuate the influence of the Scindia royal family in contemporary Gwalior and Madhya Pradesh
politics. As a member of the Lok Sabha, she brought the family's prominence
to an All-India level, and as a BJP vice-president to an international visibility.
Arguably, the new system of electoral politics allows ex-princes to have more

public authority and influence over a much greater constituency than their earlier princely territories, particularly when participating in parliamentary politics. As a former Zenana woman, Vijaya Raje married into a princely home where there was strict *pardah*. Like Gayatri Devi, a political moment pushed her towards a lifetime commitment to democratic politics. After she became a widow, she changed party affiliation to the Jan Sangh and began her political career in earnest. In many ways, Vijaya Raje's childhood was a humble one in comparison to Gayatri Devi's girlhood in anglicized Cooch Behar, and it was her marriage to the powerful Scindia monarch, which would catapult her to prominence in post-Independence India.

Vijaya Raje was born in the same year as Gayatri Devi on 12 October 1919.[76] The daughter of a Rajput nobleman and the aristocratic Rana family of Nepal, which had connections with the Nepalese Crown, she had little thought as a young woman that she would one day marry a Maratha ruler.[77] Furthermore, her mother's family had been expelled from Nepal and were trying to find secure footing in India.

She grew up surrounded by educated female role models and empowered widows. Vijaya Raje's mother was taught at home and later became the first Nepalese girl to pass the university matriculation exams.[78] She married a petty Rajput nobleman but died in childbirth. Thereafter, Vijaya Raje was brought up almost solely by her maternal grandmother, a tough Rana lady, who was also a widow. Like Gayatri Devi, she saw early on the power possible for a woman independent of her husband, and the reverence and respect given to a widowed woman within the family hierarchy.

It was this grandmother who gave her a religious identity, which would influence Vijaya Raje throughout her life and drive her politics.[79] She was drawn most to religion over her studies, and became a Krishna *bhakt*. As she notes, 'Krishna who played the flute, tended his cows, stole butter from irate housewives and slew dragons, became my private god'.[80] She sang the devotional songs of Mirabai, a sixteenth-century Rajput princess who had become a Krishna devotee and relinquished her husband, the ruler of Mewar, for the wandering life of an ascetic. This early foundation in Hindu ideology and the admiration for a Rajput royal woman who had given up family for god may have influenced Vijaya Raje's later decision to choose her allegiance to the BJP party over her own family ties.

Originally home tutored, she later studied in Vasantha College, Benares, and Isobella Thoburn College, Lucknow.[81] After university, her family began to look for possible marital partners. Following four proposals, which for various reasons were unacceptable, she was married to Jivajirao Scindia, Maharaja of Gwalior, a large Maratha state in Madhya Pradesh in February 1941.[82]

Like Gayatri Devi's experience in Jaipur, her entrance into the Gwalior Zenana was not without restrictions. Although her life within the palace was more informal, she was veiled when travelling within the environs of Gwalior proper. She recalls this introduction to *pardah* life as a new bride:

> If I went to the cinema, I went in a car with tinted windows and slipped into our box
> through a corridor of screens held in position by attendants. But whenever we were
> outside the borders of our state, I did not have to observe purdah at all, except in
> gatherings in which other princes or their families might be present.[83]

While she did not have to observe *pardah* outside Gwalior state, her emergence from the zenana had a particularly symbolic meaning for her husband's people. In 1947, Vallabhai Patel visited Gwalior to perform the ceremony of integration whereby the kingdom was incorporated into the then new state of Madhya Bharat, which later became Madhya Pradesh. When Vijaya Raje greeted him, he requested that she give a speech of introduction, but without the screen of *pardah* and before a mixed group of men and women. In her memoirs, she recounts his words to her: 'If you call yourself the mother and father [Ma-Bap] of the people, how can you bear to have a veil between them and you?' To honour her guest she appeared at the Gwalior Town Hall, unveiled, and gave a short speech. In her autobiography, she notes the significance of this moment: 'it was quite plain that the majority of people had come not to see [Vallabhai Patel] explaining the transfer of power, but to see what their Maharani, whom they had never seen, looked like'.[84]

Her entrance into politics less than ten years later in 1956 was similarly inadvertent. While her husband was Rajpramukh of Madhya Bharat, she was approached by numerous members of the central cabinet to stand for Parliament.[85] Trying to protect her husband, who had openly criticized the Congress party, she was pressured by then Prime Minister Jawaharlal Nehru to run on a local Congress ticket. The opposing party, the Mahasabha, had strong support in Gwalior, and state Congress leaders feared the Maharaja of Gwalior would support it. Vijaya Raje knew that criticism from an ex-prince would be unfavourably looked upon for 'to join the opposition would be something in the nature of high treason'.[86] Spurred by the advice of her associates, she sought to explain to Nehru that the rumours her husband was joining the Mahasabha were baseless.

When she was able to speak with the Prime Minister in New Delhi, he pressed her to run on a Congress ticket, ignoring her many hesitations. Her husband was disconcerted by what had happened, but decided that it was 'prudent' for her to accept the offer. Although she participated in the elections at the time, she was uninterested in her parliamentary position and her vote was 'available' to the Congress party when it was politically expedient.[87] As the former BJP party president Shashikant 'Kushabhau' Thakre suggests, as she long as she remained in the Congress, she remained 'dormant' as a politician.[88]

It was only later, after she became a widow, that her political career began in earnest. On 17 September 1966, riots broke out around Gwalior, resulting in the arrests of students by the police. Vijaya Raje felt a responsibility to be politically involved after a student delegation asked for her support.[89] However, D.P. Mishra, the head of the Congress-ruled government in Madhya Pradesh, refused to accept her candidacy for her own seat in Gwalior.[90] Appalled by the state of affairs, she decided to run on non-Congress tickets: first as a Jan Sangh candidate for the legislative assembly of Madhya Pradesh and then as a Swatantra candidate for Parliament. As she notes in her autobiography, she won her place with 200,000 votes over her Congress rival, about 50,000 votes more than Gayatri Devi's record.[91] She put together a non-Congress coalition which ruled the state for nearly two years.

With the Emergency ten years later, life drastically changed. Vijaya Raje describes that 'overnight India was transformed into a police state in which any petty official could settle a private grudge by having his adversary thrown into jail'.[92] The first reports of the 1975 Emergency came over a BBC Broadcast; the All India Radio news bulletins making no mention of it. No newspapers came that day. One of her friends, Mr Surinderlal Dewan, took it upon himself to hide Vijaya Raje from arrest. As she would be identifiable in her white widow's clothes, she wore colourful saris for the first time after thirteen years.

After hiding in various places in Delhi, she retreated to the foothills of the Himalayas near Nepal. Although within a few hours of the Nepalese border where her son, Madhavrao, the young Maharaja of Gwalior, had taken refuge, she decided to return to Gwalior and give herself up to the government. It was a moment of revelation:

> Now I had made the decision. I could not bring myself to run away, seeking safety and leaving others to face the music – I, who called myself a leader and who had been accepted as such by a large number of people. Leaders do not run away.[93]

This was an integral moment in Vijaya Raje's life both as a descendant of a dynastic family and as a democratic politician. Brought up on stories of Rajput honour and courage, she was addressing a concept of leadership founded on dharmic principles of duty. For her, this moment might have seemed reminiscent of a Rani of Jhansi dilemma, where the female leader fled or stood her ground in the face of adversity. Returning to India was the correct political choice to make. It was a decision she knew instinctively was based on an ancestral code of conduct. Furthermore, this decision fitted well with the BJP ideology. On the official BJP web site, martial Kshatriya kings are cited as inspiration for the party's Hindu philosophy, including Maratha ruler Shivaji and Rajput prince Rana Pratap, who fought against Muslim forces and withstood aggression.[94]

After giving herself up to the Congress Government, Vijaya Raje was sent to Tihar Jail. There she met her compatriot and fellow Maharani, Gayatri Devi. She described their greeting: We bowed to each other and folded our hands as we would have at a social occasion but the greeting she came out with was one of agonized concern: 'Whatever made you come here? This is a horrible place!'[95]

As the months passed, it only grew worse. She described the environs of the jail:

> A stench that was thick as a vapour, flies which we had to ward off with one hand to be able to eat our meals with the other, and a cacophony of noise that may have been especially designed as some kind of torture – can hell be much different? When the flies went to sleep at night, the mosquitoes and other insects came in their place; the noise that may have been especially designed as some kind of torture – can hell be much different? When the flies went to sleep at night, the mosquitoes and other insects came in their place; the noise and the stench seemed to remain constant. Sandwiched as we were between the men's and women's wards, we were subjected to a dual set of barked orders, of hobnailed boots slithering on the flagstones, of hawking and spitting and the howling of children, of slanging bouts and political slogans, midnight bursts of song, screams or maniacal laughter.[96]

Later, she was allowed to bring items into her jail cell. She asked her daughters for children's clothes, medicines and shelter, which she distributed to the inmates.[97] Her eldest daughter Usha Raje, whose husband was a Minister in the Nepalese government, persevered with Delhi to arrange her mother's bail, and her son threatened to give up politics if she was not released.[98] Finally Vijaya Raje was let out of Tihar on the grounds of ill health.

In the following years, Vijaya Raje became an important player in Indian politics. From her earlier affiliation with the Jana Sangh, she later became a senior member of the BJP, and is described as the 'most powerful figure that the Bharatiya Janata Party [had] since the mysterious death of Jan Sangh leader Deendayal Upadhyay in the late sixties'.[99] Along with Atal Bihari Vajpayee and L.K. Advani, she formed the inner core of the party elders.[100] From 1980 until 1998, she served as one of the vice-presidents of the party, until she stepped down for health reasons. She played a key role in propagating the BJP's stance on Ayodhya and was considered a party hard-liner.[101] In 1992, she was present in Ayodhya at the demolition of the Babri Masjid.[102] Opposing Vajpayee's line of ideology, she declared that adopting Gandhian socialism in the party's philosophy would only make the BJP a 'photocopy' of Indira Gandhi's Congress.[103] She served on several government committees, including the Ministry of Human Resource Development, and the Committees on Society and Technology, Environment and Food Technology. For forty years, she was the President of the All India Women's Conference in the Gwalior Branch, and has received numerous honorary doctorates for her government service and works (from Vikram, Ujjain and Sagar universities).[104]

Her agenda as a politician was deeply tied with the Hindutva movement. Amrita Basu describes Vijaya Raje Scindia as one of three influential women who emerged as the 'most powerful orators of Hindu Nationalism'.[105] The image of sobriety and asceticism associated with widowhood, Basu argues, presented Vijaya Raje as a potent figure in a religiously defined political movement. She suggests that chastity 'heightens [Vijaya Raje's] iconic status for it is deeply associated in Hinduism with notions of spirituality, purity and otherworldliness; these qualities also make these women reliable spokespersons for the future Hindu *rashtra* (nation)'.[106] This conception of Vijaya Raje as politician also relates to her private motivations within her highly politicized family. Her well-publicized alienation from her only son made her more identifiable with the notion of nation, with the Hindu *rashtra*, rather than the private world of the family, Basu suggests.

The year of 2001 was an *annus horribilis* for the Gwalior family. In January, Vijaya Raje passed away after an ambitious career in politics, and her son, Maharaja Madhavrao Scindia, who was a leading member of the rival Congress party, died in a plane crash in September. Considered a forward-looking, meritocratic princely politician, there were high hopes he might one day become Prime Minister. His political record was, in many ways, as impressive as his mother's. He held the distinction of holding a Lok Sabha seat for 30 years, and, in 1984, defeated 'political heavyweight', former Prime Minister Atal Bihari Vajpayee, in a famous victory from Gwalior. Under Rajiv Gandhi's administration, he was made Minister of State for the Railways, and served in the Civil Aviation and Human Resources Development Ministries.[107]

Arguably, Vijaya Raje's greatest political legacy to modern India is through her children: three of whom have been elected members of the Indian Parliament or held senior posts in recent years, and the fourth whose husband is a Minister in Nepal.[108] As she notes in her memoirs, her family's commitment to politics is merely a continuation of their traditional duties as descendents of a ruling lineage. Thus the domestic nature of the courtly family enters a public, politicized arena. The fractured relationship between Vijaya Raje and her son, Madhavrao Scindia, demonstrates vividly the continued interrelationship between the 'private' world of household rivalry and the 'public' desire for political power among postcolonial dynastic elites. In such moments, 'palace politics become public'.[109]

According to Vijaya Raje, tension with her son began during her 1975 incarceration. As she recounts in her memoirs, Madhavrao encouraged her to flee with him to Nepal, where he was living with his Nepalese Rana wife. Her close advisor and kinsman to her deceased husband, Sardar Angre, was with her at that time. She remembers him rebuking Madhavrao for not remaining in India during the Emergency, and thereby dishonouring his duty as the titular leader of his people:

> 'Tell our Maharaja that we and those who were his father's subjects look upon him as the Scindia; that it is not proper for him to think of his own safety and show fear of the sort of people that have taken over the running of the country'.[110]

Later, she would note that her son had not come to her aid when she was in jail, and in contrast would highlight how often her three daughters had helped her. This split within the private realm of the family in due course was exacerbated by political choices. According to her, Madhavrao was forced to join the Congress Party, the very party which had placed her in jail. He argued that his entrance into the party had served as barter for her freedom. As she describes in her memoirs, he replied to her in anguish: 'Amma, it was like giving with one hand to be able to take with the other. I just had to go along with them to be able to secure your release'.[111] For Vijaya Raje, this was an inexcusable expression of weak character. Their divergent political views only heated with time. He continued his career in the Congress Party, while she remained in the BJP. In the last pages of her memoirs, she describes this final parting of ways with her son:

> Then I appealed to him to accept that although we were now in opposite camps politically, it did not mean that we should become estranged, too ... My son did not see it that way. His revisionist zeal, his eagerness to prove that his loyalty to the hierarchy was beyond question, and, I suspect, his fear of retribution, gave his attitude a narrowness that I found hard to accept. 'But Amma, you leave me no choice!' he protested. 'As far as I am concerned, this is the parting of ways for us'.[112]

In later years, she notes that her son used violent means to contest her authority. She accused him of having raided one of her properties in 1983 during her absence under the allegation of theft, that he made false criminal cases against those loyal to her, and that he locked her out of her own home. She described him as 'opportunistic', with a lust for power and prestige. So deep was the rift between them that Vijaya Raje excluded him from her will, gifting her property and wealth to her daughters, and even tried to prevent him from performing his final duty as a Hindu son in lighting her funeral pyre.

The Maharaja of Dhrangadhra suggests that the schism between mother and son may have occurred much earlier than the Emergency, but rather shortly after Madhavrao's return from Oxford as a young man. His depiction of their relationship discredits not the 'cowardly son' of Vijaya Raje's autobiography but a power-hungry, Machiavellian mother. He writes:

> I was cautiously bringing the subject up, when [Madhavrao] blurted out, 'Maharaj, do you think I should go into politics?' She cottoned on at once. 'Now I know why this meeting has been called! You want His Highness to tell me that you shouldn't go into

politics, isn't it?' – We have a full journal record of this most unhappy happenstance. – As she got worked up she started hitting the arm of her chair, weeping, and shouting, 'You coward, you coward, you coward' ... The parting of ways was in the offing. At my last meeting of the Committee which was dealing with Govt, after I had made over its chairmanship to him and he was leaving, I happened to say something about his 'illustrious house'. He turned at the door and said, 'My illustrious house, your Highness? Have you read what my mother has said about me in her book?' He stood there, tears welling up in his eyes, hand on the doorknob. He was a stalwart in my battle against Indira Gandhi. His joining her and her Congress (our mortal enemy) later on was a matter of terror, of compulsion, of expedience, pure and simple.[113]

Tragically, the rift between mother and son was never healed. They were two dramatically divergent personalities. In his obituaries, Madhavrao emerges as a prince with a disinclination towards the dirtier side of politics. As journalist Rashmi Saksena suggests 'his aristocratic background made him feel that realpolitik was beneath his dignity'.[114] Perhaps, this was in part because he had been born a royal, the heir to a large and powerful erstwhile princely state. His mother, in contrast, had grown up in a smaller, modest Rana home, which had a marginal place in India, and had she selected her first suitor, she might have been the wife of an ICS officer not a Maharaja. She became a fighter in part because she had learned to assert herself by moving up the socio-political and socio-economic ranks. It is possible that her son, in contrast, was accustomed to the greater gentility of noblesse oblige. Like the fatalistic outcomes of a modern day *Mahabharata*, they were not long parted in death. This story of alienation between mother and son, Rajmata and Maharaja, has deeper inclinations. It is not just a family history, but also a telling narrative of the ambitions of erstwhile royal families with political motivations.

The Princess as Politician: The Journey from *Pardah* to Parliament

Traditionally, the custom of *pardah* has been interpreted as removing Zenana women from a political sphere. However, women from within the zenana walls were not merely passive agents, but in some instances were wielders of significant political power. While the mid-twentieth century saw the wane of the princely order and the zenana as an institution with the rise of the nation state, *rajvanshi* men and women continue to engage in the political arena. Indeed, democratic ideas of consensus building were not foreign to Indic kingship and the aristocratic politician often entered electoral politics out of a dharmic duty to service their former *praja*.

In certain cases, ex-princes have public influence over a larger constituency than that of their former princely states, which may have only been a small segment of the region they now represent as Chief Ministers, Members of Parliament or All-India level cabinet ministers. This trend reflects the popularity for dynastic leadership in postcolonial South Asian electoral politics. Just as Indira Gandhi came to power as the daughter of a former prime minister who then exercised her own power and personality, so did these former Zenana women engage in democratic politics at times eclipsing the male members of their families.

The life histories of Rajmata Gayatri Devi of Jaipur and Rajmata Vijaya Raje Scindia of Gwalior are striking examples of former queens who became elected politicians. Both were driven into democratic politics because of their opposition towards the ruling Congress party. Using the platforms of open discourse, they entered a 'public sphere' of dialogue, exposing not only their faces from behind the veil, but also their political and personal lives as former Maharanis and contemporary politicians. They have emerged as individuals, beyond merely a familial identity, and have wielded a public clout on an equal (and sometimes more influential) level than their male counterparts. Multi-party politics furthermore allow various members of the courtly family to hold visible political power, not just the erstwhile ruler. In this way, the intergenerational and cross-gendered nature of palace politics during the colonial and pre-colonial periods, conducted within the households of the zenanas, continues to be played in a new and larger arena. The family disputes which occurred behind the palace walls and courtyards have now entered the public space of partisanal politics, as witnessed in the conflict between Vijaya Raje Scinda and her son.

In addition, these accounts question the conventional portrait that widowed women in Hindu society retire to a life of asceticism and deprivation after the death of their husbands. In contrast, these women had successful years in politics long after their spouses were dead and left behind them the legacy of their children and grandchildren as powerful players in the new nation. Thus, these women engaged in two dramatic revolutions of twentieth-century South Asian history, unlike their male counterparts: the transition from princely state to modern republic and the move from *pardah* to parliament.

EPILOGUE

In early June 2001, the Nepalese royals convened at the state residence in Kathmandu for a family dinner as they did every third Friday of the month.[1] As in the past, the event was to be a leisurely private affair with the playing of billiards, rounds of cards and the enjoyment of food, liquor and conversation. It was a chance for the members of the large extended family, both old and young, to come together for an evening's entertainment in the spirit of tradition, duty and unity. What, however, began as a routine gathering soon turned into a tragic blood bath, when rounds of gunfire reverberated through the palace halls. Several members of the royal family were shot to death suddenly and inscrutably. Bringing to mind historic images of the brutal demise of the Romanovs, the Nepalese media initially presumed the massacre to be the handiwork of leftwing, Maoist radicals who were attempting to overthrow the monarchy. In actuality, the insurgency had occurred within the ranks of the royal family itself. Crown Prince Dipendra had shot his father, King Birendra, his mother, Queen Aishwarya, his brother, sister and several other relations, before turning his weapon upon himself. As one news outlet described the 'brief and violent incident':

> The rampage lasted some one and a half minutes, during which the crown prince walked in and out of the room where the royal family was gathered, firing his weapon continuously.
> At one point, Shahi said, Dipendra aimed at his mother, Queen Aishwarya. The crown prince's younger brother stepped in the way, pleading for Dipendra to stop, but Dipendra instead shot his brother several times in the back and then fired the fatal shots at the queen.[2]

Later media coverage of the happenings exposed the role of courtly women, marriage politics and intra-clan rivalry as motivations for the violence. According to eyewitness accounts, the Eton-educated Dipendra had wished to marry the daughter of a prominent Nepalese Minister and aristocrat, Devyani Rana, who was herself actively engaged in her father's campaigns. Devyani had strong political and dynastic connections in India, being the granddaughter of Vijaya Raje Scindia, the last Rajmata of Gwalior and leading member of the BJP party, and the niece of Vasundaraje, the present Chief Minister of Rajasthan, Yeshodaraje, a BJP Member of Parliament, and Madhavrao Scindia, who was a senior minister in the earlier Rajiv Gandhi- led, Congress government. Despite Devyani's prominent connections to political and royal families in South Asia, Queen Aishwarya, the Crown Prince's mother, was nonetheless troubled by her pedigree and thwarted Dipendra's marital ambitions. According to her, Vijaya Raje Scindia, also a Nepalese Rana, was descended from an 'undesirable' strain of the family who supposedly had as their ancestress a royal courtesan or a lower-ranked wife. Devyani was thus classified as being from the 'C Class' Ranas whereas the Shah Nepalese royals ordinarily only married 'A Class' Ranas. This 'tainted' blood was part of Queen Aishwarya's objection towards Devyani as a prospective daughter-in-law. In addition, it was reported that she was not on the most amicable terms with the girl's mother, Usharaje Rana, who alienated the Queen, by claiming that her birth and wealth as a Gwalior princess trumped the prestige of the 'backward' Nepalese royalty.[3]

Such events make clear the continued relevance of palace politics, zenana intrigue and the role of power and purity in marriage alliance making in twenty-first century South Asia. This narrative highlights the heteroglossic, cosmopolitan and volatile world within the female court, where the private and the public were never separate spheres. On the one hand, this is an intergenerational tale of personal conflict between a son and his parents over love marriage; on the other hand, it falls into a larger historical canvas, which illuminates the role of courtly women, as queens, princesses, mothers, wives and lovers, in controlling dynastic marriage, royal succession and relationships of degree within the royal household. The prince was up against various zenana players: his mother as the queen, his lover, an aristocrat, ambitious to become the mother of a future reigning prince and his lover's mother, a princess from another formidable royal lineage with its own sets of contacts and allegiances. In this world, his choices appear incidental and secondary, and ultimately overawed, by the desires of these women to retain, augment and finesse power as they jostled for power against each other. Heavy, indeed, is the head, which bears the crown. Like many of the indigenous male elites in this book, prince Dipendra was unable to penetrate and ultimately reconstruct the zenana hierarchies for his own purposes, and failed in a last show of bravado.[4]

In contrast to these narratives, British imperial and South Asian nationalist historiographies have largely portrayed courtly women as politically impotent. They have appeared either the frivolous and licentious members of an orientalized *seraglio*, ensconced in an indulgent world of sexual depravity and personal jealousies, or the secluded and docile *pardahnashins*, hidden behind latticed windows and locked doors from engagement with the affairs of state. They have been portrayed as constrained by seclusion, tradition and the dominating forces of men, both indigenous and European. In contrast to this image of the cloistered, *pardah* ladies, who remain largely the figures of exploitation and desire by Eastern princely males[5] or the subject of reform and rescue by the liberating, 'heroic' British officer,[6] this book has argued that courtly women were not precluded access from a public sphere of power and were much more active agents than has been earlier presupposed. These women were neither docile, demure, feminized, chaste or pure characters on the one hand nor the sexualized, demonized, plotting, secretive creatures of male fantasy on the other. In contrast to the image of the absent woman caught between imperialism and patriarchy, tradition and modernity,[7] Zenana females were proactive participants in the delicate dance of power both within the colonial Indian kingdom and in its relationship with British paramountcy.

In the historiography of colonial India, scholars have neglected the study of courtly women for two reasons. First, because until more recently, South Asian historians have focused on the histories of the directly governed British Indian provinces over those of princely Indian states in gauging how imperial India was governed; and second, because of the perceived inaccessibility of Zenana archives. While there has been a growing literature on the role of the Indian princes, there have been no comparable works examining the female members of these courtly households, both elite and non-elite. This perceived paucity of sources seemed to suggest to scholars that there was no historical agency for these indigenous women. As Durba Ghosh has countered, scholars must be critical of historical documents that deny native women existed and new methodologies must be introduced for reading texts where historical subjects are marginally or partially named.[8] In contrast, this book has argued that the colonial archive of the zenana paints a very different portrait: one of women's empowerment, resistance and strategy, thereby complicating the story of the contact zone between British political officials and traditional Indian rulers.

This book in effect debunks a number of myths regarding the apparent lack of agency for Zenana women in influencing how colonial India was governed. These women engaged in power plays at various levels: through the explicit or implicit governance of the princely state, the securing of political marriage alliances both as agents and objects and as educators and social reformers. They were feisty resisters to imperial and nationalist hegemonies and their resistance was multi-tiered in its proximity to them. Women fought amongst each other behind the walls of the palace; they struggled against patriarchal, traditional elites within the boundaries of the kingdom or princely state; and they circumvented the intervention of external dominant entities, whether that of the colonial state or the republican nation, for their own ends. Tracing events from the mid nineteenth to the late twentieth centuries, this book examines the vital intersection between royal authority, gender and sexuality in late imperial and postcolonial India.

After the East India Company emerged as the single paramount power with the defeat of the Marathas and the Pindaris during the decline of the Mughal

Empire, the Indian states formed treaties with the British during the early 1800s, relinquishing their pre-colonial identities as martial states. Thus the time under review canvassed an era when Indian kingdoms metamorphosed from warrior states to administrative ones. With the change from Company to Crown rule after the Mutiny of 1857, the map of India was again vibrantly redrawn: princely India standing alongside the Queen's dominions as part of the larger British Empire. Princely India was vast, diverse and multifarious in its attributes: from the desert plains of the Maratha and Rajput states in Gujarat and Rajasthan in the west to the hilly, riverine kingdom of the Buddhist Chakmas in eastern Bengal. These several hundred kingdoms had distinct religious, ethnic, regional, linguistic and legal histories. As an entity, it was by no means a homogenous whole to be classified with sharp, defining brushstrokes. The zenanas within individual kingdoms served, in certain instances, to provide the nucleus whereby the customs, histories and religious practices of different kingdoms and parts of British India could intermingle.

While seclusion and isolation were practised, courtly women themselves saw their world as porous, dynamic and constantly changing. Just as the princely states were heterogeneous and defied universalizing definitions, so were the female courts within them. These Zenana courts were multi-caste, multi-religious, hierarchical communities where women vied for ascendancy. In this domain, women exercised the piety of religious life, refined their aesthetic sensibilities, celebrated the arts, and lived the ideals of duty and service to their people. In part, this cosmopolitanism and diversity was created through marital alliances and differentiating social components in which courtly women saw themselves as originating somewhere else – sometimes coming from quite distant kingdoms, or from the hinterlands of the kingdom itself. Thus this book has shown that the zenana embodied a paradox: on the one hand it was removed, bounded, secluded and isolated; on the other hand this bounded world was heteroglossic, defined through generations of women who had come from disparate places and whose allegiances were continually being negotiated and renegotiated. While its architecture emphasized enclosure and seclusion, its culture and worldview exuded porosity, differentiation and multi-facetedness. In addition, the very sequestered space – architectural and cultural – of the zenana permitted women to resist the gaze and intrusion both of colonial officials and local males into their affairs. These narratives raise questions of hybridity, broadly defined by religion, race and class, which emphasize the multiple complications of locating communities within traditional definitions of gender in colonial and postcolonial South Asia and underline that these women were adroit players in this complex geography and landscape.

Within the ambit of politics, courtly women affected the governance of the state as regents and advisors to male rulers and controlled succession disputes or aided in rewriting succession law. In the area of knowledge appreciation, they themselves had a more multicultural and dynamic education than has been perceived earlier. They were instructed in regional and Indic forms of learning, customary religious practice and European subject disciplines. They were among the first Indian women to write their autobiographies in English, to study at university and to travel abroad, to Europe, America and East Asia. Overseas, these women influenced powerful constituencies, both social and political. They were early founders of schools and colleges for women in India and were active in advocating for the rights of women, even as they fought for their own voices, leading women's societies and social movements, locally and nationally.

In the arena of sexuality, their roles as wives, lovers and mothers were integral for the effective running of the state, whether in matters of dynastic marriage, the production of royal heirs, influence over royal spouses or the upbringing of royal children. In addition, the 'wrong type' of woman either as bride or courtesan could vitally undermine a male ruler's sovereignty or legitimacy to rule. In such cases, the very presence of the woman could emasculate the power of the prince.

Nonetheless, the historian cannot make broad generalizations. As each princely state was distinct, so were the female courts within them. In addition, notable paradoxes emerged, both in relationship to the definition of the princely female and the nature of colonial intervention. While British imperialists and indigenous male reformers advocated legislation relating to women, such as anti-Sati laws and widow remarriage acts, and encouraged women to come out of *pardah*, certain colonial officials promoted the practice of seclusion and decried the woman who broke with the veil. Similarly, while the British endorsed anglicized, educated, high-caste Indian women as brides for Indian princes, they were appalled when rulers crossed the racial boundary and wed European, Australian and American women themselves.

Such problematic results underline the 'colonial confusion' over the role of courtly females in the upbringing of princes, which is one of the main theoretical contributions of this book. The British, in an attempt to extract young males from the nefarious influences of the zenana, sent them away to public schools in India or Britain: the very places where they cultivated their 'transgressive' interests in Caucasian women which defied the rules of colonial racial propriety and decorum. In the process of 'purifying' the prince of the negative influences of the zenana, the British created perhaps far greater problems than what had existed earlier by paving the way for interracial marriages. In such incidences, the very institution that they had tried to undermine and devalue, the female sphere, came back to haunt them by playing a more prominent role in state politics. In addition, it can be argued that the prince in being extracted from the world of his female relations when sent to a distant, alien environment emerged sometimes as a quixotic, confused character unable to comfortably exist in any cultural context. This outcome did not equate with the colonial ambition of creating an indigenous monarch, who simultaneously epitomized the best of both the East and West. This question of 'cultural confusion' begs the observation that the study of princely India, which has often been neglected in mainstream South Asian historiography, needs to be vitally reassessed. By bringing courtly women back into the picture, this study argues that the 'problem' of the zenana was a constant source of frustration and anxiety for racial, class, legal and sexual regulation by colonial officials in imperial India.

The spread of occidental views on romance fostered new kinds of 'love marriage' in the late nineteenth and early twentieth century within royal Indian circles. At the same time, the emerging 'idea of India', which developed under the Pax Britannica, permitted novel forms of political marriage between dynasties which ordinarily did not intermarry. British officials and royals became involved in the unions of Indian princes, while courtly women simultaneously used the language of western conjugality and love to break earlier alliances and combat local male patriarchies by incorporating colonial intervention for their own ends. Contrary to the idea that Indian male elites and the paramount power predominantly agreed in their attitudes towards Indian women,[9] several of the histories in this book suggest that the colonial state and its administrators were often found supporting courtly women in resisting indigenous patriarchies, such as in the marriage disputes involving the Rani of Rajkot and the Rani of Palitana at the turn of the twentieth century in Saurashtra or during the rewriting of succession law in Bastar, Bhopal or Indore. At the same time, the paramount power did try its best to curtail the influence of Zenana women in situations where it wished to dominate. Courtly women, like Rani Kalindi of the Buddhist Chakma Raj, combated the interference of colonial administrators through diplomatic measures and armed force. At other times, Zenana women, when frustrated by the obstructions of local British political agents or Residents, actively and successfully petitioned higher levels of the imperial bureaucracy, moving from regional levels upwards to the Governors, the Viceroy, the India Office in London and sometimes even the British monarch.

In addition, contrary to the perception that Anglo-Indian law empowered indigenous Brahmanic lawyers and Victorian judges to extend their power over women,[10] Ranis, Rajkumaris and princely courtesans utilized the colonial legal courts or lawyerly advice to incriminate Indian men, including rulers, as Mumtaz Begum did in the Malabar Hill Murder trial of Maharaja Tukoji Rao of Holkar, or questioned historical legal precedent, as Begum Sultan Jahan did in upturning primogeniture as the succession practice in the state of Bhopal. Theses accounts do not portray these women as weak or unable but quite the reverse.

Women who lived in zenanas also influenced the larger cultural world outside the palace perimeters. The underworld of the princely courtesans affected the development of Hindi film music and the narratives of Bollywood and Hollywood cinema, most notably with the romantic tragedy of Tukoji Rao Holkar's mistress, Mumtaz Begum, played out on the big screen.[11] Further forays into this subtopic suggest that courtly aesthetics, music, dance and dress have influenced and continue to shape Indian popular culture.

Contrary to the perception that princely females have no place in republican India, this book argues that, while small in numbers, they have been and are major players in the contemporary public life of the subcontinent, at regional, national and international levels. After India became Independent in 1947, erstwhile princes, both male and female, became active in democratic, electoral politics. Courtly Indian women campaigned, ran for political office and made substantial contributions to party politics such as Vijaya Raje Scindia and Gayatri Devi. In some notable instances, they defied prescriptive stereotypes, which required that Hindu widows should withdraw from public life or that Zenana women were precluded access beyond the limitations of a *pardah* culture. They still upheld traditional ideas of *rajadharma, ramarayja* and Rajwada ideology even as they engaged in electoral politics, transforming themselves into leaders who now served their people as democratic representatives out in the open rather than hereditary rulers hidden from view. In certain situations, *rajvanshi* politicians have more political power today than in their previous roles as princes, especially when they represent larger constituencies as elected leaders than those of their erstwhile princely states or play a prominent role on the national or international stage. In addition, electoral politics has allowed female dynasts to engage in public displays of power, alongside those of traditional male members of the courtly family, further bringing zenana domestic politics out into the larger discourse of national life.

Finally, it can be asked, is the historical agency of Zenana women less relevant today because they are members of the royal and the elite? Has their significance lapsed with the dissolution of monarchy? These accounts suggest not. This history of the women's world within princely India is a telescope not only into the past and the present but also very possibly into the future, as women from the subcontinent gain more political recognition and higher positions in the executive, judicial and legislative arenas of government. Today, in 2008, there is the rising phenomena of dynastic political families where women are vitally engaged, whether Benazir Bhutto and her descendents in Pakistan or Hillary Rodham Clinton in the United States. These histories of the women of the zenana have left a legacy that has much to teach us about shifting political landscapes and the role of dynastic women for the twenty-first century, which remains as salient today as ever.

In larger part, it is the differing source material incorporated in this project, which has yielded such a multiplicity of voices and life histories. Letters from colonial records, official reports, political speeches, biographies, memoirs, and oral histories mine the colonial and postcolonial archives, attempting to bring to life the women who have been excluded from histories of princely India and modern South Asia. There are still many more narratives yet to emerge from the historical archive. In the late colonial period and the twentieth century, courtly women were regents, rulers, politicians, educators, entrepreneurs, patrons of art, culture and religious institutions; they were also wives, mothers, daughters and lovers of courtly men. Fusing the public and the private, these women brought local epistemologies of knowledge, sexual politics, *realpolitik* strategy, religious power and sacredness and the manipulation of Anglo-Indian law into their roles as members of the courtly household. They crossed boundaries – cultural, ethnic, religious, caste, class and racial – in these domestic yet simultaneously politicized identities. They have been located at the margins of history when in fact they were integral actors in the relationships between indigenous courts and the British as well as traditional leadership and nationalist elites.

NOTES

Introduction

1. Sir W. Barton, *The Princes of India* (New Delhi: Cosmo Publications, 1983), p. 85.
2. E. M. Forster, *The Hill of Devi* (New York: Harcourt, Brace and Company, 1953), p. 37.
3. J. Nehru, *The Discovery of India* (1946; Delhi: Oxford University Press, 1998), p. 243.
4. T. Metcalf, *Ideologies of the Raj* (Cambridge: Cambridge University Press, 1995), p. 94.
5. I. Copland, *The Princes of India in the Endgame of Empire, 1917–1947* (Cambridge: Cambridge University Press, 1997), p. 8.
6. B. Ramusack, *The Indian Princes and Their States* (Cambridge: Cambridge University Press, 2004), p. 10.
7. Copland, *The Princes of India*, p. 8.
8. Ramusack, *The Indian Princes*, p. 34.
9. See M. Rai's *Hindu Ruler, Muslim Subjects* (2004) for a history of pre-colonial and colonial Kashmir.
10. R. Jeffrey (ed.), *People, Princes and Paramount Power: Society and Politics in the Indian Princely States* (Delhi: Oxford University Press, 1978), p. 6.
11. S. R. Ashton, *British Policy towards the Indian States, 1905–1909* (London: Curzon Press, 1982), p. 7.
12. 'Reports of the committee on the relationship between the paramount power and the states' (Butler Committee), *Parliamentary Papers* (Great Britain, Reports of Commissioners, pp. 1928–9), vol. VI, Cd. 3302.
13. W. Lee-Warner, *The Native States of India* (London: Macmillan and Co, 1910), pp. 201–2.
14. Ramusack, *The Indian Princes*, p. 2.
15. Ashton, *British Policy towards the Indian States*, p. 7.
16. Ramusack, *The Indian Princes*, p. 87. She suggests that the Indian rulers are thus 'an excellent prism' to view the complex hierarchies of the British Raj in India. It was a system of indirect rule, which served as a model in other areas of the Empire, including Malaya and Africa.
17. GOI, Foreign Department, Despatch No. 43A to S/S, 30 April 1860, PCI, 1792–1874, vol. 85, in Ashton, *British Policy towards the Indian States*, p. 17.
18. Ashton, *British Policy towards the Indian States*, p. 17.
19. D. Cannadine, *Ornamentalism: How the British Saw Their Empire* (Oxford: Oxford University, 2001), p. 44.

20. B. Cohn, 'Representing Authority in Victorian India', in *An Anthropologist among the Historians and Other Essays* (Delhi: Oxford University Press, 1987), pp. 632–82, on p. 648.

21. C. A. Bayly, *Indian Society and the Making of the British Empire* (Cambridge: Cambridge University Press, 1988), p. 197.

22. L. I. Rudolph and S. H. Rudolph, *Essays on Rajputana* (New Delhi: Concept Publishing Company, 1984), p. 4.

23. K. Fitze, *Twilight of the Maharajas* (London: John Murray, 1956), p. 33.

24. Maharaja of Dhrangadhra, personal correspondence with the author, via letter, dated 16 April 2005.

25. Hansard's *Parliamentary Debates*, 3rd series, ccxxvii (1876), p. 409.

26. B. Cohn, 'Representing Authority in Victorian India', p. 653.

27. M. Rai, *Hindu Rulers, Muslim Subjects: Islam, Rights and the History of Kashmir* (Princeton: Princeton University Press, 2004), p. 89.

28. Lytton to Queen Victoria, 21 April 1876, IOLR, E218/518/1.

29. Lytton to Queen Victoria, 4 May 1876, IOLR, E218/518/1.

30. Cohn, 'Representing Authority in Victorian India', p. 660.

31. Bayly, *Indian Society*, p. 197.

32. Viceroy Lord Lytton's speech at the state banquet during the imperial assemblage, reprinted in James Talboys Wheeler, *The History of the Imperial Assemblage at Delhi* (London: Longmans, Green, Reader & Dyer, 1877), pp. 83–4.

33. Cannadine, *Ornamentalism*, p. 90.

34. Ramusack, *The Indian Princes*, p. 90.

35. Cannadine, *Ornamentalism*, pp. 12–13.

36. J. McLeod, *Sovereignty, Power, Control: Politics in the States of Western India, 1916–1947* (Leiden: Brill, 1999), p. 251.

37. M. Bhagavan, *Sovereign Spheres: Princes, Education and Empire in Colonial India* (Oxford: Oxford University Press, 2003), p. 61.

38. Rudolph and Rudolph, *Essays on Rajputana*, pp. 6–7.

39. Ramusack, *The Indian Princes*, p. 8.

40. Copland, *The Princes of India*, p. 10.

41. Ibid.

42. Note enclosed in Indore to Baroda 21 October 1916, GSAB, Baroda, Pol. Dept. 341, p. 3, cited in Copand, *Princes of India*, p. 10.

43. B. Ramusack, *The Princes of India in the Twilight of Empire: Dissolution of a Patron-Client System, 1914–1939* (Columbus, OH: University of Cincinnati Press, 1978), p. xv.

44. Rudolph and Rudolph, *Essays on Rajputana*, p. 18.

45. Copland, *The Princes of India*, p. 2.

46. V. Joshi, *Polygamy and Pardah* (Jaipur: Rawat Publications, 1995), pp. 87–8.

47. R. Lal, 'The "Domestic World" of the Mughals in the Reigns of Babur, Humayan and Akbar, c. 1500–1605' (unpublished D.Phil. dissertation, University of Oxford, 2000), p. 179.

48. Ibid., pp. 123–7.

49. N. Ziegler, 'Some Notes on Rajput Loyalties During the Mughal Period', in J. F. Richards (ed.), *Kingship and Authority in South Asia* (Madison, WI: University of Wisconsin-Madison Publication Series, 1978), pp. 215–51, on p. 235.

50. I have discussed this heterogeneous and hierarchical world of the zenana further in my thesis, 'Opening the Lotus: Reflections on the Lives of Royal Indian Women' (unpublished Senior Thesis, Harvard University, 2000).

51. L. Peirce, *The Imperial Harem* (Oxford: Oxford University Press, 1993), p. 28.

52. R. Lal, 'The "Domestic World" of Peripatetic Kings: Babur and Humayun, c. 1494–1556', *The Medieval History Journal*, 4:1 (2001), pp. 43–82, on p. 81.

53. S. Lambert-Hurley, 'Out of India: The Journeys of the Begam of Bhopal, 1901–1930', in *Women's Studies International Forum*, 21:3 (1998), p. 264.

54. S. Devi, *Autobiography of an Indian Princess: Memoirs of Maharani Sunity Devi of Cooch Behar* (New Delhi: Vikas Publishing House, 1995), p. 11.

55. Chimnabai II, Maharani of Baroda, *The Position of Women in Indian Life* (Delhi: Neeraj Publishing House, 1981).

56. V. R. Scindia, *The Last Maharani of Gwalior: An Autobiography* (Albany, NY: State University of New York, 1987), p. 16.

57. Rajmata Krishna Kumari of Jodhpur was pivotal in schooling her son when he was a minor ruler in the 1940s and 1950s.

58. S. Devi, *Autobiography of an Indian Princess*, p. 49.

59. Ibid., pp. 58–9.

60. W. Dalrymple's *White Mughals: Love and Betrayal in Eighteenth-Century India* (London: Flamingo, 2004) chronicles the story of Khair-un-Nissa, the niece of the Diwan of Hyderabad who married James Achilles Kirkpatrick, the British Resident.

61. See C. Younger, *Wicked Women of the Raj: European Women Who Broke Society's Rules and Married Indian Princes* (New Delhi: HarperCollins Publishers, 2003)

62. R. O'Hanlon, 'Gender in the British Empire', in J. Brown and W. R. Louis (eds), *The Oxford History of the British Empire, Twentieth Century* (Oxford: Oxford University Press, 1999), pp. 379–97, on p. 388.

63. To provide some examples, contemporary women politicians include: Chandresh Kumari, princess of Jodhpur, who was President of the All-India Mahila Congress and her mother, Rajmata Krishna Kumari of Jodhpur, who came out of *pardah* when she won her seat to parliament. Urvashi Devi, princess of Baria (Congress), the daughters of Vijaya Raje Scindia, the former Maharani of Dholpur Vasundhara Raje (BJP) who is the current Chief Minister of Rajasthan, and her sister Yashodara Raje, princess of Gwalior (BJP), and the former Maharani of Bharatpur (BJP) are or have been elected leaders of government.

64. Cannadine, *Ornamentalism*, pp. xv–xvi; N. Peabody, *Hindu Kingship and Polity* (Cambridge: Cambridge University Press, 2003), p. 169.

65. Cannadine, *Ornamentalism,* pp. xv– xvi.

66. E. Said, *Orientalism* (New York: Vintage Books, 1979), p. 57.

67. As N. Dirks wrote of Pudukkottai: 'Colonialism purposefully preserved many of the forms of the old regime, nowhere more conspicuously than in the indirectly ruled Princely State ... but these forms were frozen, and only the appearances of the old regime – without its vitally connected political and social processes – were saved'. N. Dirks, *The Hollow Crown: Ethnohistory of an Indian Kingdom* (Cambridge: Cambridge University Press, 1987), p. 6.

68. J. P. Waghorne argues in her religious history of the colonial state of Pudukkottai that the princely states were structured within an intricate code of 'ornamentation', regal display and pageantry in the 'performance' of the 'durbar', which necessitated a form of exchange with the paramount power. She notes that the Indian kingly tradition of ornamentation

absorbed both European styles of ceremonial as well as allowed the 'British to experience their own intense fascination with the same kind of sacredness', J. P. Waghorne, *The Raja's Magic Clothes: Re-visioning Kingship and Divinity in England's India* (University Park: The Pennsylvania State Press, 1994), p. 12.

69. See P. Price, *Kingship and Political Practice in Colonial India* (Cambridge: Cambridge University Press, 1996); McLeod, *Sovereignty, Power, Control*; Peabody, *Hindu Kingship and Polity*; Rai, *Hindu Ruler, Muslim Subjects*.

70. McLeod, *Sovereignty, Power, Control*, p. 27.

71. Bhagavan, *Sovereign Spheres*, p. 7.

72. See Copland, *The Princes of India*; Ramusack, *The Indian Princes*.

73. Cannadine, *Ornamentalism*, p. 179.

74. D. Cannadine points out an example of this distinction between race and class from Paul Scott's series of novels, the *Raj Quartet*: 'Major Ronald Merrick, whose social background was relatively low, believed that the 'English were superior to all races, especially black'. But the Cambridge-educated Guy Perron feels a greater affinity with the Indian Hari Kumar, who went to the same public school as he did, than he does with Merrick, who is very much his social inferior'. Ibid., p. 9.

75. Ibid., p. 10.

76. B. Cohn, 'Society and Social Change under the Raj', in *An Anthropologist among the Historians*, pp. 172–99, on p. 188.

77. S. Bose and A. Jalal, *Modern South Asia: History, Culture, Political Economy* (London: Routledge, 1998), p. 167. In addition, see N. Dirks's reading of caste: 'it is increasingly clear that colonialism in India produced new forms of society that have been taken to be traditional, and that caste itself as we now know it is not a residual survival of ancient India but a specifically colonial form of civil society', in N. Dirks, 'Castes of Mind', *Representations*, 37 (1992) pp. 56–80, on p. 59.

78. R. Inden, *Imagining India* (Oxford: Basil Blackwell, 1990), introduction.

79. Bayly, *Indian Society*, p. 158.

80. N. Peabody, 'Tod's "Rajasth'an" and the Boundaries of Imperial Rule in Nineteenth-Century India', *Modern Asian Studies*, 30:1 (1996), pp. 185–220, on p. 201.

81. Inden, *Imagining India*, p. 174.

82. J. Tod, *Annals and Antiquities of Rajasth'an* (New Delhi: M. N. Publishers, 1978), p. 112.

83. V. Joshi, *Polygamy and Pardah* (Jaipur: Rawat Publications, 1995), p. 32.

84. Inden, *Imagining India*, p. 175.

85. Peabody, 'Tod's "Rajasth'an"', p. 186.

86. G. Prakash expands the binary opposition at the heart of orientalism to articulate the difference between India and the Occident: 'In other words, orientalist textual and institutional practices created the spiritual and sensuous Indian as an opposite of the materialistic and rational British, and offered them as justifications for the British conquest'. G. Prakash, 'Writing Post-Orientalist Histories of the Third World: Perspectives from Indian Historiography', in *Mapping Subaltern Studies and the Postcolonial* (London: Verso, 2000), pp. 163–90, on p. 165.

87. N. Peabody suggests that Tod's work is 'inhabited by a multiplicity of 'essences' which are non-congruent, divergent, or discrepant ... which opens up the text to multiple, often strategically deployed, interpretations'. Peabody, 'Tod's "Rajasth'an"', p. 191; for a similar response, see D. Washbrook and R. O'Hanlon, 'After Orientalism: Culture, Criticism

and Politics in the Third World', in V. Chaturvedi (ed.), *Mapping the Subaltern and the Postcolonial* (London: Verso, 2000), pp. 191–219, on p. 193.

88. D. A. Washbrook, 'Orients and Occidents: Colonial Discourse Theory and the Historiography of the British Empire', in R. W. Winks (ed.), *The Oxford History of the British Empire, Historiography* (Oxford: Oxford University Press, 1999), pp. 596–611, on p. 604.

89. K. Sangari and S. Vaid (eds), *Recasting Women: Essays in Indian Colonial History* (New Brunswick, NJ: Rutgers University Press, 1990), p. 10.

90. L. Mani, 'Contentious Traditions: The Debate on *Sati* in Colonial India', in Sangari and Vaid (eds), *Recasting Women*, pp. 88–126, on p. 90.

91. Ibid., p. 115.

92. Ibid., p. 111.

93. Ibid., p. 117–18. Refer also to D. Ghosh, *Sex and the Family in Colonial India*, pp. 16–17; K. Visweswaran, 'Small Speeches, Subaltern Gender: Nationalist Ideology and its Historiography', *Subaltern Studies*, 9 (1996), pp. 83–125, on p. 89; J. Nair, 'On the Question of Agency in Indian Feminist Historiography', *Gender and History*, 6 (1994), pp. 82–100, on p. 86.

94. G. Spivak, 'Can the Subaltern Speak?', in C. Nelson and L. Grossberg (eds), *Marxism and the Interpretation of Culture* (Illinois: Illini Books, 1988), pp. 271–313, on p. 306.

95. P. Chatterjee, *The Nation and Its Fragments: Colonial and Postcolonial Histories* (Princeton, NJ: Princeton University Press, 1993), p. 120.

96. O'Hanlon, 'Gender in the British Empire', p. 386.

97. Chatterjee, 'The Nationalist Resolution of the Women's Question', in Sangari and Vaid (eds), *Recasting Women*, pp. 233–53, on p. 249.

98. D. Ghosh, 'Decoding the Nameless: Gender, Subjectivity, and Historical Methodologies in Reading the Archives of Colonial India', in K. Wilson (ed.), *A New Imperial History: Culture, Identity and Modernity in Britain and the Empire, 1660–1840* (New York: Cambridge University Press. 2004), pp. 297–316, on p. 299.

99. Chatterjee does note however that it would be limiting to perceive the woman as completely passive in the discourse, and he argues for the use of new source material, such as family histories, autobiographies, songs and pictures, which will allow women's voices to be heard ('The Nationalist Resolution', p. 250).

100. T. Sarkar, 'The Hindu Wife and the Hindu Nation: Domesticity and Nationalism in Nineteenth Century Bengal', *Studies in History*, 8:2 (1992), pp. 213–35, on p. 224.

101. Ghosh, *Sex and the Family in Colonial India*, p. 17.

102. Ibid., p. 22.

103. L. I. Rudolph and S. H. Rudolph, *The Modernity of Tradition: Political Development in India* (Chicago, IL: University of Chicago Press, 1967), p. 6.

104. S. Dube, *Stitches on Time: Colonial Textures and Postcolonial Tangles* (Durham, NC: Duke University Press, 2004), pp. 184–5.

105. Chakrabarty notes 'as happens in the relation between humans and language, I am to some extent a tool in the hands of pasts and traditions; they speak through me even before I have chosen them critically or approached them with respect'. Chakrabarty, D., *Habitations of Modernity: Essays in the Wake of Subaltern Studies* (Chicago, IL: University of Chicago Press, 2002), p. 46.

106. D. Chakrabarty, *Provincializing Europe: Postcolonial Thought and Historical Difference* (Princeton, NJ: Princeton University Press, 2000), pp. 224–8.

107. S. Joshi, *Fractured Modernity: Making of a Middle Class in Colonial North India* (New Delhi: Oxford University Press, 2001), p. 8.

108. Ibid., pp. 18, 74.

109. Ibid., p. 93.

110. Ibid., p.18.

111. B. Cohn, 'Representing Authority in Victorian India', p. 633.

112. Ibid.

113. Ramusack, *The Indian Princes*, pp. 174–9; see the construction of universities at Baroda and Mysore in Bhagavan's *Sovereign Spheres* and James Manor's analysis on representative assemblies in Mysore in *Political Change in an Indian State: Mysore 1917–1955* (New Delhi: Manohar, 1977).

114. L. Moore's *Maharanis: The Lives and Times of Three Generations of Indian Princesses* (London: Penguin Books, 2004) gives several examples of such 'anglicized' princes, and, in particular, the problem of alcoholism for certain royal families.

115. Consider the story of Maharaja Martanda Bhairava Tondaiman of Pudukkottai in N. Dirks' *Hollow Crown*, pp. 389–97. A ward of the British, he had a Cambridge-educated tutor and was taken on tours of Europe as a boy. By the time he was a young man, he was often absent from his kingdom on European visits. During one such trip, he fell in love with and married the Australian Molly Fink to the chagrin of his British advisors. Rather than accepting the prohibitions of the British, Martanda went ahead with his marriage, even though it was not clear if his mixed issue would ever be able to succeed to the *gaddi*. This particular succession dispute will be addressed in greater depth in Chapter 2.

116. See J. W. Scott's 'Women's History', in *Gender and the Politics of History* (New York: Columbia University Press, 1988).

117. A. Burton, *Dwelling in the Archive: Women Writing House, Home and History in Late Colonial India* (New York: Oxford University Press, 2003), p. 4.

118. B. Cohn, 'Anthropology and History in the 1980s: Towards a Rapprochement', in *An Anthropologist Among the Historian*, pp. 50–77, on p. 42.

119. M. Chamberlain and P. Thompson, eds. *Narrative and Genre* (London: Routledge, 1998), p. 3.

120. Ibid.

121. P. Price, *Kingship and Political Practice in Colonial India* (Cambridge: Cambridge University Press, 1996).

122. Joshi, *Polygamy and Pardah*.

123. L. Harlan, *Religion and Rajput Women: The Ethics of Protection in Contemporary Narratives* (Berkeley, CA: University of California Press, 1992)

124. R. Lal, *Domesticity and Power in the Early Mughal World* (Cambridge: Cambridge University Press, 2005); S. Lambert-Hurley, *Muslim Women, Reform and Princely Patronage: Nawab Sultan Jahan Begam of Bhopal* (London: Routledge, 2006).

125. Ghosh, *Sex and the Family in Colonial India*.

126. Ramusack, *The Indian Princes*, p. 182.

127. W. Dalrymple, *White Mughals: Love and Betrayal in Eighteenth Century India* (London: Flamingo, 2003); C. Campbell, *The Maharajah's Box: An Imperial Story of Conspiracy, Love and a Guru's Prophecy* (London: HarperCollins *Publishers*, 2000); C. Younger, *Wicked Women of the Raj: European Women Who Broke Society's Rules and Married Indian Princes* (New Delhi: HarperCollins, 2003); Moore, *Maharanis*; A. Willesee and M. Whittaker, *Love and Death in Kathmandu: A Strange Tale of Royal Murder* (London: Rider, 2003).

128. See the autobiographies of Gayatri Devi, Maharani of Jaipur, Vijayaraje Scindia, Maharani of Gwalior, Sunity Devi, Maharani of Cooch Behar, Sucharu Devi, Maharani of Mayurbhanj and Chimnabai, Maharani of Baroda as well as the oral histories of Brinda, princess of Kapurthala and Anita Delgado, Maharani of Kapurthala.

129. G. Mehta, *Raj: A Novel* (New York: Fawcett Columbine, 1989); R. Mehta, *Inside the Haveli* (New Delhi: Penguin Books, 1977).

130. R. P. Jhabvala, *Heat and Dust* (London: J. Murray, 1975); M. M. Kaye, *The Far Pavilions* (London: Allen Lane, 1978).

1 Palace Politics

1.   Major-Gen. G. Le Grand Jacob, *Western India: Before and During the Mutinies* (London: Henry S. King & Co., 1871), p. 13.

2.   A. Morrow, *Highness: The Maharajas of India* (London: Grafton Books, 1986), p. 161.

3.   A. Loomba, *Colonialism/Postcolonialism* (New York: Routledge, 2005), p. 130.

4.   R. Kabbani, *Imperial Fictions: Europe's Myths of the Orient* (London: Pandora, 1994), p. 19.

5.   Ibid.

6.   R. O'Hanlon, *A Comparison between Women and Men: Tarabai Shinde and the Critique of Gender Relations in Colonial India* (Madras: Oxford University Press, 1994), p. 50.

7.   R. Lewis, *Rethinking Orientalism: Women Travel, and the Ottoman Harem* (London: I.B. Tauris, 2004), pp. 182–3.

8.   Ibid., p. 183.

9.   J. W. Scott, *Gender and the Politics of History* (New York: Columbia University Press, 1988), pp. 49–50.

10. O'Hanlon, *A Comparison between Women and Men*, p. 49.

11. Harlan, *Religion and Rajput Women*, p. 196.

12. Ramusack, *The Indian Princes*, p. 181.

13. O'Hanlon, *A Comparison between Women and Men*, pp. 49–50.

14. Ramusack, *The Indian Princes*, pp. 49–50.

15. Joshi, *Polygamy and Pardah*, p. 19.

16. A. Jhala, 'Opening the Lotus, Reflections on the Lives of Royal India Women: A Narrative History of the Rajput Zenana' (Undergraduate Honours Thesis, Departments of Sanskrit and History, Harvard University, Cambridge, 15 August 2000), pp. 28–9.

17. Ramusack, *The Indian Princes*, pp. 49–50.

18. G. H. Ojha, *Bikaner Rajya Ka Itihas (History of Bikaner State)* (Ajmer, 1940), p. 266.

19. Peabody, *Hindu Kingship and Polity*, p. 169.

20. A. McClintock, *Imperial Leather: Race, Gender and Sexuality in the Colonial Conquest* (New York: Routledge, 1995), p. 15.

21. Bhagavan, *Sovereign Spheres*, p. 175.

22. M. Fisher, *Indirect Rule in India: Residents and the Residency System, 1764–1858* (Delhi: Oxford University Press, 1991), p.8.

23. Ibid., p.9.

24. C. Dewey, *Anglo-Indian Attitudes: The Mind of the Indian Civil Service* (London: The Hambledon Press, 1993), p.3.

25. J. Brown, 'India', in Brown and Louis (eds), *The Oxford History of the British Empire, Twentieth Century*, pp. 421–46, on p. 423.

26. Ramusack, *The Indian Princes*, pp. 48–9.

27. E. J. Thompson, *The Making of the Indian Princes* (Oxford: Oxford University Press, 1943), p. v.
28. D. Gilmour, *The Ruling Caste: Imperial Lives in the Victorian Raj* (New York: Farrar, Straus & Giroux, 2005), p. 177.
29. Ramusack, *The Indian Princes*, p. 106.
30. Ibid.
31. Gilmour, *The Ruling Caste*, pp. 17–18.
32. Copland, *The Princes of India*, p. 16.
33. Gilmour, *The Ruling Caste*, p. 19.
34. D. B. Srivastava, 'Constitutional Significance of the Treaty Relations between the Indian States and the Paramount Powers', in R. P. Vyas (ed.), *British Policy towards Princely States of India* (Jodhpur: Rajasthan-Vidya Prakashan, 1991), pp. 1–5, on p. 4.
35. Ramusack, *The Indian Princes*, p. 92.
36. Ibid., p. 90.
37. Cohn, 'Representing Authority in Victorian India', pp. 656–61.
38. D. Cannadine, *Aspects of Aristocracy* (New Haven, CT: Yale University Press, 1994), pp. 78–9.
39. Ibid., p. 79.
40. Ibid., p. 83.
41. Ibid., p. 85.
42. Ibid.
43. Ibid., p. 88.
44. Ibid., p. 110.
45. Cannadine, *Ornamentalism*, p. 89.
46. These aristocratic Viceroys included Viscount Canning, Lord Elgin, Sir John Lawrence, Lord Mayo, Lord Northbrook, Lord Lytton, Lord Ripon, Lord Dufferin, Lord Lansdowne, Lord Elgin, Lord Curzon, Lord Minto, Lord Hardinge, Lord Chelmsford, Lord Reading, Lord Irwin, Lord Wilingdon, Lord Linlithgow, Lord Wavell and Lord Mountbatten. David Cannadine, *The Decline and the Fall of the British Aristocracy* (New Haven, CT: Yale University Press, 1990), p. 723.
47. Fisher, *Indirect Rule in India*, p. 32.
48. *Queen Victoria's Proclamation*, 1 November 1858, in Harlow and Carter, *Imperialism and Orientalism*, p. 210.
49. Gilmour, *The Ruling Caste*, pp. 1–5.
50. For example, Queen Victoria served as godmother to the son of Maharaja Nripendra of Cooch Behar in 1888, being a close friend of his wife, Maharani Sunity Devi. Their son, Victor, was named in honour of the Empress. Moore, *Maharanis*, pp. 106–7.
51. Gilmour, *The Ruling Caste,* p. 4.
52. Ramusack, *The Indian Princes*, pp. 130–31; Copland, *The Princes of India*, p. 33.
53. Copland, *The Princes of India*, p. 21.
54. Ibid., p. 24.
55. Ibid., p. 22.
56. Ibid., p. 24; *The Times of India*, 19 November 1929.
57. Gilmour, *The Ruling Caste*, p. 178.
58. Ibid., p. 179.
59. Ibid.
60. L. P. Mathur and L. Sukhwal, 'British Interference in the Internal Sovereignty of Princely States (1858–1885)', in Vyas (ed.), *British Policy towards Princely States of India*, pp. 23–40, on p. 28.

61. Ibid., p. 31.
62. Ibid., p. 33.
63. Vyas (ed.), *British Policy towards Princely States of India*, p. xii.
64. W. Lee-Warner, 'The Native States of India', *British Empire Series, Volume 1: India, Ceylon, Straits Settlements, British Northern Borneo, Hong-Kong* (London: Kegan Paul, Trench, Trubner & Co, 1899), pp. 270–94, on p. 271.
65. McLeod, *Sovereignty, Power, Control*, p. 55.
66. Ibid.
67. V. R. Scindia, *The Last Maharani of Gwalior*, p. 144.
68. Copland, *The Princes of India*, p. 35.
69. Ibid., p. 41.
70. Ramusack, *The Indian Princes*, p. 98.
71. Ibid., pp. 97–8.
72. C. Disman, 'The Princely States before Independence: The Indian Princes as Political Successors to the British Raj', Honors Thesis, San Francisco State University, 2004. http://userwww.sfsu.edu/~cdisman//Honors%20thesis,%20'The%20Princely%20States%20before%20Independence'.htm
73. J. Manor, 'The Demise of the Princely Order', in Jeffrey (ed.), *People, Princes and Paramount Power*, pp. 306–28, on pp. 306–23.
74. S. M. Burke and S. Al-Din Quraishi, *The British Raj in India: An Historical Review* (Karachi: Oxford University Press, 1995), p. 282–4; D. A. Low, 'Laissez-Faire and Traditional Rulership in Princely India', in Jeffrey (ed.), *People, Princes and Paramount Power*, pp. 372–87, on p. 373; R. J. Moore, *The Crisis of Indian Unity 1917–1940* (Oxford: Oxford University Press, 1974) ch. 3.
75. Copland, *The Princes of India*, p. 10.
76. Ramusack, *The Princes of India in the Twilight of Empire*, p. 186.
77. I. Copland, 'The Other Guardians: Ideology and Performance in the Indian Political Service', in Jeffrey (ed.), *People, Princes and Paramount Power*, pp. 275–305, on p. 296.
78. McLeod, *Sovereignty, Power, Control*, p. 56.
79. Ibid.
80. Burke and Quraishi, *The British Raj in India*, pp. 283–4.
81. Ibid., p. 574.
82. McLeod, *Sovereignty, Power, Control*, p. 57.
83. Ibid., p. 58.
84. Ibid., pp. 58 9.
85. Ibid., p. 60.
86. V. B. Kulkarni, *Princely India and the Lapse of British Paramountcy* (Bombay: Jaico Publishing, 1985), p. 85.
87. Fisher, *Indirect Rule in India*, p. 456.
88. Brown, 'India', p. 423.
89. Kulkarni, *Princely India*, p. 85.
90. Sir C. Corfield, *The Princely India I Knew: From Reading to Mountbatten* (Madras, 1975), p. 17.
91. Fitze, *Twilight of the Maharajas*, p. 33.
92. S. A. Pataudi, *The Elite Minority: The Princes of India* (Lahore: Syed Mobin Mahmud & Co., 1989), p. 57.
93. Ibid., p. 59.
94. Ibid., p. 56.

95. Kulkarni, *Princely India*, p. 86.
96. Ibid., pp. 85–6.
97. Ibid., p. 86.
98. Pataudi, *The Elite Minority*, p. 60.
99. Dewey, *Anglo-Indian Attitudes*, p. 5.
100. Ibid.
101. T. C. Coen, *The Indian Political Service: A Study in Indirect Rule* (London: Chatto, Windus, 1971), p. 35.
102. Pataudi, *The Elite Minority*, pp. 61–2.
103. P. Mason, *The Men Who Ruled India* (London: Jonathan Cape, 1985), p. 208.
104. Gilmour, *The Ruling Caste*, p. 64.
105. Ibid., p. 52.
106. Ibid. In 1894, the Viceroy and the Governors of Madras and Bombay were not only all Eton graduates but had also been students under the same housemaster, Mr Warre. Wenlock to Elgin, 6 June 1894, Elgin Papers.
107. Ibid., pp. 181–2.
108. Fitze, *Twilight of the Maharajas*, p. 6.
109. Ibid., p. 7.
110. Ibid., pp. 7–8.
111. Ibid., p. 10.
112. Pataudi, *The Elite Minority*, p. 60.
113. Fisher, *Indirect Rule in India*, p. 456.
114. Dewey, *Anglo-Indian Attitudes*, pp. 13–14.
115. Ibid., pp. 148–50.
116. Ibid., p. 178.
117. Pataudi, *The Elite Minority*, p. 61.
118. Gilmour, *The Ruling Caste*, p. 51.
119. Quoted in L. S. S. O'Malley, *The Indian Civil Service: 1601–1933* (London: Frank Cass, 1965), p. 160.
120. Pataudi, *The Elite Minority*, pp. 60–1.
121. Gilmour, *The Ruling Caste*, p. 51.
122. Ibid., p. 182.
123. Pataudi, *The Elite Minority*, p. 58.
124. Morrow, *Highness: The Maharajas of India*, p. 166.
125. Gilmour, *The Ruling Caste*, p. 184.
126. Coen, *The Indian Political Service*, p. 32.
127. Bhagavan, *Sovereign Spheres*, p. 176.
128. Ramusack, *The Indian Princes*, p. 105.
129. Joshi, *Polygamy and Pardah*, ch. 3.
130. Fitze, *Twilight of the Maharajas*, p. 28.
131. W. Sleeman, *Rambles and Recollections of an Indian Official* (London: 1893), vol. 1, p. 310.
132. There are, however, some significant exceptions to this rule, such as the matrilineal Hindu kingdoms of Travancore and Cochin in South India as well as the Muslim state of Bhopal.
133. Foreign and Political, A Proceedings, March 1882, nos. 396–429.
134. Ramusack, *The Indian Princes*, p. 108.

135. Ibid.
136. Joshi, *Polygamy and Pardah*, p. 87.
137. Fisher, *Indirect Rule in India*, pp. 280–95.
138. Ibid., p. 130.
139. V. C. Prinsep, *Glimpses of Imperial India* (Delhi: Mittal Publications, 1878), pp. 78–9.
140. Joshi, *Polygamy and Pardah*, p. 24.
141. G. Devi, *A Princess Remembers* (Calcutta: Rupa & Co., 1995).pp. 167–70.
142. Joshi, *Polygamy and Pardah*, pp. 114–15.
143. K. M. Ashraf, *Life and Conditions of the People of Hindustan* (New Delhi: 1970), p. 55.
144. Reet Bahi, Rani Pado, Raniji Shri Sohagdeoji, p. 66.
145. Ibid.
146. Raja Patta Abhishek, letters 21B, 22B, Mewar Oriental Research Institute, Udaipur; Joshi, *Polygamy and Pardah*, p. 87.
147. Joshi, *Polygamy and Pardah*, pp. 115, 158–9.
148. Ibid., p. 159.
149. Ibid., p. 123.
150. L. K. Chundavat (ed.), *Rajwari Lokgeet (Folk Songs of the Royal Houses)* (Jaipur: Sheetal Printers, 1985), p. 87.
151. L. K. Chundavat, *Gir Uncha Garh Unch Ghana* (Jaipur: Sheetal Printers, 1966), pp. 157–9; Joshi, *Polygamy and Pardah*, p. 125.
152. R. T. Roy, *The Departed Melody* (Islamabad: PPA Publications, 2003), p. 39.
153. Ibid.
154. Ibid., p. 41.
155. Ibid.
156. Ibid.
157. Ibid., p. 43.
158. Le Grand Jacob, *Western India*, p. 18.
159. R. Stern, *Cat and the Lion: Jaipur State in the British Raj*, Leiden: Brill, 1988, p. 7.
160. Ramusack, *The Indian Princes*, p. 108.
161. Lee-Warner, *The Native States of India*, p. 328.
162. *Parliamentary Papers*, vol. 41, 1850, p. 514.
163. *Parliamentary Papers*, vol. 41, 1850, p. 448.
164. Moore, *Maharanis*, pp. 30–1.
165. P.C (A) July 1875, No. 379, Para 9, in A. Neogy, *The Paramount Power and the Princely States of India, 1858–1881* (Calcutta: K.P. Bagchi, 1979), p. 51.
166. Moore, *Maharanis*, p. 35.
167. Le Grand Jacob, *Western India*, p. 22.
168. Ibid., p. 23.
169. Ibid.
170. Ibid., p. 27.
171. Ibid., p. 30.
172. Ibid., pp. 30–1.
173. Ibid., p. 36.
174. Fitze, *Twilight of the Maharajas*, p. 35.
175. Le Grand Jacob, *Western India*, p. 44.
176. Ibid., p. 45.
177. Ibid.
178. Ibid., pp. 45–6.

179. Ibid., p. 47.
180. Ibid., p. 49.
181. Ibid., p. 50.
182. Ibid., pp. 56–7.
183. Fitze, *Twilight of the Maharajas*, p. 123.
184. Forster, *Hill of Devi*, p.37.
185. Ibid., p. 61.
186. Ibid., p. 97.
187. Ibid., p. 64.
188. Fitze, *Twilight of the Maharajas*, p. 124.
189. Ibid., pp. 124–5.
190. Ibid., p. 125.

2 Reading the Role of Women in Succession Disputes

1.   Fitze, *Twilight of the Maharajas*, p. 6.
2.   *Hansard's Parliamentary Debates, Third Series, Volume CCXXVII* (London: Cornelius Buck, 1876), p. 409.
3.   K. Fitze, 'A Review of Modern Practice in Regard to Successions in Indian States', in R/2/(136/45), Box 136, p. 19, Crown Representative's Residency Reports, India Office Library, London.
4.   Ibid., pp. 2–3.
5.   Maharaja of Dhrangadhra, letter to the author, via email, 26 March 2005.
6.   Fitze, *A Review of Modern Practice*, p. 3.
7.   Ibid.
8.   Ibid.
9.   Ibid., p. 4.
10. J. Dunn, *Elizabeth and Mary: Cousins, Rivals, Queens*. New York: Alfred Knopf, 2003.
11. R. O'Hanlon, 'Gender in the British Empire', pp. 383–4.
12. Ibid., p. 383.
13. Dirks, *Hollow Crown*, pp. 389–90.
14. K. R. Venkatarama Ayyar, *A manual of the Pudukkottai state, vol. 2, part 1* (Pudukkottai: Sri Brihadamba State Press, 1940), p. 873.
15. Dirks, *Hollow Crown*, p. 391.
16. Ibid.
17. K. Nagarajan Papers. Volume II, 1900–1957. South Asian Institute Library, University of Cambridge, p. 80.
18. Ibid.
19. Dirks, *Hollow Crown*, p. 391.
20. Younger, *Wicked Women of the Raj*, p. 117.
21. Ibid., pp. 115–19.
22. Fitze, *A Review of Modern Practice*, p. 4.
23. Younger, *Wicked Women of the Raj*, p. 120.
24. Ibid., p. 119.
25. Ibid., p. 120.
26. K. Nagarajan Papers, vol. II, pp. 181–2.
27. Younger, *Wicked Women of the Raj*, p. 123.
28. Dirks, *Hollow Crown*, p. 392.

29. Nagarajan papers, vol. II, p. 181.
30. Younger, *Wicked Women of the Raj*, p. 127.
31. Dirks, *Hollow Crown*, p. 396.
32. Fitze, *Review of Modern Practice,* p. 4.
33. Younger, *Wicked Women of the Raj*, p. 123.
34. Fitze, *Review of Modern Practice,* p. 5.
35. Ibid.
36. Ibid.
37. Curzon to Lord Hamilton, 1 October 1900, MSS EUR 111/159 as quoted in R. Visram, *Ayahs, Lascars and Princes: Indians in Britain 1700–1947* (London, 1986), p. 176.
38. P. Chowdhry, *Colonial India and the Making of Empire Cinema: Image, Ideology and Identity* (Manchester: Manchester University Press, 2000), pp. 205–10.
39. Ramusack, *The Indian Princes*, p. 135.
40. Fitze, *Review of Modern Practice*, p. 5.
41. Younger, *Wicked Women of the Raj*, pp. 131–4.
42. Fitze, *A Review of Modern Practice*, p. 5.
43. N. Sundar, *Subalterns and Sovereigns: An Anthropological History of Bastar, 1854–1996* (Delhi: Oxford University Press, 1997), p. 192.
44. E. Hyde, *Autobiographical Memoir: 'India, First Person Singular',* Edgar Hyde Papers, South Asian Institute Library, University of Cambridge.
45. Ibid.
46. For. & Pol. F. no.305-P, 1924–7, NAI cited in Sundar, *Subalterns and Sovereigns*, p. 192.
47. Hyde, *Autobiographical Memoir: 'India, First Person Singular'.*
48. Ibid.
49. F. no 84-P(S)/1936, Acc. No. 353, Reel 2, CRR, ESA, Confidential Notes on Diary and letters by Pol. Sec. GOI; Burton to H.A.F. Metcalfe, F & P, GOI, 25 June 1931, NAI, cited in Sundar, *Subalterns and Sovereigns*, p. 192.
50. F. no. 617-P, 1934, For. & Pol. Dept., Acc. 357, CRR, ESA, Article in *The New Statesman and Nation, The Weekend Review*, 1 September 1934, cited in Sundar, *Subalterns and Sovereigns*, p. 193.
51. F. no 84-P(S), Confidential Note by Pol. Sec., B. Glancy on meeting with Prafulla, 20 November 1936, cited in Sundar *Subalterns and Sovereigns*, p. 193.
52. Hyde, *Autobiographical Memoir: 'India, First Person Singular.*
53. F. no. 23 (3) – P/40-(Sec) of 1940, Pol. Dept. Pol. Branch, Col. Barton, Res., ESA, to C.G. Herbert, Pol. Advisor to Crown Representative, 27 November 1940, NAI, cited in Sundar, *Subalterns and Sovereigns,* p. 193.
54. Sundar, *Subalterns and Sovereigns,* p. 193.
55. S. M. Khan, *The Begums of Bhopal: A Dynasty of Women: Rulers in Raj India* (London: I.B. Tauris Publishers, 2000), pp. vii–x.
56. C. Peckel, *Begums of Bhopal* (New Delhi: Roli Books, 2000), p. 10.
57. Ibid., quote on the back flap of the book.
58. Khan, *The Begums of Bhopal*, p. 155.
59. Ibid., p. 156.
60. Ibid., p. 158.
61. Ibid., p. 169.
62. Ibid., pp. 168–71.
63. Ibid., p. 180.

64. Ibid., p. 189.
65. Ibid.
66. Fitze, A Review of Modern Practice, p. 9.
67. Ibid.
68. Khan, *The Begums of Bhopal*, p. 192.
69. Ibid., p. 199.
70. Ibid., pp. 200–1.
71. Ibid., p. 202.
72. Fitze, *A Review of Modern Practice*, p. 11.
73. Khan, *The Begums of Bhopal*, p. 205.
74. O'Hanlon, 'Gender in the British Empire', p. 384.
75. K. Mittal, *History of Bhopal State: Development of Constitution, Administration and National Awakening, 1901–1949* (Delhi: Munshiram Manoharlal Publishers Pvt. Ltd., 1990), p. 91.
76. Fitze, *Review of Modern Practice*, p. 11.
77. Ibid.
78. Ibid., p. 18.
79. Ibid., p. 19.

3 A Discourse on Desire

1. S. Devi, *Autobiography of an Indian Princess*, pp. 54–5.
2. Shruti Kapila provides a fascinating exposition on the colonial regulation of Indian princely sexuality in her article, 'Masculinity and Madness', including the British arrangement of political marriages for courtly men and women. S. Kapila, 'Masculinity and Madness: Princely Personhood and Colonial Sciences of the Mind in Western India, 1871–1940', *Past and Present*, 187 (May 2005), pp. 121–56.
3. The British advisors of M. Shivaji IV of Kolhapur arranged his state marriage to a minor Khirke royal in 1878 in 'an untypical fashion that adhered more to the demands of British political authority than the pomp usually associated', in part due to their fears that he had an 'irregular' taste for the company of other men and also because of pressure from the royal household, who would not agree to his education in an Indian public school, Rajkumar College, unless he was first married. Kapila, 'Masculinity and Madness', p. 127.
4. Moore, *Maharanis*, pp. 55–8.
5. D. Ali, 'Courtly love and the Aristocratic Household in Early Medieval India', in F. Orsini (ed.), *Love in South Asia* (Cambridge: Cambridge University Press, 2006), pp. 43–60, on p. 44; D. Ali, *Courtly Culture and Political Life in Early Medieval India* (Cambridge: Cambridge University Press, 2004), p. 43.
6. Chatterjee, *The Nation and its Fragments*, p. 120.
7. Ibid., pp. 51–2.
8. The *sa-gotra* marriage of Diya Kumari, princess of Jaipur, in 1997, led to friction between the Rajput nobility in Rajasthan and the Kacchava royal family. In marrying a member of her same clan (*kul*), the princess was accused of violating Rajput precepts for appropriate marriage; a practice close to incest. P. Kaushal, 'Rajput Snap Ties with Royals', *Indian Express*, 12 August 1997; 'Royal vignettes: Jaipur: In touch with reality'. *The Hindu*, 20 October 2002; S. Bose, 'Jaipur Maharaja to adopt grandson', *The Hindustan Times*, 22 November 2002; K. Bora, 'Jaipur's royal family has an heir', Rediff.com, 23 November

2002. In addition, note the familial opposition to the secret engagement between Prince Dipendra of Nepal and Devayani Rana, a Nepalese aristocratic and granddaughter of the Maharaja of Gwalior, which resulted in the young scion killing several of his relatives, including his parents, in June 2001. See A. Willesee and M. Whittaker, *Love and Death in Kathmandu.*

9. Frances Taft Plunkett and Barbara Ramusack, while they have been valiant in attempting to address the issue of political marriages among Zenana women in colonial North India, are themselves aware of the need for greater discussion. Jayasinhji Jhala has written on Rajput marriages and ideology among aristocratic and royal dynasties but not more broadly on marriage patterns across princely India. See F. T. Plunkett, 'Royal Marriages in Rajasthan', *Contributions to Indian Sociology*, n.s. 7(1973), pp. 64–80; B. Ramusack, 'Princes as Men, Women, Rulers, Patrons and Oriental Stereotypes', in *The Indian Princes*; J. Jhala, 'Marriage, Hierarchy and Identity in Ideology and Practice: An Anthropological Study of Jhala Rajput Society in Western India, against a historical background, 1090–1990 AD' (PhD dissertation, Harvard University, Anthropology Department, 1991).

10. J. E. Howard and P. Rackin, *Engendering a Nation: A Feminist Account of Shakespeare's English Histories* (London: Routledge, 1997), p. 5.

11. Plunkett, 'Royal Marriages in Rajasthan', p. 66.

12. Ibid., p. 71.

13. Joshi, *Polygamy and Pardah*, p. 41.

14. Peirce, *The Imperial Harem*, p. 28.

15. Ibid.

16. B. Kumari, interview with the author, Suraj Mahal Palace, Dhrangadhra, 12 August 2002.

17. Letter to Umrao Singh (Nimrana) to Agent for the Governor General, 10 December 1932, Crown Representative Records, RZ/A91, India Office Library.

18. Plunkett, 'Royal Marriages in Rajasthan', p. 66.

19. L. Dumont, *Homo Hierarchicus: The Caste and Its Implications* (Chicago: University of Chicago Press, 1966), pp. 117–18.

20. G. Buhler (trans.), *The Laws of Manu* (Oxford: Clarendon Press, 1886), introduction.

21. Joshi, *Polygamy and Pardah*, p. 23.

22. Plunkett, 'Royal Marriages in Rajasthan', p. 67.

23. C. Hurtig, *Les Maharajahs et la politique dans L'Inde contemporaine* (Paris: Presses de la Fondation nationale des sciences politiques, 1988), pp. 284–5.

24. J. McLeod, 'Towards the Analysis of Hindu Princely Genealogy in the British Period, 1850–1950', *South Asia Research*, 6:2 (November 1986), pp. 181–93.

25. Mehta, *Raj*, p. 261.

26. E. M. Collingham, *Imperial Bodies: The Physical Experience of the Raj, c. 1800–1947* (Cambridge: Polity Press, 2001), p. 50.

27. J. Jhala, 'Marriage, Hierarchy and Identity in Ideology and Practice: An Anthropological Study of Jhala Rajput society in western India, against a historical background, 1090–1990. A.D', Ph.D. Dissertation, Harvard University, Anthropology Department, 1991, ch. 7, pp. 70–1.

28. Ali, *Courtly Culture and Political Life*, p. 144.

29. In *Meghaduta*, the poet describes the 'darkening evening light on a hill' as 'like a breast'. S. Kaviraj, 'Tagore and Transformations in the Ideals of Love', in Orsini (ed.), *Love in South Asia*, pp. 161–82, on pp. 165–6.

30. Ali, *Courtly Culture and Political Life*, p. 215.

31. Ibid.
32. A. Krishna, 'Beauty in the Human Form in Sixteenth Century Hindi Poetry and the Evolution of *Ek Chashma Chehra* in Rajasthani Painting', in H. Dehejia and M. Paranjape (eds), *Saundarya: The Perception and Practice of Beauty in India* (New Delhi: Samvad India Foundation, 2003), pp. 73–80, on pp. 73–4.
33. Ibid., p. 74.
34. Lal, *Domesticity and Power*, p. 62.
35. M. Alam and S. Subrahmanyam, 'Love, Passion and Reason in Faizi's *Nal-Daman*', in Orsini (ed.), *Love in South Asia*, pp. 109–41, on p. 121.
36. G. W. Bernard, *The King's Reformation: Henry VIII and the Remaking of the English Church* (New Haven, CT: Yale University Press, 2005), p. 547.
37. Ghosh, *Sex and the Family in Colonial India*, p. 62.
38. In G. Mehta's novel *Raj*, a newly married Rajasthani princess conforms to the westernized tastes of her Europeanized royal husband by bobbing her hair, tweezing and sculpting her eyebrows and removing facial hair. G. Mehta, *Raj,* pp. 196–204.
39. C. Allen and S. Dwivedi, *Lives of the Indian Princes* (New York: Crown Publishers, 1984), p. 34; B. Kumari, interview with the author, 27 July 1999; Sita Devi, interview with the author, 27 June 1999.
40. Morrow, *Highness*, p. 45.
41. B. Kumari, interview with the author, Suraj Mahal Palace, Dhrangadhra, 3 August 2002.
42. B. Kumari, 'Time Table', *Exercise Notebooks*, Umed Palace School, Jodhpur, India, 1942.
43. K. Kumari, interview with the author, Umaid Bhavan Palace, Jodhpur, 2 July 1999.
44. Maharaja of Dhrangadhra, Commentary on Michael Goater's Jack Meyer of Millfield, 1993, 'An Indian Travesty: Dhrangadhra Rajshala Revisted', p. 20.
45. S. Devi, interview with author, St Helen's Cottage, Mussoorie, India, 27 June 1999.
46. Ibid., interview with the author, St Helen's Cottage, Mussoorie, India, 24 June 1999.
47. B. Kumari, interview with the author, Suraj Mahal Palace, Gujarat, India, 17–19 July 1999.
48. Morrow, *Highness: The Maharajas of India*, p. 48.
49. Krishna Kumari, interview with the author, Umaid Bhavan Palace, Jodhpur, 2 July 1999.
50. Brijraj Kumari, interview with the author, Suraj Mahal Palace, Dhrangadhra, 17–19 July 1999.
51. Jhala, 'Opening the Lotus', p. 70.
52. K. Kumari, interview with the author, Umaid Bhavan Palace, Jodhpur, 2 July 1999. K. Kumari's husband did later maintain two mistresses who became his wives in the palace zenana: Sandra McBryde, an English nurse, and Zubeida, a Muslim nautch girl.
53. Ali, *Courtly Culture and Political Life*, pp. 75 –7.
54. Ibid., pp. 223–4.
55. I. Grewal, *Home and Harem: Nation, Gender, Empire and the Cultures of Travel* (Durham: Duke University Press, 1996), p. 45.
56. Many high ranked British politicals kept Indian mistresses and domestic households such as David Octerlony, Resident to Delhi in the early nineteenth century who apparently had thirteen wives, or Colonel James Skinner who was alleged to have had fourteen wives and eighty children. See R. Hyam, 'The Sexual Life of the Raj', in R. Hyam (ed.), *Empire and Sexuality* (Manchester: Manchester University Press, 1992), pp. 115–36, on pp. 115–18.

57. See D. Ghosh's *Sex and the Family in Colonial India* for a detailed historical study of cohabitation between Indian men and British women in the early years of the British Empire.

58. Hyam, 'The Sexual Life of the Raj', p. 118.

59. Ibid., p.119.

60. D. Ghosh argues in *Sex and the Family in Colonial India* that native or indigenous women were key members of the eighteenth-century contact zone between Britons and Indians, particularly as romantic partners for the *nabob* while in India. During the early phase of colonial rule in the eighteenth century, Englishmen went native by learning local languages, local dress, maintaining a household with Indian women and having children from them. She suggests that while these female members of Anglo-Indian households remained 'marginal' to colonial society, their marginality was a key site from which colonial authority was articulated and consolidated.

61. Margaret MacMillan, *Women of the Raj* (Thames and Hudson, 1988), p. 12.

62. Ibid., pp. 107–8.

63. Ibid., pp. 108–9.

64. Ibid., pp. 12–13.

65. Ibid., p. 61.

66. Scindia, *The Last Maharani of Gwalior*, p. 18.

67. Ibid., p. 36.

68. Ibid., pp. 48–9.

69. Ibid., pp. 50–7.

70. Ibid., p. 131.

71. Ibid., p. 120.

72. Ibid., p. 65.

73. Chapter 6 will elaborate upon V. R. Scindia's career as an elected politician.

74. S. Devi, interview by author, video recording, Mussoorie, St Helen's Cottage, Mussoorie, 24 June 1999.

75. Maharaja of Dhrangadhra, personal communication with the author, via email, 9 February 2003.

76. S. Devi, interview by author, video recording, Mussoorie, St Helen's Cottage, Mussoorie, 24 June 1999.

77. H.C. Batra, *The Relations of Jaipur State with East India Company* (Delhi: S. Chand & Co., 1958), pp. 174–5.

78. Roy, *The Departed Melody*, pp. 84–6.

79. Ibid., pp. 86–7.

80. C. Campbell, *The Maharajah's Box: An Imperial Story of Conspiracy, Love and a Guru's prophecy* (London: HarperCollins Publishers, 2001), p. 47.

81. Phipps to Login, 5 September 1854, in E. D. Login, *Lady Login's Recollections: Court and Camp Life 1820–1904* (London: Smith, Elder, 1916).

82. Ibid.

83. M. Alexander and S. Anand, *Queen Victoria's Maharajah: Duleep Singh, 1838–93* (London: Weidenfeld and Nicolson, 1980), p. 64.

84. Ibid., p. 77.

85. Ibid., p. 81.

86. Moore, *Maharanis*, p. 57.

87. Ibid., p. 44.

88. Gilmour, *The Ruling Caste*, pp. 4–5.
89. Moore, *Maharanis*, p. 103.
90. Ibid., p. 104.
91. Ibid., p. 105.
92. Ibid., pp. 106–7.
93. Ibid., p. 108. Later, this would be a cause for criticism by the Baroda family when their daughter married into Cooch Behar.
94. Ibid., p. 79.
95. Ibid., p. 80.
96. Gilmour, *The Ruling Caste*, p. 4.
97. S. Anand, *Indian Sahib: Queen Victoria's Dear Abdul* (London: Duckworth, 1996), pp. 14–15.
98. Ibid., pp. 82–3.
99. In December 1893, Queen Victoria wrote to the Munshi on the advice of her doctor that his wife might have hurt 'something inside' by twisting her leg: 'If this is so, it can only be found out by her being examined (felt) by the hand of this Lady Doctor. Many, many 1000 ladies have to go through this with a Doctor, which is very disagreeable – but with a Lady Dr there can be no objection, and without that you can not find out what is the matter'. Ibid. p. 45; RA Add. U104/10.
100. Ibid., p. 77; IOR Eur. F84/126a, 27 April 1897, Fritz Posonby to H. Babbington-Smith.
101. Alexander and Anand, *Queen Victoria's Maharajah*, p. 301. It is important to note that Queen Victoria had not encouraged miscegenation a generation earlier when Maharaja Duleep Singh showed interest in a high ranked Englishwoman.
102. Even though Maharaja Sayajirao Baroda is well remembered for his resistance to the British, his sons fell victim to many of the many vices of western excess. A number died of alcohol-related complications before the age of thirty-five as did the sons of Maharani Sunity Devi of Cooch Behar, and it is surmised that the boys' schooling in Britain and America may have strongly contributed to this trend. For more on this topic, see Moore's *Maharanis*.
103. D. Chakrabarty, 'The Difference-Deferral of a Colonial Modernity: Public Debates on Domesticity in British Bengal', in D. Arnold and D. Hardiman (eds), *Subaltern Studies VIII* (Oxford: Oxford University Press, 1994), pp. 50–88, on p. 51.
104. Moore, *Maharanis*, p. 15.
105. Ibid., pp. 9–23.
106. B. Ramusack, 'Fairy Tales, Soap Operas, or Expressions of Individuality: Autobiographies of Indian Princesses' (unpublished paper), p. 9.
107. Devi, *A Princess Remembers*, p. 28.
108. Moore, *Maharanis*, p. 11.
109. Devi, *A Princess Remembers*, p. 142.
110. Ibid., p. 102.
111. D. Kanwar, *Rajmata Gayatri Devi … Enduring Grace* (Delhi: Lustre Press/Roli Books, 2004), p. 41.
112. Jhala, *Marriage, Hierarchy and Identity*, p. 71.
113. Maharaja of Dhrangadhra, letter to the author, via email, dated 17 April 2005.
114. Kanwar, *Enduring Grace*, p. 41.

115. Moore, *Maharanis*, p. 205.
116. K. Ballhatchet, *Race, Sex and Class under the Raj: Imperial Attitudes and Policies and Their Critics, 1793–1905* (London: Weidenfeld and Nicolson, 1980), pp. 116–17.
117. Brinda, Maharani of Kapurthala, *Maharani: The Story of an Indian Princess*, as told to Elaine Williams (New York, 1953), pp. 112–13.
118. Corfield, *The Princely India I Knew*, p. 17.
119. Copland, *Princes of India*, pp. 193–4.
120. Style and Status of Foreign wives married by Indian princes (two American wives married to Holkar) Style of Sita Devi wife of the Maharaja of Baroda, 1940, in R/2 (163/227), India Office Library, London.
121. The following are two examples of these marriages from the eighteenth century. In the late 1790s, W. L. Gardner, who served in the Nizam of Hyderabad's army, married Begum Mah Munzel ul-Nissa, daughter of the Nawab of Cambay, and converted to Islam for the purpose of the wedding. He first saw his future wife during the interminable functions requisite for signing a treaty, from behind a curtain, and was instantly smitten. Dalrymple, *White Mughals*, p. 120. In 1800, the British Resident Lieutenant Colonel James Achilles Kirkpatrick married Khair un-Nissa, the grand-niece of the diwan of Hyderabad. Fulfilling ambassadorial duties at the Hyderabadi court from 1797 to 1805, Kirkpatrick allegedly had 'turned native', taking on local forms of dress, toilette and customs. They were wed according to Muslim law, although their marriage was not approved by the British Indian government and created a furor at the time. Dalrymple, pp. 188–90; Ghosh, *Sex and the Family in Colonial India*, pp. 69–109.
122. Alexander and Anand, *Queen Victoria's Maharajah*, p. 85.
123. Moore, *Maharanis*, pp. 164–5.
124. Rajkumari Moitri Hume, interview with the author, private residence, Cambridge, Massachusetts, 5 August 2005.
125. Jhala, ' Marriage, Hierarchy and Identity in Ideology and Practice', Ch. 7, pp. 17–19; N. Dirks, 'The Invention of Caste: Civil Society in Colonial India', in 'Identity, Consciousness and the Past: The South Asian Scene', ed. H. L. Seneviratne, Special Issue series of *Social Analysis: Journal of Culture and Social Practice*, 25 (1989), pp. 42–52, on p. 42.
126. Ibid., ch. 7, p. 22.
127. Ibid., ch. 7, p. 26.
128. Scindia, *The Last Maharani of Gwalior*, p. 254.
129. It is useful to note as well that there has been much less of a taboo against divorce or separation in Indian royal families since the 1970s.
130. Sixteenth-century English property-owning classes wed according to the precepts of family and kin connections. In marriage, 'past lineage associations, political patronage, extension of lineage connections, and property preservation and accumulation were the principal considerations'. L. Stone, *The Family, Sex and Marriage: In England 1500–1800* (New York: Harper & Row Publishers, 1977), p. 87. This was best achieved 'by vigorous, even combative, self assertion, military glory in the field, a scrupulous maintenance of good faith, backed by good lineage origins and good marriage connections'. Ibid., p. 90.
131. Some British aristocrats achieved this by allying with the daughters of businessmen from the City (L. Stone, *The Crisis of the Aristocracy, 1558–1641* (Oxford: Oxford University Press, 1967), pp. 282–8). From the mid-sixteenth century to the mid-seventeenth cen-

tury, noble families sought out heiresses, who brought in generous inheritances, vital to support diminishing estates (ibid., p. 79). This trend of marrying into wider and wider pools would resurface in the late nineteenth and early twentieth centuries, when British nobles and notables wed the daughters of British industrialists and American plutocrats. The depreciating value of land compelled some members of the aristocracy to look to alternate methods for wealth enhancement in order to maintain traditional lifestyles. Marriage was one of them. Between 1870 and 1914, for instance, 10 per cent of British aristocratic marriages were with brides from overseas, particularly from the United States. Perhaps the case which garnered the greatest publicity was that of Edward VIII's marriage to Baltimore-based Wallis Simpson (Cannadine, *Decline and Fall of the British Aristocracy*, p. 347).

132. B. Kumari, interview with the author, Suraj Mahal Palace, Dhrangadhra, 27 July 1999.
133. Scindia, *The Last Maharani of Gwalior*, pp. 62–6.

4 Breaking (Male) Hearts

1. Appendix III. Letter from Sorabahah Hormasjee, Manager, Rajkot State to the Assistant Political Agent Jhalawar, Wadhwan Camp. 'Case of the Rani of Rajkot', in R/2 (732/181), Crown Representative's Residency Reports, India Office Library, London.
2. Note from Political Agent, Kathiawar, No 4303 of 2-8-1901, Rajkot, 6 August 1901. 'Case of the Rani of Rajkot'.
3. *Kathiawar Times*, 30 September 1897.
4. *Kathiawar News*, 2 October 1897.
5. *Kathiawar Times*, 30 September 1897.
6. *Kathiawar News,* 2 October 1897.
7. *Bombay Gazette*, 13 October 1897.
8. *Bombay Gazette*, 17 May 1898.
9. *Kathiawar Times*, 9 May 1899.
10. Letter from Kamdar Amratlal Premchand to His Excellency the Right Honourable Henry Stafford Baron Northcote of Exeter, C.B. K.G.C.I., Governor and President in Council, Bombay, 15 August 1901. 'Case of the Rani of Rajkot'.
11. Ibid., p. 3.
12. Letter from R. R. B. S. Hajuba to Colonel W. P. Kennedy, Political Agent, Kathiawar, dated 23 August 1901. 'Case of the Rani of Rajkot'.
13. Letter from Rajkot Kunvari Shri to the Assistant Political Agent, Halar Pranth, 19 July 1901. 'Case of the Rani of Rajkot'.
14. Letter from Assistant Political Agent, Halar Pranth, 19 July 1901. 'Case of the Rani of Rajkot'.
15. Letter from Rajkot Rani to the Assistant Political Agent, Halar Pranth, 20 July 1901. 'Case of the Rani of Rajkot'.
16. Confidential, Bombay Caste, Letter from J. L. Jenkins, Esq. M. A., ICS, Acting Secretary to the Government of Bombay, to the Political Agent, Kathiawar, 10 September 1901.
17. Ibid.
18. Ibid.
19. Letter from Samatsingji of Palitana to his Excellency the Right Honourable George Nathaniel Baron Curzon of Keldeston, Viceroy and Governor-General of India, Calcutta, 9 September 1901, from Rajkot, p. 2. 'Case of the Rani of Rajkot'.

20. Ibid., p. 12.
21. Ibid., p. 6.
22. Ibid.
23. Ibid., p. 9.
24. Consider Rajmata Indira Devi of Cooch Behar's hesitation when her daughter, Gayatri Devi, was considering marrying the Maharaja of Jaipur as a third wife (mentioned in the last chapter); Jhala, *Marriage, Hierarchy and Identity*, ch. 5, pp. 75–6.
25. Letter from Samatsingji of Palitana to Curzon, 9 September 1901, p. 14. 'Case of the Rani of Rajkot'.
26. Ibid., p. 15.
27. Ibid., p. 10.
28. Ibid.
29. Ibid., p. 12.
30. Ibid., p. 11.
31. Ibid.
32. Letter from Samatsingji of Palitana to Right Honourable Lord Northcote of Exeter, CGIE CB Governor and President in Council, Poona, 5 July 1901, 13. 'Case of the Rani of Rajkot'.
33. Appendix C. Letter from Samatsingji of Palitana to Colonel W.P. Kennedy, Political Agent, Kathiawar, Camp, Porbandar, 23 June 1901, Confidential, 8. 'Case of the Rani of Rajkot'.
34. Letter from Samatsingji to Curzon, 9 September 1901, 11. 'Case of the Rani of Rajkot'.
35. Ibid., p. 19.
36. Letter from Samatsingji to Curzon, 5 July 1901, p. 2. 'Case of the Rani of Rajkot'.
37. Rudolph and Rudolph, *The Modernity of Tradition*, p. 270.
38. Ibid., p. 279.
39. Appendix C, Letter from Samatsingji of Palitana to Political Agent of Kathiawar, Kennedy, 23 June 1901, 8. 'Case of the Rani of Rajkot'.
40. Letter from Samatsingji to Curzon, 9 September 1901, p.15. 'Case of the Rani of Rajkot'.
41. Letter from Kunvari Shri of Rajkot to the Meherban Assistant, Political Agent, Prant Halar, 17 February 1902, Rajkot. Translated from Gujarati. 'Case of the Rani of Rajkot'.
42. No. 302. Letter from P.S.V. Fitzgerald, CSI Agent to the Governor, Kathiawar, to the Acting Secretary to the Government, Political Department, Bombay, 14 March 1908. 'Protest by Palitana Rani to alliance with Dhrangadhra's Ganshyamsinhji', in R/2 (676/26), Crown Representative's Residency Reports, India Office Library, London.
43. Letter From HH Ajitsinhji Jaswantsinhji, Raj Saheb of Dhrangadhra to Fitzgerald, Agent to the Governor, Kathiawar, 27 February 1908. 'Protest by Palitana Rani to alliance with Dhrangadhra's Ganshyamsinhji'.
44. Appendix P. Letter from Tudor Owen to Palitana Rani, 22 November 1907. 'Protest by Palitana Rani to alliance with Dhrangadhra's Ganshyamsinhji'.
45. Appendix E. Letter from W.T. Owen, to Vansdavala Rani Saheb, Bombay, 1 December 1907, pp. 2–3. 'Protest by Palitana Rani to alliance with Dhrangadhra's Ganshyamsinhji'.
46. Ibid., p. 2.
47. It is possible that Samatsingji may have helped her in drafting this letter as she uses arguments similar to those he confronted when dealing with the Rajkot Rani.

48. Letter from Palitana Rani to His Excellency, the Honourable Sir George Sydenham Clarke, GCIE, GCMG &c, Governor and President in Council, Bombay, 11 January 1908, drafted by her lawyer, barrister at law, 1. 'Protest by Palitana Rani to alliance with Dhrangadhra's Ganshyamsinhji'.
49. Ibid., p. 3.
50. Ibid., p. 4.
51. Appendix K. Letter from Major Beale to Palitana Rani, 12 September 1907, translation from Gujarati. 'Protest by Palitana Rani to alliance with Dhrangadhra's Ganshyamsinhji'.
52. Ibid., p. 5.
53. Ibid., p. 21.
54. Ibid., p. 23.
55. Ibid., p. 7.
56. Ibid., p. 12.
57. Ibid., p. 13.
58. Ibid., pp. 18–19.
59. Ibid., p. 29.
60. Ibid., p. 30.
61. Ibid.
62. Ibid., pp. 14–15.
63. Ibid., p. 30.
64. Ibid., p. 22.
65. Appendix U. Outward No. 8, from Palitana Rani to Tudor Owens, 21 December 1907. 'Protest by Palitana Rani to alliance with Dhrangadhra's Ganshyamsinhji'.
66. 'Protest by Palitana Rani to alliance with Dhrangadhra's Ganshyamsinhji', 12 September 1907, p. 32.
67. Ibid.

5 Troubles in Indore, the Maharaja's Women

1. Copland, *Princes of India*, p. 193.
2. Cohn, 'Some Notes on Law and Change in North', in *An Anthropologist Among the Historians*, pp. 554–74, on p. 569.
3. Price, *Kingship and Political Practice in Colonial India*, p. 66.
4. Lambert-Hurley, *Muslim Women, Reform and Princely Patronage*, p. 146.
5. S. Lateef, *Muslim Women in India: Political and Private Realities, 1890s–1980s* (New Delhi: Kali for Women, 1990), p. 55.
6. Lambert-Hurley, *Muslim Women, Reform and Princely Patronage*, p. 146.
7. Ibid.
8. Lateef, *Muslim Women in India*, p. 56.
9. Ibid., p. 59.
10. Ibid., p. 62.
11. Lambert-Hurley, *Muslim Women, Reform and Princely Patronage*, p. 146.
12. Lateef, *Muslim Women in India*, p. 90.
13. Ibid., p. 75.
14. Ibid., p. 62.
15. Ibid., p.78.
16. Ibid., p. 84.

17. Ibid., p. 86.
18. Appendix A. Letter from R.I. R. Glancy, The AGG to Central India regarding Indore Affairs, dated 6 January 1925 in R/2 (418/14) Crown Representative's Residency Records, India Office Library, London.
19. Ibid.
20. Maharaja of Dhrangadhra, personal correspondence with the author, via letter, 16 April 2005.
21. Bawla Murder Trial, Part I. From Monday 27 April 1925 to Thursday 7 May 1925, 1-206 in R/2 (418/14). Crown Representative's Residency Reports, India Office Library, London.
22. Ibid., p. 3.
23. Ibid., p. 53.
24. Ibid., p. 12.
25. Ibid., p. 3.
26. Ibid., p. 12.
27. Ibid., p. 13.
28. Ibid.
29. Ibid., p. 16.
30. Ibid., p. 20.
31. Ibid., p. 14.
32. Ibid.
33. Ibid., pp. 15–16.
34. Ibid., p. 41.
35. Ibid.
36. Much of the existing archive on women and law in colonial India has emerged more in regions of British India, such as the Bengal presidency, than the princely states. J. Nair, *Women and Law in Colonial India: A Social History* (Delhi: Kali for Women, 1996), p. 17.
37. Ibid., p. 8.
38. Ibid., pp. 21–4.
39. As J. Nair notes, religion was 'considered the prime mover of Indian society throughout history'. Ibid., p. 21.
40. Ibid., p. 27.
41. Ibid., p. 24.
42. Ibid., pp. 28–9.
43. Ibid., p. 29.
44. Ibid.
45. Ibid., pp. 29–30.
46. Bose and Jalal, *Modern South Asia*, p. 83.
47. Ibid., p. 109.
48. Bawla Murder Trial, Part I. From Monday 27 April 1925 to Thursday 7 May 1925, 1-206 in R/2 (418/14). Crown Representative's Residency Reports, India Office Library, London, p. 27.
49. Ibid., p. 34.
50. Ibid., p. 91.
51. Ibid., p. 40.
52. Ibid., p. 27.
53. Ibid., p. 36.

54. Ibid., p. 37.
55. Ibid., p. 48.
56. Ibid., p. 39.
57. Ibid.
58. Ibid., p. 40.
59. Ibid., p. 6.
60. Ibid., p. 16.
61. Ibid., p. 85.
62. Ibid., p. 57.
63. Ibid., p. 74.
64. Ibid., p. 58.
65. Maharaja of Dhrangadhra personal correspondence with the author, via letter, 16 March 2005.
66. Ibid.
67. Bawla Murder Trial, Part I. From Monday 27 April 1925 to Thursday 7 May 1925, 1-206 in R/2 (418/14). Crown Representative's Residency Reports, India Office Library, London, p. 9.
68. Ibid., pp. 9–10.
69. Ibid., p. 10.
70. Ibid., p. 125.
71. Ibid., pp. 126–8.
72. Ibid., p. 136.
73. See G. Spivak's famous line on sati: 'white men saving brown women from brown men'. Spivak, 'Can the Subaltern Speak?', p. 297.
74. Younger, *Wicked Women of the Raj*, p. 150.
75. K. Bhaumik, 'The emergence of the Bombay film industry, 1913–1936' (Unpublished D.Phil. thesis, University of Oxford, 2001), p. 88.
76. Political Report from R.I.R, Glancy, Confidential Branch, Central India on 31 January 1925, 35. 'Malabar Hill Outrage (murder of Mr Bawla) and the Alleged Connection of H.H. the Maharaja Holkar with it', in R/2 (421/15), Crown Representative's Residency Reports, India Office Library, London.
77. Ibid.
78. McLeod, *Sovereignty, Power, Control*, p. 55.
79. Letter from Tukoji Rao to R. I. R. Glancy, CSI, CIE, Agent to the Governor General in Central India, Camp Bijasani, 26 February 1926, p. 1. 'Minority Administration of Holkar State', in R/2 (435/107), Crown Representative's Residency Reports, India Office Library, London.
80. Ibid.
81. Ramusack, *The Indian Princes*, p. 119.
82. Ashton, *British Policy towards the Indian States*, p. 24.
83. Letter from Tukoji Rao to R. I.R. Glancy 26 February 1926, 1. 'Minority Administration of Holkar State'.
84. Ramusack, *The Indian Princes*, p. 52.
85. Letter from Major Ramprasad Dube, Rai Bahadur, Chief Minister to H.H. The Maharaja Holkar, to The First Assistant to the Agent to the Governor General in Central India, Indore, Darbar Office, Indore, 16 December, 1918, 2 in 'Minority Administration of Holkar State'.
86. Ibid.
87. Maharaja of Dhrangadhra, correspondence with the author, via letter, 16 April 2005.

88. Letter from Major Ramprasad Dube to the Agent to the Governor General, 16 December 1918, pp. 2–3. 'Minority Administration of Holkar State'.
89. Ibid., p. 3.
90. Ibid.
91. Ibid., p. 9.
92. Ibid., p. 15.
93. Ibid.
94. Ibid.
95. Letter from R.I. R. Glancy to H.H. Maharajadhiraja Raj Rajeswar Sawai Shri Tukojirao Holkar, G.C.I.E, Indore, 26 February 1926. 'Minority Administration of Holkar State'.
96. Terms Proposed by His Highness the ex-Maharaja Tukoji Rao Holkar. 'Minority Administration of Holkar State'.
97. Ibid., pp. 1–2.
98. Ibid., p. 2.
99. Confidential Letter, 9 March 1926, Re: Minority Administration in Indore State From the Hon'ble Mr J. P. Thompson, CSI, Political Secretary to the Government of India, Delhi, 4. 'Minority Administration of Holkar State'.
100. Ibid., p. 6.
101. Ibid., p. 7.
102. Ibid., p. 8.
103. Telegram from Political Office, India to Central India, Indore, 2 March 1926. 'Minority Administration of Holkar State'.
104. Programme of Rajyabhishek ceremony on Thursday, 11 March 1926. 'Minority Administration of Holkar State'.
105. The princes of the Punjab, Patiala, Jind, Kapurthala, Rampur, Tikari Koh Fort, Jaora, Palanpur, Jodhpur, Bahwalpur, Udaipur and Hyderabad married Caucasian women, among others. See C. Younger's *Wicked Women of the Raj.*
106. Ibid., p. 150.
107. Ibid., p. 151.
108. Ibid.
109. Letter Regarding the Marriage of H.H. the Ex-Maharaja of Indore, 13 March 1928, from The Hon'ble Mr C. C. Watson, CSI, CIE, ICS, Political Secretary to the Government of India. '1928 Marriage of Tukoji Rao Holkar', in R/2 (435/106), Crown Representative's Residency Reports, India Office Library, London.
110. Note by R.I.R. Glancy of an interview with H.H., the Ex-Maharaja of Indore. '1928 Marriage of Tukoji Rao Holkar'.
111. Very Confidential Report from the Residency Indore, 16 April 1928. '1928 Marriage of Tukoji Rao Holkar'.
112. Kapila, 'Masculinity and Madness', p. 131.
113. Note by R. I. R. Glancy of an Interview with H.H., the Ex-Maharaja of Indore, 1. '1928 Marriage of Tukoji Rao Holkar'.
114. Ibid.
115. Ibid., p. 2.
116. Very Confidential Report from the Residency Indore, 16 April 1928. '1928 Marriage of Tukoji Rao Holkar'.
117. Kapila, 'Masculinity and Madness', p. 142.
118. Very Confidential Report from the Residency Indore, 16 April 1928. '1928 Marriage of Tukoji Rao Holkar', p. 2.

119. Ibid.
120. Ibid.
121. Younger, *Wicked Women of the Raj*, pp. 152–9.
122. Allen and Dwivedi, *Lives of the Indian Princes*, p. 259.
123. Speech delivered by the Hon'ble R. I. R. Glancy, CSI, CIE, AGG in C. I. at the Darbar of Occasion of M.R. Yeshwant Rao Holkar at Manikbagh Indore on 12 March 1926, 1, in R/2 (435/107), Crown Representative's Residency Reports, India Office Library, London.
124. Ibid., pp. 1–2.
125. Ibid., p. 2.
126. *Evening Standard*, 28 March 1939.
127. Rajkumar Martand Singh, verbal communication with the author, 6 April 2005.
128. Morrow, *Highness: The Maharajas of India*, pp. 71–2.
129. Younger, *Wicked Women of the Raj*, p. 190.
130. Kapila, 'Masculinity and Madness', p. 126; see also D. Newsome, *Godliness and Good Learning: Four Studies on a Victorian Ideal* (London 1961).
131. Younger, *Wicked Women of the Raj*, p. 190.
132. Copland, *Princes of India*, p. 194.
133. Indore Affairs 1939. Secret file/notes written by K.S. Fitze between 10.3.39–13.3.39 (Fitze notes on 10.3.39), p.1. 'Marriage of His Highness the Maharaja Holkar, 1939', in R/2 (422/18), Crown Representative's Residency Reports, India Office Library, London.
134. For more on succession disputes in Bhopal, see Chapter 2.
135. Copland, *Princes of India*, p. 194.
136. Letter by Fitze. Confidential, Central India Agency, Indore, 28 March 1939, Subject: Indore Affairs, 5. 'Marriage of Maharaja Holkar 1939'.
137. Ibid.
138. Fitze, Secret Notes, 3.17.39. 'Marriage of Maharaja Holkar 1939'.
139. Ibid.
140. Confidential, Demi-Official, 25 March 1939, Subject: Indore Affairs, Kenneth Fitze to Bertrand Glancy, KCIE, CSI, Political Advisor to His Excellency the Crown Representative, New Delhi. 'Marriage of Maharaja Holkar 1939'.
141. Ibid., pp. 1–2.
142. Letter from Dinanath, Minister in Attendance, Indore state, to Fitze, from Manik Bagh Palace, Indore, 26 March 1939. 'Marriage of Maharaja Holkar 1939'.
143. Letter from Dinanath to Fitze, Manik Bagh Palace, Indore, 27 March 1939. 'Marriage of Maharaja Holkar 1939'.
144. Transcript of Yeshwant Rao Holkar's official announcement of his marriage to Miss Marguerite Lawler, pp. 3–4. 'Marriage of Maharaja Holkar 1939'.
145. Ibid., p. 4.
146. Ibid., p. 8.
147. Ibid., p. 11.
148. Confidential, Demi-Official, 25 March 1939, p.3, 'Marriage of Maharaja Indore 1939'.
149. Ibid., p. 4.
150. Fitze letter, Confidential, Central India Agency, Indore, 28 March 1939, Subject: Indore Affairs, p.2. 'Marriage of Maharaja Indore 1939'.
151. Ibid., p. 3.
152. *Evening Standard*, 29 March 1939.

153. Very Confidential, The Residency Indore, 10 June 1939. Re: Indore Affairs. To Bertrand Glancy, Political Advisor to His Excellency the Crown Representative, Simla, 2. 'Marriage of Maharaja Holkar 1939'.
154. Younger, *Wicked Women of the Raj*, p. 189.
155. Report by Fitze on 3 April 1939. Secret. Indore Affairs. 'Marriage of Maharaja Holkar 1939'.
156. Unnamed American newspaper from 1939 with the caption: 'Minneapolis Bride Budgets 'Rajah'.
157. Younger, *Wicked Women of the Raj*, p. 191.
158. Confidential, Central India Agency, Indore, 15 April 1939. Subject: Indore Affairs, p. 2. 'Marriage of Maharaja Holkar 1939'
159. Very Confidential. The Residency Indore, 12 June 1939. Re: Indore Affairs, pp. 3–4. 'Marriage of Maharaja Holkar 1939'.
160. Ibid., p. 4.
161. Confidential. The Residency, Indore, 6 May 1939, Letter from Kenneth Fitze to Glancy, 2. 'Marriage of Maharaja Holkar 1939'.
162. Ibid., p. 3.
163. Ibid.
164. Ibid.
165. Letter from Hamington-Hawes, Political Department, New Delhi, 4 November 1939, Confidential to Fitze, p. 1. 'Marriage of Maharaja Holkar 1939'.
166. Ibid., pp. 1–2.
167. Ibid., p. 2.
168. Very Confidential. The Residency Indore, 12 June 1939. Re: Indore Affairs. 'Marriage of Maharaja Holkar 1939'.
169. Ibid., p. 2.
170. Indore Affairs. 3 April 1939. Secret. 'Marriage of Maharaja Holkar 1939'.
171. Very Confidential, The Residency Indore, 10 June 1939. Re: Indore Affairs. To Bertrand Glancy, Political Advisor to His Excellency the Crown Representative, Simla, 2. 'Marriage of Maharaja Indore 1939'.
172. 'Rajah and Minneapolis Bride Building 'Kidnap-proof Fortress', Unnamed American newspaper, 10 November 1939.
173. Ibid.
174. Younger, *Wicked Women of the Raj*, p. 192.
175. Ibid.
176. Copland, *Princes of India*, p. 194.
177. Younger, *Wicked Women of the Raj*, p. 193.
178. Ibid.
179. Ibid., p. 194.
180. Ibid.
181. Ibid., p. 196. Again, madness refigures as an explanation for deviant sexual or marital practice. See also Kapila, 'Masculinity and Madness', pp. 154–5.
182. Younger, *Wicked Women of the Raj,* pp. 196–7.
183. Ibid.
184. Ibid., p. 198.
185. Ibid.
186. Ibid., pp. 198–9.

187. Ibid., p. 200.
188. Kapila, 'Masculinity and Madness', p. 185.

6 From 'Pardah to Parliament'

1. This expression is taken from S. Ikramullah's book of the same tittle, *From Purdah to Parliament*, London, 1964.
2. Rudolph and Rudolph, *Essays on Rajputana*, p. 50.
3. Copland, *The Princes of India*, p. 8.
4. W. L. Richter, 'Traditional Rulers in Post-Traditional Societies: The Princes of India and Pakistan', in Jeffrey (ed.), *People, Princes and Paramount Power*, pp. 329–54.
5. L. I. Rudolph and S. Rudolph, 'Toward Political Stability in Underdeveloped Countries: The Case of India', *Public Policy*, 9 (1959), pp. 149–78, on p. 152.
6. Bose and Jalal, *Modern South Asia*, p. 152.
7. Cannadine, *Ornamentalism,* p. 54.
8. Rudolph and Rudolph , *Essays on Rajputana*, p. 3.
9. P. Brass, *The Politics of India Since Independence* (Cambridge: Cambridge University Press, 1990), p. 10.
10. To read more in regards to princes (particularly in Rajasthan) and tourism, see B. Ramusack's article, 'Tourism and Icons: The Packaging of Princely States in Rajasthan', in C. B. Asher and T. R. Metcalf (eds), *Perceptions of South Asia's Visual Past* (New Delhi: Oxford and IBH Publishing Co., 1994), pp, 235–55.
11. H. Tinker, *India and Pakistan: A Political Analysis* (London, 1967), p. 40.
12. Copland, *The Princes of India*, pp. 267–8; Ramusack, *The Princes of India at the Twilight of Empire*, pp. 244–6; Cannadine, *Ornamentalism*, p. 174.
13. Richter, *Traditional Rulers in Post-Traditional Societies*, pp. 335–7.
14. 'Rajasthan's royal affair', 3 February 1998, Rediff.com.
15. F. G. Bailey, 'Politics in Orissa-VIII: The Ganatantra Parishad', *The Economic Weekly*, 24 October 1959, pp.1469–76.
16. Further examples include: Bhairon Singh Shekawat, a Rajput nobleman from Jaipur, who had been a long standing Chief Minister of Rajasthan; the former Raja of Raghu Gadh is the present Chief Minister of Madhya Pradesh; and the former Maharaja of Patna was the principal opposition to the Congress Chief Minister in Orissa.
17. Copland, *The Princes of India*, p. 268.
18. Richter, *Traditional Rulers in Post-Traditional Societies*, p. 333.
19. I. Narain and P. C. Mathur, 'The Thousand Year Raj: Regional Isolation and Rajput Hinduism in Rajasthan Before and After 1947', in F. Frankel and M. S. Rao (eds), *Dominance and State Power in Modern India, Vol. 2* (Delhi: Oxford University Press, 1990), pp. 1–58, on pp. 24–5.
20. J. McLeod, personal communication with the author, via email, 9 May 2002.
21. Maharaja of Dhrangadhara, personal correspondence with author, via email, 3 May 2002.
22. Narain and Mathur, 'The Thousand Year Raj', p. 32.
23. Tod, *Annals*, introduction.
24. Ibid., vol. 1, p. 261.
25. During the Raj tilak ceremony, the Rajput king is anointed with a tikka of blood from a Bhil on his forehead.
26. Narain and Mathur, 'The Thousand Year Raj', p. 47.

27. Richter, 'Traditional Rulers in Post-Traditional Societies', p. 342.
28. Ibid., p. 343.
29. S. Khilnani, *The Idea of India* (New York: Farrar, Straus, Giroux, 1997), p. 43.
30. Ibid., p. 45.
31. Note S. Gandhi's current ascendancy as the head of the Congress party, continuing the family legacy, despite her foreign nationality and race.
32. Devi, *A Princess Remembers*, p.315.
33. Sawnet bio: Gayatri Devi. http://sawnet.org/whoswho/?Devi+Gayatri.
34. S. Devi, *Autobiography of an Indian Princess*, p.11.
35. Ibid., p. 1.
36. Ibid., p. 7.
37. Ibid., p. 49.
38. Ibid., p. 29.
39. S. Lambert-Hurley, 'Out of India: The Journeys of the Begam of Bhopal, 1901–1932'. *Women's Studies International Forum*, 21:3 (1998), pp. 263–76, on p. 266.
40. S. Devi, *Autobiography of an Indian Princess*, p. 101.
41. Ibid., p. 128.
42. Richter, 'Traditional Rulers in Post-Traditional Societies', p. 339.
43. Maharani of Baroda, *The Position of Women in Indian Life*, p. viii.
44. Ibid., pp. xiii–xiv. This is a view similarly expressed by her contemporary, the female rule of Bhopal, Sultan Jahan Begum.
45. Devi, *A Princess Remembers*, p. 19.
46. Ibid., p. 57.
47. Ibid., p. 142.
48. Ibid., pp. 167–70.
49. Ibid., p.179.
50. Ibid., p. 202.
51. Ibid., p. 241.
52. Ibid., p. 255.
53. Ibid., p. 260.
54. Ramusack, 'Tourism and Icons', p. 244.
55. Brass, *The Politics of India*, p. 83.
56. Devi, *A Princess Remembers*, p. 272.
57. Ibid., p. 289.
58. Ibid., p. 293.
59. Ibid., p. 302.
60. Ibid., p. 321.
61. Moore, *Maharanis*, p. 269.
62. Ibid., p. 271.
63. Devi., *A Princess Remembers*, p. 370.
64. Ibid.
65. Ibid., p. 378.
66. Moore, *Maharanis*, p. 286.
67. Devi, *A Princess Remembers*, p. 382.
68. Narain and Mathur, 'The Thousand Year Raj', p. 21.
69. G. Devi, interview by author, video recording, 20 June 1999, Cadogan Square, London.
70. Ibid.
71. Moore, *Maharanis*, p. 295.

72. Kanwar, *Enduring Grace*, p. 116.

73. P. Bhandari, 'Rajmata's 'Enduring Grace' is put under falsity pressure', *Times of India-Ahmedabad*, 22 June 2004.

74. T. Sahay, 'Ramata was Tender yet Tough: Vajpayee', Rediff.com, 25 January 2001 (www.rediff.com/news/2001/jan/25tara.htm).

75. R. Menon, 'Thousands pay homage to Rajmata', Rediff.com, 26 January 2001 (www.rediffcom/news/2001/Jan26raje.htm).

76. Scindia, *The Last Maharani of Gwalior*, p. 20.

77. The connections to the Nepalese crown continue in the family to this day. Vijaya Raje Scindia's granddaughter, Devayani Rana, has been associated as the love interest of Crown Prince Dipendra of Nepal, who in 2001 allegedly assassinated his parents and numerous members of the royal family in Kathmandu on the grounds that they would not accept her as his choice for a bride.

78. Scindia, *The Last Maharani of Gwalior*, p. 16.

79. Ibid., p. 26.

80. Ibid., p. 27.

81. 'Vijayaraje Scindia dies', Rediff.com, 25 January 2001 (www.rediff.com/news/2001/jan/25raje.htm).

82. Scindia, *The Last Maharani of Gwalior*, p. 131. See Chapter 3 for a critical analysis of Vijaya Raje's marital options.

83. Ibid., p. 132.

84. Ibid., pp. 162–3.

85. Richter, 'Traditional Rulers in Post-Traditional Societies', p. 340.

86. Scindia, *The Last Maharani of Gwalior*, p. 172.

87. Richter, 'Traditional Rulers in Post-Traditional Societies', p. 340.

88. K. Thakre, 'She wept for the poor', Rediff.com, 25 January 2001 (www.rediff.com/news/2001/Jan/25onkar.htm).

89. Scindia, *The Last Maharani of Gwalior*, p. 193.

90. C. Jaffrelot, *The Hindu Nationalist Movement and Indian Politics: 1925 to the 1990s* (London: Hurst & Company, 1993), p. 216.

91. Scindia, *The Last Maharani of Gwalior*, p.196. It is worth noting that throughout their memoirs, there is a constant sense of competition between these two women.

92. Ibid., p. 219.

93. Ibid., p. 227.

94. See the history section of the official home page of the BJP party: http://www.bjp.org/history.htm.

95. Scindia, *The Last Maharani of Gwalior*, p. 242.

96. Ibid., p. 244.

97. Ibid., p. 248.

98. Ibid., p. 249.

99. R. Menon, 'Madhavrao had no business to die', Rediff.com, 30 September 2001.

100. Y. K. Malik and V. B. Singh, *Hindu Nationalists in India: The Rise of the Bharatiya Janata Party* (Oxford: Westview Press, 1994), p. 143.

101. 'Vijayaraje dies', Rediff.com, 15 January 2001 (www.rediff.com/news/2001/jan/25raje.htm).

102. C. Jaffrelot, *The Hindu Nationalist Movement*, p. 457.

103. Malik and Singh, *Hindu Nationalists in India*, p. 44.

104. Biographical Sketch of Member of XII Lok Sabha (http://alfa.nic.in/lok12/biodata/12mp04.htm).

105. A. Basu, 'Feminism Inverted: The Real Women and Gendered Imagery of Hindu Nationalism', *Bulletin of Concerned Asian Scholars*, 25:4 (1992), pp. 25–36, on p. 25.

106. Ibid., p. 27.

107. 'Madhavrao Scindia, 1945–2001', *The Hindu*, 2 October 2001 (www.hinduonnet.com/thehindu/2001/10/02/stories/05022511.htm).

108. Her third daughter Vasundhara Raje is the BJP Chief Minister of Rajasthan, and her youngest daughter Yashodhara Raje is a BJP MLA in Madhya Pradesh. Her second daughter, Usha Raje, is married to Rana Pashupati Shamsher who is a Minister in Nepal. Her grandson, Jyotriaditya, is also a Congress MP.

109. Such schisms among princely families in politics were not uncommon. William Richter notes similar family feuds in the Muslim dynasties of Rampur and Bhopal, 'Traditional Rulers in Post-Traditional Societies', p. 339.

110. Scindia, *The Last Maharani of Gwalior*, p. 224.

111. Ibid., p. 258.

112. Ibid., p. 262.

113. Maharaja of Dhrangadhra, personal correspondence with the author, via email, 31 January 2002.

114. Rashmi Saksena, 'Fair well maharaj', *The Week*, 14 October 2001 (www.the-week.com/21oct14/events1.htm).

Epilogue

1. Willesee and Whittaker, *Love and Death in Kathmandu*, p. 226.

2. 'Witness says drunk prince "was the killer"', 7 June 2001, Cnn.com/world. http://archives.cnn.com/2001/WORLD/asiapcf/south/06/07/nepal.shooting.02/

3. Willesee and Whittaker, *Love and Death in Kathmandu*, p. 184–7.

4. It is worth noting here that six years after the 2001 massacre of the Nepalese royal family, Devyani Rana went on to marry a Rajput aristocrat and grandson of Indian Human Resources Minister (Congress), Arjun Singh, in February 2007. Several Indian royal families, leading members of the elected government and foreign dignitaries attended the marriage. The event reveals the continued relevance of political marriage alliance making in Devyani's choice of a bridegroom, who had both a courtly pedigree as well as connections to postcolonial, democratic elites. *The Hindu*, 26 February 2007. http://www.hindu.com/2007/02/26.

5. W. Barton, *The Princes of India* (Reprint Cosmo Publications, 1983); R. Kabbani, *Imperial Fictions: Europe's Myths of the Orient* (London: Pandora, 1994); Reina Lewis, *Rethinking Orientalism: Women, Travel, and the Ottoman Harem* (London: I.B. Tauris, 2004); A. Loomba, *Colonialism/Postcolonialism* (New York: Routledge, 2005); A. Morrow, *Highness: The Maharajas of India* (London: Grafton Books, 1986); O'Hanlon, *A Comparison between Women and Men*.

6. L. Mani, *Contentious Traditions: The Debate on Sati in Colonial India* (Berkeley, CA: University of California Press, 1998); Spivak, 'Can the Subaltern Speak?'; J. Singh, *Colonial Narratives/Cultural Dialogues: Discoveries of India in the Language of Colonialism* (London; Routledge, 1996).

7. Spivak, 'Can the Subaltern Speak?', p. 306.

8. Ghosh, *Sex and the Family in Colonial India*, p. 252.

9.   O'Hanlon, *A Comparison between Women and Men*, p.3.

10. R. O'Hanlon, 'Issues of Widowhood: Gender, Discourse and Resistance in Colonial Western India', in D. Haynes and G. Prakash (eds), *Contesting Power: Resistance and Everyday Social Relations in South Asia* (Berkeley, CA: University of California Press, 1991), pp. 62–108, on p. 75.

11. Bhaumik, 'The Emergence of the Bombay Film Industry, 1913–1936', p. 88.

WORKS CITED

Manuscript and Archival Sources

Centre for South Asian Studies, University of Cambridge

    Edgar Hyde Papers, Autobiographical Memoir: 'India, First Person Singular'.

    K. Nagarajan Papers, 1900–1957.

India Office Records and Library, British Library London

    Crown Representative's Records, Political Department, R/1.

    Crown Representative's Residency Reports, R/2.

Private Collections

Raja Patta Abhishek, Mewar Oriental Research Institute, Udaipur.

Dhrangadhra Raj Private Archives.

Dhrangadhra Raj Private Archives – 'Dhrangadhra Rajshala Revisited'.

Jodhpur Raj Private Archives.

Brijraj Kumari. Exercise Notebooks, Umed Palace School, Jodhpur, India, 1942.

Official Publications – Published Government Records

Hansard's *Parliamentary Debates*, 3rd series, ccxxvii (1876).

Parliamentary Papers, 41 (1850).

'Reports of the Committee on the Relationship between the Paramount Power and the States' (Butler Committee), *Parliamentary Papers*, 6, Cd. 3302.

Lytton to Queen Victoria, 21 April 1876, IOLR, E218/518/1.

Lytton to Queen Victoria, 4 May 1876, IOLR, E218/518/1.

Oral Archives

Brinda, Maharani of Kapurthala, 'Maharani: The Story of an Indian Princess', as told to Elaine Williams (New York, 1953).

Oral Interviews

Gayatri Devi, Rajmata of Jaipur (London, 1999).

Sita Devi, Ranisaheb of Kapurthala (Mussoorie, 1999).

Rajkumari Moitri Hume, Princess of the Chakma Raj (Cambridge, MA, 2005).

Brijraj Kumari, Maharani of Dhrangadhra (Dhrangadhra, 1999–2002).

Krishna Kumari, Rajmata of Jodhpur (Jodhpur, 1999).

Rajkumar Martand Singh of Kapurthala (New Delhi, 2005).

Personal Correspondence with the Author

Maharaja of Dhrangadhra, 2002–5.

John McLeod, 2002.

Newspapers and Periodicals

Kathiawar News, 1897

Kathiawar Times, 1897

Bombay Gazette, 1897–1898

The Hindu, 2001–2

Indian Express, 1997

Rediff.com, 1998–2003

Times of India-Ahmedabad, 2004

The Week, 2001

Internet Resources

Sawnet bio: Gayatri Devi, http://www.umiacs.umd.edu/users/sawweb/sawnet/people/gayatri_devi.html

History section of the official home page of the BJP party, http://www.bjp.org/history.htm.

Biographical Sketch of Member of XII Lok Sabha, http://alfa.nic.in/lok12/biodata/12mp04.htm.

Performances

Tittman, B., and J. Bethell, *The Great Game or How Cricket Saved the Empire: A Musical Drama in Two Acts*. Performed at The Tavern Club, Boston, 30–1 March 2005.

Printed Primary Sources

Ayyar, K. R. Venkatarama, *A Manual of the Pudukkottai State, vol. 2, part 1* (Pudukkottai: The Sri Brihadamba State Press, 1940).

Barton, Sir W., *The Princes of India* (New Delhi: Cosmo Publications, 1983).

Chimnabai, Maharani of Baroda, *The Position of Women in Indian Life* (Delhi: Neeraj Publishing House. 1981 Reprint).

Corfield, Sir C., *The Princely India I Knew: From Reading to Mountbatten* (Madras, 1975).

Devi, G., *A Princess Remembers* (Calcutta: Rupa & Co., 1995).

Devi, S., *Autobiography of an Indian Princess: Memoirs of Maharani Sunity Devi of Cooch Behar (*New Delhi: Vikas Publishing House, 1995).

Fitze, K., *Twilight of the Maharajas* (London: John Murray, 1956).

Forster, E. M. *The Hill of Devi* (New York: Harcourt, Brace and Company, 1953).

Le Grand Jacob, Major-Gen. G., *Western India: Before and During the Mutinies* (London: Henry S. King & Co., 1871).

Lee-Warner, W., 'The Native States of India', *British Empire Series, Volume 1: India, Ceylon, Straits Settlements, British Northern Borneo, Hong-Kong* (London: Kegan Paul, Trench, Trubner & Co., 1899), pp. 270–94.

—, *The Native States of India* (Macmillan and Co., London, 1910).

Nehru, J., *The Discovery of India* (1946; Delhi: Oxford University Press, 1998).

Ojha, G. H., *Bikaner Rajya Ka Itihas (History of Bikaner State)* (Ajmer, 1940).

Prinsep, V. C., *Glimpses of Imperial India* (Delhi: Mittal Publications, 1878).

Roy, R. T., *The Departed Melody* (Islamabad: PPA Publications, 2003).

Scindia, V. R., *The Last Maharani of Gwalior: An Autobiography* (Albany, NY: State University of New York, 1987).

Sleeman, W., *Rambles and Recollections of an Indian Official* (London: Constable, 1893), vol. 1.

Thompson, E. J., *The Making of the Indian Princes* (Oxford: Oxford University Press, 1943).

Tod, J., *Annals and Antiquities of Rajasth'an* (New Delhi: M. N. Publishers, 1978).

Queen Victoria's Proclamation, 1 November 1858, in B. Harlow and M. Carter, *Imperialism and Orientalism: A Reader* (Oxford: Blackwell, 1999), p. 210.

Wheeler, J. T., *The History of the Imperial Assemblage at Delhi* (London: Longmans, Green, Ryder & Dyer, 1877).

Secondary Sources

Alam, M., and S. Subrahmanyam, 'Love, Passion and Reason in Faizi's *Nal-Daman*', in Orsini (ed.), *Love in South Asia*, pp. 109–41.

Alexander, M., and S. Anand, *Queen Victoria's Maharajah: Duleep Singh, 1838–93* (London: Weidenfeld and Nicolson, 1980).

Ali, D., *Courtly Culture and Political Life in Early Medieval India* (Cambridge: Cambridge University Press, 2004).

—, 'Courtly Love and the Aristocratic Household in Early Medieval India', in Orsini (ed.), *Love in South Asia*, pp. 43–60.

Allen, C., and S. Dwivedi, *Lives of the Indian Princes* (New York: Crown Publishers, 1984).

Anand, S., *Indian Sahib: Queen Victoria's Dear Abdul* (London: Duckworth, 1996).

Ashraf, K. M., *Life and Conditions of the People of Hindustan* (New Delhi: Munshiram Manoharlal, 1970).

Ashton, S. R., *British Policy towards the Indian States, 1905–1909* (London: Curzon Press, 1982).

Bailey, F. G., 'Politics in Orissa-VIII: The Ganatantra Parishad,' *The Economic Weekly* (24 October 1959), pp. 1469–76.

Ballhatchet, K., *Race, Sex and Class Under the Raj: Imperial Attitudes and Policies and Their Critics, 1793–1905* (London: Weidenfeld and Nicolson, 1980).

Basu, A., 'Feminism Inverted: The Real Women and Gendered Imagery of Hindu Nationalism', *Bulletin of Concerned Asian Scholars*, 25:4 (1992), pp. 25–36.

Batra, H. C. *The Relations of Jaipur State with East India Company* (Delhi: S. Chand & Co., 1958).

Bayly, C. A. *Indian Society and the Making of the British Empire* (Cambridge: Cambridge University Press, 1988).

Bernard, G. W. *The King's Reformation: Henry VIII and the Remaking of the English Church* (New Haven, CT: Yale University Press, 2005).

Bhagavan, M., *Sovereign Spheres: Princes, Education and Empire in Colonial India* (Oxford: Oxford University Press, 2003).

Bhaumik, K. 'The emergence of the Bombay film industry, 1913–1936' (D.Phil. dissertation, University of Oxford, 2001).

Bose, S., and A. Jalal, *Modern South Asia: History, Culture, Political Economy* (London: Routledge, 1998).

Brass, P., *The Politics of India Since Independence.* (Cambridge: Cambridge University Press, 1990).

Brown, J., 'India', in Brown and Louis (eds), *The Oxford History of the British Empire, Twentieth Century*, pp. 421–46.

Brown, J., and W. R. Louis (eds), *The Oxford History of the British Empire, Twentieth Century* (Oxford: Oxford University Press, 1999).

Buhler, G. (trans.), *The Laws of Manu* (Oxford: Clarendon Press, 1886).

Burke, S. M., and S. Al-Din Quraishi, *The British Raj in India: An Historical Review*. (Karachi: Oxford University Press, 1995).

Burton, A., *Dwelling in the Archive: Women Writing House, Home and History in Late Colonial India* (New York: Oxford University Press, 2003).

Campbell, C., *The Maharajah's Box: An Imperial Story of Conspiracy, Love and a Guru's Prophecy* (London: HarperCollins Publishers, 2001).

Cannadine, D., *The Decline and the Fall of the British Aristocracy* (New Haven, CT: Yale University Press, 1990).

—, *Aspects of Aristocracy* (New Haven, CT: Yale University Press, 1994).

—, *Ornamentalism: How the British Saw Their Empire* (Oxford: Oxford University Press, 2001).

Chakrabarty, D., 'The Difference-Deferral of a Colonial Modernity: Public Debates on Domesticity in British Bengal', in D. Arnold and D. Hardiman (eds), *Subaltern Studies VIII* (Oxford: Oxford University Press, 1994), pp. 50–88.

—, *Provincializing Europe: Postcolonial Thought and Historical Difference* (Princeton, NJ: Princeton University Press, 2000).

—, *Habitations of Modernity: Essays in the Wake of Subaltern Studies* (Chicago, IL: University of Chicago Press, 2002).

Chamberlain, M., and P. Thompson (eds), *Narrative and Genre* (London: Routledge, 1998).

Chatterjee, P., 'The Nationalist Resolution of the Women's Question', in Sangari and Vaid (eds), *Recasting Women*, pp. 233–53.

—, *The Nation and Its Fragments: Colonial and Postcolonial Histories* (Princeton, NJ: Princeton University Press, 1993).

Chowdhry, P., *Colonial India and the Making of Empire Cinema: Image, Ideology and Identity* (Manchester: Manchester University Press, 2000).

Chundavat, L. K., *Gir Uncha Garh Unch Ghana* (Jaipur: Sheetal Printers, 1966).

— (ed.), *Rajwari Lokgeet (Folk Songs of the Royal Houses)* (Jaipur: Sheetal Printers, 1985).

Coen, T. C., *The Indian Political Service: A Study in Indirect Rule* (London: Chatto & Windus, 1971).

Cohn, B., *An Anthropologist among the Historians and Other Essays* (Oxford: Oxford University Press, 1987).

—, 'Anthropology and History in the 1980s: Towards a Rapprochement', in *An Anthropologist among the Historians*, pp. 50–77.

—, 'Representing Authority in Victorian India', in *An Anthropologist among the Historians*, pp. 632–82.

—, 'Society and Social Change Under the Raj', in *An Anthropologist among the Historians*, pp. 172–99.

—, 'Some Notes on Law and Change in North India', in *An Anthropologist among the Historians*, pp. 554–74.

Collingham, E. M., *Imperial Bodies: The Physical Experience of the Raj, c.1800–1947* (Cambridge: Polity Press, 2001).

Copland, I., 'The Other Guardians: Ideology and Performance in the Indian Political Service', in Jeffrey (ed.), *People, Princes and Paramount Power*, pp. 275–305.

—, *The Princes of India in the Endgame of Empire 1917–1947* (Cambridge: Cambridge University Press, 1997).

Dalrymple, W., *White Mughals: Love and Betrayal in Eighteenth-Century India* (London: Flamingo, 2003).

Dewey, C., *Anglo-Indian Attitudes: The Mind of the Indian Civil Service* (London: The Hambledon Press, 1993).

Dirks, N., *The Hollow Crown: Ethnohistory of an Indian Kingdom* (Cambridge: Cambridge University Press, 1987).

—, 'Castes of Mind', *Representations*, 37 (1992), pp. 56–80.

—, 'The Invention of Caste: Civil Society in Colonial India', in H. L. Seneviratne (ed.), 'Identity, Consciousness and the Past: The South Asian Scene'. Special Issue series of *Social Analysis: Journal of Culture and Social Practice*, 25 (1989), pp. 42–52.

Disman, C., 'The Princely States Before Independence: The Indian Princes as Political Successors to the British Raj' (Honors Thesis, San Francisco State University, 2004).

Dumont, L., *Homo Hierarchicus: The Caste System and Its Implications* (Chicago, IL: University of Chicago Press, 1966).

Dube, S., *Stitches on Time: Colonial Textures and Postcolonial Tangles* (Durham, NC: Duke University Press, 2004).

Dunn, J., *Elizabeth and Mary: Cousins, Rivals, Queens* (New York: Random House, 2003).

Fisher, M., *Indirect Rule in India: Residents and the Residency System, 1764–1858* (Delhi: Oxford University Press, 1991).

Ghosh, D., 'Decoding the Nameless: Gender, Subjectivity, and Historical Methodologies in Reading the Archives of Colonial India', in K. Wilson (ed.), *A New Imperial History: Culture, Identity and Modernity in Britain and the Empire, 1660–1840* (New York: Cambridge University Press. 2004), pp. 297–316.

—, *Sex and the Family in Colonial India* (Cambridge: Cambridge University Press, 2006).

Gilmour, D., *The Ruling Caste: Imperial Lives in the Victorian Raj* (New York: Farrar, Straus & Giroux, 2005).

Grewal, I., *Home and Harem: Nation, Gender, Empire and the Cultures of Travel* (Durham, NC: Duke University Press, 1996).

Harlan, L., *Religion and Rajput Women: The Ethics of Protection in Contemporary Narratives* (Berkeley, CA: University of California Press, 1992).

Howard, J. E., and P. Rackin, *Engendering a Nation: A Feminist Account of Shakespeare's English Histories* (London: Routledge, 1997).

Hurtig, C., *Les Maharajah et la Politique dans L'Inde Contemporaine* (Paris: Presses de la Fondation nationale des sciences politiques, 1988).

Hyam, R., 'The Sexual Life of the Raj', in R. Hyam (ed.), *Empire and Sexuality* (Manchester: Manchester University Press, 1992), pp. 115–36.

Ikramullah, S., *From Purdah to Parliament* (London: Cresset Press, 1964).

Inden, R., *Imagining India* (Oxford: Basil Blackwell, 1990).

Jaffrelot, C., *The Hindu Nationalist Movement and Indian Politics: 1925 to the 1990s* (London: Hurst & Company, 1993).

Jeffrey, R. (ed.), *People, Princes and Paramount Power: Society and Politics in the Indian Princely States* (Delhi: Oxford University Press, 1978).

Jhabvala, R. P., *Heat and Dust* (London: J. Murray, 1975).

Jhala, A., 'Opening the Lotus: Reflections on the Lives of Royal Indian Women' (Undergraduate Honors Thesis, Departments of Sanskrit and History, Harvard University, 2000).

Jhala, J., 'Marriage, Hierarchy and Identity in Ideology and Practice: An Anthropological Study of Jhala Rajput Society in Western India, Against a Historical Background, 1090–1990 AD' (PhD dissertation, Anthropology Department, Harvard University, 1991).

Joshi, S., *Fractured Modernity: Making of a Middle Class in Colonial North India* (New Delhi: Oxford University Press, 2001).

Joshi, V., 'Zenana Deorhi: A Study of the Davree System (With Special Reference to Mewar)' (Dissertation, University of Rajasthan, 1988).

—, *Polygamy and Pardah* (Jaipur: Rawat Publications, 1995).

Kabbani, R., *Imperial Fictions: Europe's Myths of the Orient* (London: Pandora, 1994).

Kanwar, D., *Rajmata Gayatri Devi ... Enduring Grace* (Delhi: Lustre Press/Roli Books, 2004).

Kapila, S., 'Masculinity and Madness: Princely Personhood and Colonial Sciences of the Mind in Western India, 1871–1940', *Past and Present*, 187 (May 2005), pp. 121–56.

Kaviraj, S., 'Tagore and Transformations in the Ideals of Love', in Orsini (ed.), *Love in South Asia*, pp. 161–82.

Kaye, M. M., *The Far Pavilions* (London: Allen Lane, 1978).

Khan, S. M., *The Begums of Bhopal: A Dynasty of Women Rulers in Raj India* (London: I.B. Tauris Publishers, 2000).

Khilnani, S., *The Idea of India* (New York: Farrar, Straus, Giroux, 1997).

Krishna, A., 'Beauty in the Human Form in Sixteenth Century Hindi Poetry and the Evolution of *Ek Chashma Chehra* in Rajasthani Painting', in H. Dehejia and M. Paranjape (eds), *Saundarya: The Perception and Practice of Beauty in India* (New Delhi: Samvad India Foundation, 2003), pp. 73–80.

Kulkarni, V. B., *Princely India and the Lapse of British Paramountcy* (Bombay: Jaico Publishing, 1985).

Lal, R., 'The 'Domestic World' of the Mughals in the Reigns of Babur, Humayan and Akbar, c. 1500–1605' (unpublished D.Phil. dissertation, University of Oxford, 2000).

—, 'The "Domestic World" of Peripatetic Kings: Babur and Humayun, c. 1494–1556', *The Medieval History Journal*, 4:1 (2001), pp. 43–82.

—, *Domesticity and Power in the Early Mughal World* (Cambridge: Cambridge University Press, 2005).

Lambert-Hurley, S., 'Out of India: The Journeys of the Begam of Bhopal, 1901–1930', *Women's Studies International Forum*, 21:3 (1998), pp. 263–76.

—, *Muslim Women, Reform and Princely Patronage: Nawab Sultan Jahan Begam of Bhopal* (London: Routledge, 2006).

Lateef, S. *Muslim Women in India: Political and Private Realities, 1890s–1980s* (New Delhi: Kali for Women, 1990).

Lewis, R., *Rethinking Orientalism: Women, Travel, and the Ottoman Harem* (London: I.B. Tauris, 2004).

Login, E. D., *Lady Login's Recollections: Court and Camp Life 1820–1904* (London: Smith, Elder, 1916).

Loomba, A., *Colonialism/Postcolonialism* (New York: Routledge, 2005).

Low, D. A., 'Laissez-Faire and Traditional Rulership in Princely India', in Jeffrey (ed.), *People, Princes and Paramount Power*, pp. 372–87.

MacMillan, M., *Women of the Raj* (London: Thames and Hudson, 1988).

Malik, Y. K., and V. B. Singh, *Hindu Nationalists in India: The Rise of the Bharatiya Janata Party* (Oxford: Westview Press, 1994).

Mani, L., 'Contentious Traditions: The Debate on *Sati* in Colonial India', in Sangari and Vaid (eds), *Recasting Women*, pp. 88–126.

—, *Contentious Traditions: The Debate on Sati in Colonial India* (Berkeley, CA: University of California Press, 1998).

Manor, J., *Political Change in an Indian State: Mysore 1917–1955* (New Delhi: Manohar, 1977).

—, 'The Demise of the Princely Order', in Jeffrey (ed.), *People, Princes and Paramount Power*, pp. 306–28.

Mason, P., *The Men Who Ruled India* (London: Jonathan Cape, 1985).

Mathur, L. P., and L. Sukhwal., 'British Interference in the Internal Sovereignty of Princely States (1858–1885)', in Vyas (ed.), *British Policy towards Princely States of India*, pp. 23–40.

McClintock, A., *Imperial Leather: Race, Gender and Sexuality in the Colonial Conquest* (New York: Routledge, 1995).

McLeod, J., 'Towards the Analysis of Hindu Princely Genealogy in the British Period, 1850–1950', *South Asia Research*, 6:2 (November 1986), pp. 181–93.

—, *Sovereignty, Power, Control: Politics in the States of Western India, 1916–1947* (Leiden: Brill, 1999).

Mehta, G, *Raj: A Novel* (New York: Fawcett Columbine, 1989).

Mehta, R., *Inside the Haveli* (New Delhi: Penguin Books, 1977).

Metcalf, T., *Ideologies of the Raj* (Cambridge, Cambridge University Press, 1995).

Mittal, K., *History of Bhopal State: Development of Constitution, Administration and National Awakening, 1901–1949* (Delhi: Munshiram Manoharlal Publishers Pvt. Ltd., 1990).

Moore, L., *Maharanis: The Lives and Times of Three Generations of Indian Princesses* (London: Penguin Books, 2004).

Moore, R. J., *The Crisis of Indian Unity 1917–1940* (Oxford: Oxford University Press, 1974).

Morrow, A., *Highness: The Maharajas of India* (London: Grafton Books, 1986).

Nair, J., 'On the Question of Agency in Indian Feminist Historiography', *Gender and History*, 6 (1994), pp. 82–100.

—, *Women and Law in Colonial India: A Social History* (Delhi: Kali for Women, 1996).

Narain, I., and P. C. Mathur, 'The Thousand Year Raj: Regional Isolation and Rajput Hinduism in Rajasthan Before and After 1947', in F. Frankel and M. S. Rao (eds), *Dominance and State Power in Modern India, Vol. 2* (Delhi: Oxford University Press, 1990), pp. 1–58.

Neogy, A., *The Paramount Power and the Princely States of India, 1858–1881* (Calcutta: K.P. Bagchi, 1979).

O'Hanlon, R., 'Issues of Widowhood: Gender, Discourse and Resistance in Colonial Western India', in D. Haynes and G. Prakash (eds), *Contesting Power: Resistance and Everyday Social Relations in South Asia* (Berkeley, CA: University of California Press, 1991), pp. 62–108.

—, *A Comparison between Women and Men: Tarabai Shinde and the Critique of Gender Relations in Colonial India* (Madras: Oxford University Press, 1994).

—, 'Gender in the British Empire', in Brown and Louis (eds), *The Oxford History of the British Empire, Twentieth Century*, pp. 379–97.

O'Malley, L. S. S. *The Indian Civil Service: 1600–1933* (London: Frank Cass, 1965).

Orsini, F. (ed.), *Love in South Asia* (Cambridge: Cambridge University Press, 2006).

Pataudi, S. A., *The Elite Minority: The Princes of India* (Lahore: Syed Mobin Mahmud & Co., 1989).

Peabody, N., 'Tod's "Rajasth'an" and the Boundaries of Imperial Rule in Nineteenth-Century India' *Modern Asian Studies* 30:1 (1996), pp. 185–220.

—, *Hindu Kingship and Polity* (Cambridge: Cambridge University Press, 2003).

Peckel, C., *Begums of Bhopal* (New Delhi: Roli Books, 2000).

Peirce, L., *The Imperial Harem* (Oxford: Oxford University Press, 1993).

Plunkett, F. T., 'Royal Marriages in Rajasthan', *Contributions to Indian Sociology*, n.s. 7 (1973), pp. 64–80.

Prakash, G., 'Writing Post-Orientalist Histories of the Third World: Perspectives from Indian Historiography', *Mapping Subaltern Studies and the Postcolonial* (London: Verso, 2000), pp. 163–90.

Price, P., *Kingship and Political Practice in Colonial India* (Cambridge: Cambridge University Press, 1996).

Rai, M., *Hindu Rulers, Muslim Subjects: Islam, Rights and the History of Kashmir* (Princeton, NJ: Princeton University Press, 2004).

Ramusack, B., 'The Princes of India and Their States' (A Volume of the New Cambridge History of India, unpublished manuscript).

—, 'Fairy Tales, Soap Operas, or Expressions of Individuality: Autobiographies of Indian Princesses' (unpublished paper).

—, *The Princes of India in the Twilight of Empire: Dissolution of a Patron-Client System, 1914–1939* (Columbus, OH: University of Cincinnati Press, 1978).

—, 'Tourism and Icons: The Packaging of Princely States in Rajasthan', in C. B. Asher and T. R. Metcalf (eds), *Perceptions of South Asia's Visual Past* (New Delhi: Oxford and IBH Publishing Co., 1994), pp. 235–55.

—, *The Indian Princes and Their States* (Cambridge: Cambridge University Press, 2004).

Richter, W. L., 'Traditional Rulers in Post-Traditional Societies: The Princes of India and Pakistan', in Jeffrey (ed.), *People, Princes and Paramount Power*, pp. 329–54.

Rudolph, L. I., and S. Rudolph, 'Toward Political Stability in Underdeveloped Countries: The Case of India', *Public Policy*, 9 (1959), pp. 149–78.

—, *The Modernity of Tradition: Political Development in India* (Chicago, IL: University of Chicago Press, 1967).

—, *Essays on Rajputana* (New Delhi: Concept Publishing Company, 1984).

Said, E., *Orientalism* (New York: Vintage Books, 1978).

Sangari, K., and S. Vaid (eds), *Recasting Women: Essays in Indian Colonial History*. (New Brunswick, NJ: Rutgers University Press, 1990).

Sarkar, T., 'The Hindu Wife and the Hindu Nation: Domesticity and Nationalism in Nineteenth Century Bengal', *Studies in History*, 8:2 (1992), pp. 213–35.

Scott, J. W., *Gender and the Politics of History* (New York: Columbia University Press, 1988).

Singh, J., *Colonial Narratives/Cultural Dialogues: Discoveries of India in the Language of Colonialism* (London; Routledge, 1996).

Spivak, G., 'Can the Subaltern Speak?', in C. Nelson and L. Grossberg (eds), *Marxism and the Interpretation of Culture* (Illinois: Illini Books, 1988), pp. 271–313.

Srivastava, D. B., 'Constitutional Significance of the Treaty Relations between the Indian States and the Paramount Powers', in Vyas (ed.), *British Policy towards Princely States of India*, pp. 1–5.

Stern, R., *Cat and the Lion: Jaipur State in the British Raj* (Leiden: Brill, 1988).

Stone, L., *The Crisis of the Aristocracy, 1558–1641* (Oxford: Oxford University Press, 1967).

—, *The Family, Sex and Marriage in England 1500–1800* (New York: Harper & Row Publishers, 1977).

Sundar, N., *Subalterns and Sovereigns: An Anthropological History of Bastar, 1854–1996* (Delhi: Oxford University Press, 1997).

Tinker, H., *India and Pakistan: A Political Analysis* (New York: 1967).

Visram, R., *Ayahs, Lascars and Princes: Indians in Britain 1700–1947* (London, 1986).

Visweswaran, K., 'Small Speeches, Subaltern Gender: Nationalist Ideology and its Historiography' *Subaltern Studies*, 9 (1996), pp. 83–125.

Vyas, R. P. (ed.), *British Policy towards Princely States of India* (Jodhpur: Rajasthan-Vidya Prakashan, 1991).

Waghorne, J. P., *The Raja's Magic Clothes: Re-visioning Kingship and Divinity in England's India* (University Park, PA: Pennsylvania State Press, 1994).

Washbrook, D., 'Orients and Occidents: Colonial Discourse Theory and the Historiography of the British Empire', in R. W. Winks (ed.), *The Oxford History of the British Empire, Historiography* (Oxford: Oxford University Press, 1999), pp. 596–611.

Washbrook, D., and R. O'Hanlon, 'After Orientalism: Culture, Criticism and Politics in the Third World', in V. Chaturvedi (ed.), *Mapping the Subaltern and the Postcolonial* (London: Verso, 2000), pp. 191–219.

Willesee, A., and M. Whittaker, *Love and Death in Kathmandu: A Strange Tale of Royal Murder* (London: Rider, 2003).

Younger, C., *Wicked Women of the Raj: European Women Who Broke Society's Rules and Married Indian Princes* (New Delhi: HarperCollins Publishers, 2003).

Ziegler, N., 'Some Notes on Rajput Loyalties During the Mughal Period', in J. F. Richards (ed.), *Kingship and Authority in South Asia* (Madison, WI: University of Wisconsin-Madison Publication Series, 1978), pp. 215–51.

INDEX